The Heart of Truth

REV. CHARLES G. FINNEY.

C. G. Finney

The Heart of Truth

Charles Finney

Finney's Lectures on Theology

BETHANY HOUSE PUBLISHERS
MINNEAPOLIS, MINNESOTA 55438
A Division of Bethany Fellowship, Inc.

The Heart of Truth
by Charles G. Finney

Published in 1976 by Bethany Fellowship, Inc.
6820 Auto Club Road, Minneapolis, Minnesota 55438

Originally issued in 1840 under the title, *Skeletons of a Course of Theological Lectures*. Issued in 1968 by Bethany Fellowship, Inc., under the title *Finney's Lectures on Theology*.

Printed in the United States of America

Library of Congress Cataloging in Publication Data:

Finney, Charles Grandison, 1792-1875.
The heart of truth.

Originally published in 1840 under title: Skeletons of a course of theological lectures.
1. Theology—Addresses, essays, lectures.
2. Christian ethics—Addresses, essays, lectures.
I. Title.
BR85.F427 1976 230 75-46128
ISBN 0-87123-226-X

PREFACE

The method of giving Theological Instruction in this Institution is as follows:

1. A series of questions is propounded for discussion, comprising an outline of a system of Natural and Revealed Theology.

2. Each of these questions comes up in order, for discussion.

3. Upon each one, every member of the class is required to make up his mind, and prepare a brief statement of his views, in writing.

4. Each student is then called upon, in order, to present his views to the class, the Professor presiding. His views and statements are then made the subject of thorough examination and discussion by the class, and by the Instructor. Questions are freely asked, and difficulties started. Answers and explanations are given, until the views of the class are settled upon the point or points discussed by him. Then another, and another are called upon in a like manner to present their views, upon which, like discussion ensues, until the class have mastered the whole subject. Here the discussion is arrested, and the Professor sums up and presents the whole subject to the class in one or more lectures. The skeletons of these lectures have heretofore been copied out by each student as a kind of memoranda, to which he might in future refer, to refresh his memory. This has cost so much labor, that the students have earnestly solicited their publication. For their use and benefit, they are therefore principally intended.

To those students and others, who may read these skeletons, it may be important to make the following remarks, explanatory of what has not, and what has been my design in preparing them for the press:

1. It has been no part of my design to relieve the student from the necessity of deep study, research, and original investigation upon every topic in Theology.

2. I have not intended to give any thing like a detailed history of the Theological opinions, that have prevailed in former ages.

3. Nor have I intended, any farther than is demanded by the nature of Polemic Theology, to give a history of the Theological Opinions that are at present entertained by different schools.

4. I have not intended so to prepare these skeletons that they can be *well understood* without deep thought, and in many instances without discussion and explanation. I have felt, that to leave them in such a state as to require much thought, was of great importance to students who would thoroughly understand Theology.

5. I have not intended to exhaust any subject of discussion; but simply, in my statements, to comprise an outline of the subject.

6. I have not intended so to prepare these skeletons, that students would, or could, on examination, barely retail my language or statements.

7. I have not intended to leave the bones of these skeletons so wholly disconnected, that students, unpracticed in Theology, would not be able, by sufficient attention and diligence, to arrange and unite them in their order.

8. Nor have I aimed so fully to unite them by statements and propositions, as to preclude the necessity of much and close thought, in order to see the connection and truth of the proposition. But,

9. I have designed to render all these subjects perspicuous to those who have given a thorough attention to Theology. They are designed as memoranda, as the summing up of previous discussions, thought, and investigation, rather than as essays from which Theological information is to be derived.

10. I have intended so to shape these skeletons, that those who understand *them*, should have a general, and pretty thorough acquaintance with Theology, as a science, so as not to be at a loss for an answer to almost any question upon Theological subjects.

11. I have intended, however, that these skeletons should be in such a form as to render it unnatural for students to fall into the habit of following exactly in my track in their statements, answers to questions, and discussions of Theological subjects.

12. These skeletons have undergone repeated revisions, enlargement, and modification. And should I live, and continue in my present employment, it is probable, that from year to year, this will continue to be the case with my Theological lectures.

13. Additions will be made to them from year to year, as the course of discussion shall render it necessary or expedient. Should these additions ever grow to a sufficient size to render their publication necessary, for the same reasons that have demanded the publication of these, they will probably be given to the public.

14. These lectures contain as full an outline of Theological Study as we have hitherto been able to fill up in our discussions and investigations, during the three years allotted to Theological Instruction in this Institution. Such additional topics of discussion will be considered from time to time, as we may be enabled to investigate, and add to the usual labors of the class.

15. It is felt that these skeletons are in an imperfect state—that many of the statements may be seen hereafter, to need modifying. I have felt it to be an exceedingly difficult thing, so to prepare these skeletons, as that their publication should be a sufficient memoranda to the graduated classes, without forestalling the studies and investigations of subsequent classes. I have done, under the circumstances, the best I could. And whether I have exactly accomplished what I have intended, can be known only by the results.

16. In some instances, I have given such *definitions* as I have, with the design to awaken thought, or suggest the inquiry why are these definitions, stated under several different heads. And why are they just as they are. If I have so stated them as to suggest these inquiries, and lead the student to search for, and find out their answer, my object in this respect, is accomplished. To the superficial and unpracticed Theologian, many things that I have said, will of course be unintelligible. But those who think, and love to think, will, I hope, be able to understand them.

My design was at first, not to publish, but barely to print a small number of copies exclusively for the use of the students. But as it was supposed that others would desire to possess them, I have consented to their publication, reminding my readers that they are a bare skeleton of the course of Theological study here pursued.

THE AUTHOR.

CONTENTS

THEOLOGY

LECTURE I.

INTRODUCTORY LECTURE.—No. 1.

I. Define the study upon which you are about to enter.
II. Notice some of the requisite personal qualifications for this study.
III. Some of the advantages to be derived from the study of Systematic Theology.
IV. Some things to be avoided.

I. *Define the study upon which you are about to enter.*

1. Theology is the science of God, and of divine things. It teaches the existence, natural and moral attributes, laws, government, and whatever may be known of God, and of our relations, duties, and responsibilities to him and to the universe. In its most comprehensive sense it embraces all knowledge.

2. It may be and generally is divided into *Natural* and *Revealed Theology.*

This distinction does not imply that natural Theology is not revealed.

(1.) NATURAL THEOLOGY is that which derives its evidence from the works of God, or from nature, as it is commonly, but erroneously expressed.

(2.) REVEALED THEOLOGY is that which derives its doctrines and evidence from the Bible.

3. Theology is again subdivided into *Didactic, Polemic, and Pastoral.*

DIDACTIC, is the system of theological doctrines with their evidences, both of Natural and Revealed Religion.

POLEMIC, is controversial. It relates to the disputed doctrines of Theology.

It consists in the controversial maintaining of them, in opposition to their opponents.

PASTORAL, relates to the relations, duties, and responsibilities of Pastors. It consists in a judicious application of the great principles of the government of God to the Pastoral relation and office.

II. *Notice some of the requisite personal qualifications for this study*

1. The ardent love of truth for its own sake.
2. The supreme and disinterested love of God.
3. An intense desire to know more of him.
4. Strong desire to make him known to others.
5. A willingness to make any personal sacrifice for this end.
6. A sense of ignorance and dependence upon divine teaching.
7. A willingness to practice as fast as you learn.
8. A fixed purpose to *know* and *do* the whole truth.
9. A state of mind that will not be diverted to make provision for the flesh.
10. Docility of mind.
11. Such humility as to be willing to expose your ignorance.
12. The love of study.
13. Sound education.
14. Industrious habits.
15. Patience and perseverance in investigation.
16. A mind so balanced as to be duly influenced by evidence.
17. Knowledge of the laws of evidence.
18. Knowledge of correct rules of biblical interpretation.
19. Knowledge of the limits of human research and investigation.

III. *Some of the advantages to be derived from the study of Systematic Theology.*

1. A constantly increasing sense of your own ignorance.
2. The highest advantages for growth in personal holiness.
3. The habit of rapid, correct, and consecutive thought.
4. System in thinking and communicating thought.
5. Facility in preparations for the pulpit.
6. Exactness in the statement of the doctrines of Christianity.
7. Facility in proving them.
8. Consistency of views and statements.
9. A settled state of mind in regard to religious truth.
10. Ability to teach the doctrines and duties of religion.

IV. *Some things to be avoided.*

1. Tempting God, by demanding an impossible or unreasonable kind or degree of evidence.
2. A caviling state of mind.
3. Defending error for the sake of argument.
4. Committing yourself to an opinion.
5. Avoid calling in question first truths.
6. Avoid attempting to prove them.
7. Avoid begging the question.
8. Avoid impatience at the ignorance or stupidity of your class-mates.
9. Avoid an ambition to excel them in study and argument.
10. Avoid a disputatious spirit.
11. Avoid stating one thing and proving another in your skeletons.

12. Avoid the use of weak and inconclusive arguments.

13. Avoid an involved method of stating your propositions.

14. Avoid stating more than you can prove.

15. Avoid leaving your propositions, until fully supported by evidence or argument.

16. Avoid the accumulation of evidence or argument after your proposition is fully established.

17. Avoid prolixity in the statement of your propositions.

18. Avoid the great error of supposing that truths which are self-evident to some minds, are so to all.

REMARKS.

1. The study of Theology demands much prayer.

2. You will never get any effectual knowledge of Theology without the illumination of the Holy Spirit.

3. Take care that your hearts keep pace with your intellects.

4. Grieve not the Holy Spirit.

LECTURE II.

INTRODUCTORY LECTURE.—No. 2.

I. Some things implied in the study of Theology.

II. Some things that we *know* of man, independently of any revelation or knowledge of God.

I. *Some things implied in the study of Theology.*

1. All reasoning implies the existence of a reasoning faculty. Hence,

2. Of a reasoner, possessing such attributes as are suited to the exercise of reasoning.

3. All study therefore assumes, or presupposes the existence and attributes of a *student*.

4. The study of Theology implies and assumes the existence and attributes of a student capable of knowing God.

5. Our first inquiry then is, on what evidence are these assumptions based?

6. That they are no mere unsupported assumptions will appear if we glance at.

II. *Some things that we* KNOW *of man, independently of any revelation or knowledge of God.*

1. The existence of man.

(1.) The fact of our existence is not an assumption without proof.

(2.) It is a direct and positive affirmation of reason, founded upon the testimony of consciousness. *Consciousness* is the mind's recognition of its own exercises or states. I am conscious of *thought*, *volition*, *emotion*, and consciousness is to my own mind the highest possible evidence.

It cannot be doubted. Upon this testimony, reason affirms and cannot doubt the fact of my own existence; or that thought implies a *thinker*; reasoning a *reasoner*, &c.

(3.) This truth is so certainly *known* by us, that to doubt it implies its truth, because doubt implies the existence of a doubter.

(4.) Pretended doubters of their own existence, therefore, always and necessarily assume the fact which they profess to doubt.

(5.) We have therefore a right to assume in the outset, the fact of our own existence.

(6.) We are conscious of certain mental impressions or states, the causes of which we necessarily refer to objects without ourselves. These states or impressions we call sensations.

(7.) Sensation informs us of the existence of those around us who exhibit the same phenomena of which we are conscious. Hence reason affirms, and cannot doubt the existence of our fellow men.

(8.) In the presence of this evidence, we can no more doubt their existence, than our own.

2. Nature of man.

(1.) Man has a body.

a. By consciousness we know that man has a *body* or a *material* habitation.

b. Of the substratum, or ultimate elements or element of body, we know nothing.

c. We call that *body* or *matter* which exhibits the phenomena of solidity, extension, form, divisibility, &c. These phenomena are all we know of matter, and our only means of knowing its nature.

d. Consciousness forces upon us the conviction that we have a body.

e. We can no more doubt it than we can doubt our existence altogether.

f. This truth never was seriously doubted, and pretended doubters have taken as much care of their bodies as others.

(2.) Consciousness itself implies or presupposes the existence of mind. We are conscious of thought—thought implies a thinker, or something that thinks. Besides, consciousness itself presupposes a subject, or that *something* is conscious.

a. We know nothing of the substratum or essence, or ultimate element of mind any more than of matter. We are in utter ignorance of what the essence of either is.

b. We call that mind, which exhibits the phenomena of *thought*, *volition*, *emotion*. &c.

c. The phenomena of matter and mind are entirely distinct and dissimilar exhibiting no evidence that their substrata are identical.

d. The phenomena of matter and mind exhibit the highest evidence that their substrata, or natures, are distinct and diverse.

e. We can no more doubt that we have mind, than that we think.

f. But some maintain that mind is only thought, volition, emotion, &c., and that these are the result of exquisite cerebral organization. In other words, that the brain, or matter, thinks, when thus organized. Their argument runs thus:

1. No thought is manifest where there is no brain.

2. But where there is living brain, there is always thought.

3. The perfection of thought, intelligence, volition, is in proproportion to the amount and perfection of the cerebral substance. Hence the inference that matter, in the form of brain, thinks.

But this only proves what all admit, that brain is the organ of mind, and the only medium through which it can manifest itself in this state of existence—that the capacities of mental development must, and do depend upon the perfection of the cerebral organization.

To the fact that the phenomena of mind and matter, are entirely distinct and dissimilar, and that therefore it is unphilosophical to infer identity of essence, they reply, that chimistry affords many illustrations and confirmations of their views. The union of chimical elements, and the action of inorganic affinities often, nay, always result in the production of substances differing entirely from either of the elements of which they are composed.

To this it may be replied,

1. That the result, so far as we have any light from chimistry, is always material and therefore does not differ *essentially*, or in *essence* from the elements of which it was composed.

2. Consciousness of continued personal identity proves that the brain is not the thinking agent or mind. It is a well settled truth, that the particles of which the human body is composed are perpetually changing, and that the substance of the entire body is changed several times during the period of an ordinary life. If then mind and matter are identical—if the brain or any other part of the body, or the whole body, is the man, the thinking agent, we are not the same person at any two moments. But consciousness testifies to our continued personal identity. The body then can only be the organ or instrument of the mind, and not the mind itself.

3. That there is nothing in natural science at all analagous to that for which they contend, the unvarying results of all combinations of matter being *material* and exhibiting only the phenomena of matter and that continually. Man therefore is a compound being, uniting in one person two distinct natures, called Body and Mind.

3. Attributes of man.

(1.) Of Body.

a. The body of man possesses all the attributes or properties of matter.

b. The attributes of an organized being.

c. The attributes of an animal body.

d. Subject to decay of course.

(2.) Attributes of mind.

The mind of man has natural and moral attributes.

THE NATURAL ATTRIBUTES are what we know of the nature of mind, some of which are.

a. Intellect, or the power to think or reason.

b. Will, or the power of volition.

c. Reason, or the power to distinguish truth from error, good from evil, or to deduce just inferences from facts or propositions.

d. Conscience, or the power to pass judgment upon the moral qualities of actions and to approve or condemn accordingly.

Consciousness testifies to the existence of these and other natural attributes of the mind of man.

Their existence cannot be doubted.

THE MORAL ATTRIBUTES of mind are its voluntary but permanent and controlling moral dispositions, or preferences, such as selfishness or benevolence, justice or injustice, &c. The existence of these is a matter of consciousness and cannot be doubted.

4. Man is an *Agent*, i. e. he originates his own actions. Proof. Consciousness.

5. Man is a *Free Agent,* i. e. he possesses intelligence with the power and liberty of choice. Proof. (1.) Consciousness.

(2.) Agency implies freedom.

(3.) The fact that men are governed by motives implies liberty of will.

(4.) We are as sure that we are free as that we exist. That we act freely as that we act at all.

6. Man is a *Moral Agent.*

Moral agency implies the possession of intellect, reason, will, conscience. A susceptibility to pleasure and pain, with some degree of knowledge on moral subjects.

Man is conscious of possessing these. He therefore knows himself to be a moral agent. The moral agency of man is further proved by the following considerations:

1. All government is founded upon the universal recognition of this truth.

2. All praise and blame which all men award to each other is founded upon the universal acknowledgment of this truth.

3. It cannot be and never was seriously disbelieved. The pretended doubters of it are as ready as others to praise or blame those around them for their actions.

4. The actual influence of moral considerations upon men, demonstrates their moral agency.

7. Man is an *Immortal Agent.*

Only a few of the proofs of this will be adduced in this place.

PROOF. 1. Life of mind is not dependent on the body, for nearly every part of the body has been destroyed in different persons, and yet the mind lived.

2. When the body is dying the mind often possesses full vigor.

3. General belief of all nations and generations.

4. Man's capacity for endlessly increasing in virtue and enjoyment.

5. If man is not immortal, his moral capabilities are inexplicable.

6. As man is capable of endless improvement, economy demands his immortality.

7. If man is not immortal, his moral powers are worse than useless.

8. If man is not immortal, God is not just, as he does not reward man here according to his conscious character.

9. Conscience refers retribution to a future state. We must not anticipate the bible argument in this place as we have proved neither the existence of God, nor the truth of the Bible.

LECTURE III.

INTRODUCTORY LECTURE.—No. 3.

I. The importance of a correct and thorough knowledge of the laws of evidence.

II. What is *evidence* and what is *proof*, and the difference between them.

III. Sources of evidence in a course of theological inquiry.

IV. Kinds and degrees of evidence to be expected.

V. When objections are not, and when they are fatal.

VI. How objections are to be disposed of.

VII. On whom lies the burden of proof.

VIII. Where proof or argument must begin.

I. *The importance of a correct and thorough knowledge of the laws of evidence.*

1. Without correct knowledge on this subject our speculations will be at random.

2. The ridiculous credulity of some, and the no less ridiculous incredulity of others, are owing to ignorance, or a disregard of the fundamental laws of evidence. E. g.: Mormonism is ridiculous *credulity*, founded in utter ignorance or a disregard of the first principles of evidence in relation to the kind and degree of testimony demanded to establish any thing that claims to be a revelation from God.

Every form of religious scepticism, on the other hand, is ridiculous *incredulity*, founded in ignorance, or a disregard of the fundamental laws of evidence, as will be shown in its place.

II. *What is* EVIDENCE *and what is* PROOF, *and the difference between them.*

1. Evidence is that which elucidates and enables the mind to apprehend truth.

2. Proof is that degree of evidence that warrants or demands belief—that does or ought to produce conviction.

3. Every degree of *evidence* is not *proof.* Every degree of light upon a subject is *evidence.* But that only is *proof* which under the circumstances can give reasonable satisfaction.

III. *Sources of evidence in a course of Theological Inquiry.*

This must depend upon the nature of the thing to be proved.

1. Consciousness may be appealed to upon questions that are within its reach, or on questions of experience, but not on other questions.

2. Sense may be appealed to on questions within the reach of our senses, but not on other questions.

3. The existence of God must be proved by his works, as an appeal to the Bible to settle this question would be *assuming* both the fact of his existence, and that the Bible is his word.

4. The Divine authority of the Bible, or of any book or thing that claims to be a revelation from God, demands some *kind* of evidence that none but God can give. Miracles, are one of the most natural and impressive kinds. Prophesy another.

5. Without God's own testimony, all other evidence would be uncertain and unsatisfactory upon such a question.

6. Appeals may also properly be made to such other evidences, external and internal, as might be reasonably expected if the revelation in question were really from God.

7. As the universe is a revelation of God, we may legitimately wander into every department of nature, science, and grace, for testimony upon theological subjects.

8. Different questions, must however draw their evidences from different departments of revelation. Some from his works and providence, others from his word, and others still from all these together.

IV. *Kinds and degrees of evidence to be expected.*

KINDS.

1. No impossible or unreasonable kind is to be expected, e. g.: The evidence of sense is not to be demanded or expected when the thing to be proved is not an object of or within the reach of sensation.

2. Nor of consciousness when the question is not one of *experience* and does not belong to the exercises of our own minds.

3. It is a sound rule that the best evidence in *kind* shall be adduced, that the nature of the case admits: for instance,

(1.) Oral testimony is not admissible where written testimony may be had to the same point.

(2.) Of course oral traditions are not to be received where there is written history to the same point.

(3.) But oral testimony is admissible in the absence of written, as then, it is the best that the nature of the case admits.

(4.) So oral traditions may be received to establish points of antiquity, in the absence of cotemporary history.

(5.) Any book claiming to be a revelation from God, should, in some way, bear his own seal as a kind of evidence at once possible and demanded by the nature of the subject.

DEGREE OF EVIDENCE.

1. Not, in general, demonstration; as this would be inconsistent with a state of probation under a moral government.

2. Not, in general, such a degree of evidence as to preclude the possibility of cavil or evasion, for the same reason.

But, 1. Such an amount of evidence on all fundamental questions as to afford reasonable satisfaction to an honest and inquiring mind.

2. Such an amount of evidence upon the face of creation itself as should gain the general assent of mankind to the facts of the Divine existence and of human accountability.

3. That the evidence chould be more or less, *Latent*, *Patent*, *Direct*, *Inferential*, *Incidental*, *Full*, *and Unanswerable* according to its relative importance in the system of Divine truth.

V. *When objections are not, and when they are fatal.*

NOT FATAL.

1. Not when they are not well established by proof.

2. Not when the truth of the objection *may* consist with the truth of the proposition which it is intended to overthrow.

3. Not when the affirmative proposition is conclusively established by testimony, although we may be unable to discover the consistency of the proposition with the objection.

4. *Not always fatal because unanswerable.*

BUT AN OBJECTION IS FATAL,

1. When it is an unquestionable reality, and plainly incompatible with the truth of the proposition against which it lies.

2. When the higher probability is in its favor.

3. When the objection is established by a higher kind or degree of evidence than the proposition to which it is opposed. E. g. Consciousness is the highest kind of evidence: an objection founded in, or supported by consciousness will set aside other testimony.

4. The testimony of *sense* is not always conclusive in the face of other testimony, and an objection founded in, and supported by sensation is not always fatal.

5. An objection is fatal, when it fully proves that the proposition in question is not merely *above*, but plainly *contrary* to the affirmations of reason.

VI. *How objections are to be disposed of.*

This depends upon their nature.

1. If mere cavils without reason or proof, they may remain unnoticed.

2. So, if they appear reasonable, if *proved*, and are yet without proof, we are not called on to reply.

3. We are not bound to explain the objection and show that it *is* consistent with the proposition against which it is alledged, but simply that if a *fact, it may be* consistent with it. It then rests with our opponent to show that if it *might* be consistent with the proposition, yet as a matter of fact it *is* not.

4. No objection is competent to set aside *first truths*, such as that a whole is equal to all its parts. A part is less than a whole &c.

5. No objection can set aside the direct testimony of consciousness.

6. Nor can an objection set aside the unambiguous testimony of God.

7. First, and self-evident truths, the affirmations of reason, consciousness, and the testimony of God, can never conflict with each other.

8. There is always a fallacy in whatever is flatly inconsistent with either of these.

VII. *Where lies the burden of proof.*

1. Always on him who makes the affirmation, unless his affirmation is sufficiently manifest without proof.

2. The *onus probandi* lies with the affirmative until the evidence fairly amounts to *proof* in the absence of opposing testimony.

3. When the affirmative evidence amounts to proof, the *onus* is upon the objector.

4. Every kind and degree of evidence that may as well consist with the negative as the affirmative of the proposition to be proved, leaves the *onus* unchanged.

5. When the evidence, or an argument, or an objection proves too much, as well as when it proves too little, it leaves the *onus* unchanged.

6. If an objection needs proof, the *onus* lies upon the objector.

VIII. *Where proof or argument must begin.*

1. Proof or argument, must commence where uncertainty commences.

2. Hence, all argument and proof take for granted such truths as need no proof but are either axioms, self-evident truths, or such as are already sufficiently apparent.

LECTURE IV.

EXISTENCE OF GOD.

First, State the several methods of proof.
Second, Show to what they amount.

First, *State the several methods of proof.*

I. Moral argument, or argument founded in the demand of our moral nature. *Short method.*

1. I am conscious of *feeling* moral obligation to do right and avoid wrong.

2. I am conscious of mental states for which I feel praise or blame-worthy, or in other words: I am conscious of having a moral character.

3. Moral character implies a moral nature or constitution.

4. It also implies a law or rule of moral action apprehended by the mind.

5. This law within implies a law without.

6. A moral constitution and moral law imply a creator, law-giver, and judge. This creator or author of my nature; this law-giver and judge, is God.

Again, 1. I cannot resist the conviction that I am accountable for my actions, not merely to myself and society, but to some law-giver.

2. This *irresistible* conviction of accountability implies, either that accountability is a dictate of my nature, or that the evidence of it is *overwhelming.*

3. I *am* therefore accountable for my conduct, or my moral nature deceives me.

4. But accountability implies a *rightful ruler.* This ruler is God.

Again, 1. My senses inform me that other men exhibit the same phenomena of which I am conscious.

2. Hence I cannot resist the conviction that they have a moral nature, and are accountable like myself.

3. Hence I cannot but award them praise or blame for their conduct.

4. This is a dictate of my moral constitution.

5. My nature then demands that I should regard them as subjects of moral government.

6. But moral government implies a moral governor. This governor is God.

7. Hence the existence of God is a dictate of my moral nature.

Rem. Upon this argument the common convictions of men in regard to the Divine existence seem to be based, as this truth is admitted previous to a knowledge of any theoretic argument whatever.

2. This argument always has insured, and always will insure the conviction of the great mass of men.

II. Physical argument, or argument from the external world. *Short method.*

1. Every event must have a cause.

2. My senses testify that the universe exists, and is a system of changes or events.

3. These events do not cause themselves. To suppose this were absurd.

4. They have not existed in an eternal series. This supposition were also absurd.

5. There must have been a first cause.

6. The first cause must have been *uncaused, self-existent, independent, and eternal.* This must be God.

Rem. This confirms the moral argument.

For answers to the atheistical objections and their arguments see *Atheism.*

III. Argument from final causes. *Short method.*

1. Means imply an end.

2. Existences sustaining the relation of means to an end, imply design.

The highest evidence of design may be manifested in two ways,

(1.) When the greatest number of beneficial results arise from the simplest means. Or from the application of one principle or power, to the production of vast and complicated events. Gravitation is an instance of this.

(2.) Where a vast and complicated mechanism is constructed for the production of a simple but highly important end. Vide. human physiology. The universe abounds with both these extremes of art, and affords a demonstration of design.

3. Design implies a designer.

4. The universe is a system of existences, sustaining the relation of means to an end.

5. It had therefore, a designer.

6. This designer is God.

Rem. This argument sets aside the doctrine of chance or fate.

IV. Historical argument. *Short method.*

1. Men have intellect and reason.

2. Therefore their opinions are based upon facts real or supposed.

3. The truth of any proposition in which all nations and ages have agreed must be highly probable.

4. But all ages and nations have agreed in the proposition, "There is a God."

5. Therefore his existence is, to say the least, highly probable.

Objection 1. The fact of this coincidence needs proof.

Answer. That this coincidence has been nearly universal is beyond doubt.

Obj. 2. If this coincidence be admitted, it proves nothing, as all men have believed other things that are false.—E. g. that the sun goes round the earth.

Ans. 1. There was high evidence of this, and the conviction was based upon nothing less than the apparent evidence of their senses.

2. The objection only proves that the historical argument may *possibly* be *inconclusive.*

3. The historical argument does prove that there is a high degree of evidence everywhere discoverable of the existence of God.

V. Argument direct from consciousness. *Short method.*

1. I *think*, therefore I *am.*
2. I was not always. Of this, there is abundant evidence.
3. I began to be, and did not create myself.
4. I descended from a race like myself.
5. This race is made up of a series of individuals.

A series of dependent events, sustaining to each other the relation of cause and effect, implies an independent first cause, for an infinite number of dependent links without an independent first, is absurd.

6. A series implies a first.
7. There must have been a first man.
8. He must have been *self-created, or self-existent, and uncreated,* or created by some other being.
9. He could not create himself.
10. Self-existence is *necessary* existence,
11. He had not a *necessary* existence, for he is dead.
12. He must have begun to be, and must have been created.
13. His Creator must have been uncaused, and eternally self-existent. This cause is God.

Again, 1. The same must be true of every series of existences.

2. Every series must have had a *distinct* self-existent cause, or all existences must have had one and the same first cause.

3. One first cause is sufficient, and it is unphilosophical to suppose more without evidence.

4. The universe as a whole is a unit, and most philosophically attributed to one first cause. This cause is God.

VI. Metaphysical argument.

1. All existences are *necessary* or *contingent.*

(1.) That existence or being is *necessary* whose non-existence is naturally impossible.

(2.) That existence is *contingent* whose non-existence is naturally possible.

2. *Ideas* of existences are *necessary* or *contingent.*

(1.) That *idea* is *necessary,* the non-existence of whose object, under the circumstances, cannot be conceived of as possible.

(2.) That *idea* is *contingent,* the non-existence of whose object may, under the circumstances, be conceived of as possible.

3. That must be a real existence of which we have a *necessary idea*, for the idea is *necessary* only because the non-existence of its object under the circumstances cannot be conceived of as naturally possible.—E. g. space, duration.

4. *Necessary ideas* need to be suggested to, or developed in the mind.—E. g. the ideas of space and duration and the idea that they are infinite are necessary ideas when once suggested. We cannot conceive that space and duration should not exist, and that they should not be infinite.

5. The idea of causality, or that every event must have a cause, is a *necessary* idea when once suggested by an event, for the mind in the presence of the event, cannot conceive that its occurrence without a cause, was naturally possible.

6. The idea of my own *present* existence is a *necessary idea* when suggested by *present* consciousness of mental action. I think, therefore, I *am*, and cannot conceive of my present nonI existence as possible.

7. The idea of the *present* existence of the universe is a *necessary idea* when suggested or developed by present conscious sensations. With this evidence before me, I cannot conceive of the *present* non-existence of the universe as possible.

8. The *idea of a first cause* is a *necessary idea* when once suggested by the events of the universe. With these events before me I cannot conceive that they had no cause, or that there was not a first cause.

9. The idea that the first cause is eternal, self-existent, and independent, is a necessary idea when once suggested to the mind.

10. The idea that this cause is *intelligent* is a *necessary* idea when once suggested by a *knowledge* of the evidences of design apparent in the universe.

11. The ideas of God's existence and attributes are therefore *necessary ideas* when suggested or developed by a knowledge of the events of the universe.

12. But necessary ideas, as above defined, are the representatives of *realities*, therefore God's existence is a reality.

Again, 1. Consciousness is the mind's cognizance of its present state or exercise.

2. We are certain of that of which we are conscious.

3. Hence our mental states or exercises are realities.

4. My existence is an affirmation or inference of reason direct from consciousness. I think, therefore, I *am*.

5. The existence of other beings is also an affirmation of reason direct from consciousness. I am conscious of sensations, the cause of which I must refer to objects external to myself. Therefore these objects *exist*.

6. The existence of God is an inference or affirmation of reason removed one step back from consciousness.

7. I think, therefore I *am*. This is the first inference. I *am*, the universe is, therefore God is, is the second step or affirmation,

the second has the same certainty as the first because it is based upon it.

8. The existence of God then is as certain as my own existence, and the existence of the universe.

SECOND.—*What these arguments amount to.*

1. If they do not amount to a demonstration, it is because the nature of the fact to be proved renders the demonstration of it to our limited faculties impossible.

2. Demonstration is that which shews that the proposition in question cannot but be true.

3. The events of the universe *being admitted* or proved, it is impossible that God should not exist.

4. The contrary supposition is an absurdity, as it assumes that the universe of events is uncaused, which is absurd.

5. The argument for the existence of God amounts to a demonstration. Other objections will be answered under the head "*Atheism.*"

LECTURE V.

ATHEISM.

FIRST. Define Atheism.

SECOND. Some of the different forms or modifications of Atheism.

THIRD. Answer the principal objections of Atheists, to Theism.

FOURTH. Point out some of the difficulties of Atheism.

FIRST.—*Define Atheism.*

Atheism is the opposite of Theism. Theism is a belief in the existence of God. Atheism is the *disbelief* of his existence.

SECOND.—*Some of the different forms or modifications of Atheism.*

I. Sceptical Atheism, or Atheistical Scepticism.

This form of Atheism professes to hold no opinion as to the existence of God, alleging that the evidence in favor of, and that against the divine existence, are too nearly balanced to afford any rational ground of conviction either way.

Hume and some others have taken this ground.

II. Speculative or Dogmatic Atheism.

This modification of Atheism, maintains that the evidence against the existence of God decidedly preponderates.

Atheists of this school either deny the existence of the material universe, or attempt to account for its existence upon principles that are consistent with the denial of the divine existence.

Atheists are however, greatly divided among themselves. Some of them maintain that the universe is all matter, and that what we call mind is only the result of cerebral organization; or, in other words, that matter is, in some forms, intelligent, especially in the form of brain.

Others maintain that the universe is all mind, and that what we call the universe is the fiction or creation of our own minds.

An extended examination of these systems of "philosophy, falsely so called," will not of course, be undertaken in these lectures. The doctrines of these self-styled philosophers will be examined no farther than is necessary to establish the truths of Theology.

III. Pantheism.

This is a *misnomer*. The name denotes a belief in the existence of God, and yet the doctrine or system denies the existence of the true God, and maintains that the universe is itself God.

To confound God with the universe, and hold that He is identical with it, is certainly Atheism, under whatever name it may attempt to conceal itself.

IV. Practical Atheism.

This admits, in words, and profession, the existence of God, but denies him in works. With this kind of Atheism, the present lecture has nothing to do.

These are the principal modifications of Atheism, both ancient and modern.

THIRD. *Answer the principal objections of Atheists to Theism.*

Obj. I. Atheists object to Theism, that it is founded in the natural credulity of the human mind.

Ans. 1. It is a notorious fact that men are not naturally credulous, but obstinately incredulous, in respect to those doctrines that rebuke their lusts.

2. The existence of the true God is an idea big with terror to depraved man.

3. Hence the general admission of God's existence, in despite of the strong prejudices of depraved human nature, is a powerful argument for its support.

Obj. II. They maintain that facts demonstrate, that the God of Theists cannot exist.

E. g. Theists maintain that God is omniscient, and also that he created the universe; but say the Atheists, before the universe existed there were no objects of knowledge. Therefore previous to creation no omniscient being could have existed.

Ans. Omniscience is the knowledge of all actual or possible events and things. This knowledge may have resided, and Theists maintain that it actually did eternally reside in the mind of God.

Obj. III. Theists maintain the immutability of God, and also that he governs the world. But, say the Atheists, we are conscious of freedom; but our freedom is inconsistent with the immutability of God as the governor of the world; therefore there can be no immutable God that governs the world.

Ans. This is a mere begging of the question. To say that God's immutability and our free agency are inconsistent with each other is bare assertion.

Again, Atheists allege that creation itself implies a change in God; and is therefore inconsistent with his immutability.

Ans. Theists maintain the immutability of God in respect to his nature and his character. Creation certainly implies no change in either of these, but only the exercise of his natural and moral attributes. If to this it be replied, that character is nothing else than the exercise of the natural attributes, and that before creation he could have had no moral character, and that the work of creation was the formation of moral character and therefore implied a change; it may be answered, that character consists in design or intention, and that God always designed or intended to create the universe; and therefore creation implies no formation or change of character in him.

Obj. IV. Theists maintain that God is a being of infinite natural and moral perfections.

To this Atheists object.

1. That the physical imperfections of the universe are entirely inconsistent with the existence of those natural and moral attributes which Theists ascribe to God.

Ans. That is perfect which is entirely suited to the end for which it was designed. Theists maintain that the universe was made and is governed for the glory of God, in the promotion of virtue and happiness; and that so far as we can see, it is in the best possible manner suited to that end.

2. To this Atheists object, that the actual existence of so much sin or moral evil, together with all the misery occasioned by it, is inconsistent with the existence either of infinite goodness, infinite knowledge, or infinite power; and that Theists may take which horn of the trilemma they please: that one of three things must be true: either God did not foresee that these evils would exist, in which case he is not omniscient, or foreseeing it, he had not power to prevent it, in which case he is not omnipotent, or, foreseeing it and being able to prevent it, he had not the goodness to do so.

Whichever of these suppositions be true, it demonstrates that the Theist's God cannot exist.

Ans. This is again begging the question. Infinite goodness, knowledge and power, imply only that if a universe were made, it would be the best that was naturally possible. This objection assumes that a better universe, upon the whole, was a natural possibility. It assumes that a universe of moral beings could, under a moral government, administered in the wisest and best manner, be wholly restrained from sin: but this needs proof, and never can be proved.

Moral agency implies freedom: freedom implies the power to resist every degree of motive that can be brought to bear upon mind. That it would have been possible to prevent sin under a moral government, or had it been possible, that it would have been wise, so to alter the administration as wholly to exclude it, is a gratuitous assumption, and any argument or objection founded upon this assumption is of no weight: as certainly it is no impeachment of the natural or moral attributes of God, that moral and natural evils exist, if their existence was, upon the whole, the less of two evils, and preferable to such an arrangement as would have entirely excluded them.

2. The force of this objection lies in the fact that there are things in the universe, all the reasons for, and uses of which, we do not understand. Suppose we are unable to account for the existence of natural and moral evil in a universe like this, is this fact to set aside the world of evidence that the universe was made and is governed by a God? Certainly nothing is more unreasonable.

Obj. V. Atheists deny that there is sufficient evidence of design in the structure of the universe to warrant a rational belief in a designer.

Ans. 1. There are two ways in which design may be most strikingly manifested. One is where a single principle, property, or law, is so applied as to produce the greatest number of beneficial results. The application of the law of gravitation is an instance of this kind. The other is, when a most complicated and labored piece of mechanism is constructed for a single but highly important end. The human frame is an instance and illustration of this. Now the universe every where abounds with instances of these two extremes of art, and affords the highest possible evidence of design.

2. This objection, if allowed, sets aside the possibility of settling any question by evidence, as it is founded in a virtual denial of *all evidence.*

Obj. VI. Atheists object that we can have no conception of such a being as the Theist's God.

Ans. There is a difference between a real and an *adequate* conception. A conception may be real so far as it goes, without including a conception of all that belongs to its object. It is plain that we can form a real, though inadequate, conception of God. If we could form *no* conception of God we could believe nothing about him. But we can and do; therefore this objection is good for nothing.

Obj. VII. Theists maintain that God created the universe out of nothing. This Atheists maintain is naturally impossible. "*Ex nihilo, nihil fit,*" is a favorite axiom of theirs, when contending against this doctrine of Theism.

Ans. 1. This is assumption.

2. The eternal existence of the matter of which the universe is formed, may be admitted without invalidating the proof of God's existence.

3. But that matter is not self-existent appears from the fact that if it is eternal it must have eternally existed, either in an elementary state or in a state of combination and consequently of change. If in an elementary state, it never could have passed into a state of combination. If in a state of combination and change its existence from eternity involves the doctrine of an infinite series, which is absurd; as will be shown in its place.

Obj. VIII. We can as well conceive of the existence of the universe in its present state without a cause, as to conceive of the existence of God without a cause.

Ans. We cannot conceive of the existence of *any event* without a cause; but the universe in its present state we know to be a stupendous series of events. God's existence is *no event* at all, as he never began to be. The difference then of the two suppositions in question, is as the supposition that myriads of events occur without any cause, and that God's existence which is *no* event is without a cause.

Obj. IX. But here they object more definitely, and say that if the universe is an exquisitely constructed machine, the mind that could create it must be still more wonderful and exquisite in its structure, and that we may as well suppose the eternal self-existence of the universe as to suppose the eternal self-existence of a being who could create it.

Ans. The universe we *know* to be continually changing and that therefore it cannot by any possibility have been eternally self-existent, for in that case either those changes have been eternally going on or they have not. If they have, then they must have occurred in an eternal series of dependent events, which is absurd and impossible. If these changes have not been eternally occurring the universe must have existed from eternity in a changeless state. In this case no change could by any possibility have taken place but by the action of some power not inherent in the universe itself; and this power must have been God. We certainly know, therefore, that the universe is not eternally self-existent. But we conceive of God, as possessing an eternal necessary self-existence, and as, therefore, unchangeable. The difficulty in the two conceptions in question, does not lie in supposing an eternal, necessary, self-existence to be impossible or unreasonable; because this supposition is not inconsistent with any first truth. It is not supposing that any event occurs without a cause; for eternal self-existence is no event; as it never begins to be. But the difficulty lies in supposing that *events* and things that *begin to be* really occur without any cause. This we cannot by any possibility conceive. Here we are brought back then to the same conclusion, that the difference in the two suppositions in question is as the supposition that myriads of events occur without a cause, and that what is no event exists without a cause.

Obj. X. To the affirmation of Theists that with the facts of the universe before us, we necessarily have the idea of a first cause, or of a God; they object, and say that as a matter of fact *they* have no such idea.

Ans. They also affirm that *they* have no idea of causality, and do not believe in the reality of it. But who does not know that this is an affirmation in the face of stubborn facts, and that they really have the idea of causality, and cannot doubt it nor act in consistency with the denial of it in any case whatever. These are the principal objections of Atheists to Theism, with brief and what are supposed to be their appropriate answers.

FOURTH. *Point out some of the difficulties of Atheism.*

I. *Difficulty.* One of the fundamental and fatal difficulties of Atheism is that it is founded upon the denial of a first truth.

1. Causality, or that every event must have a cause, is certainly a first truth. It cannot be, and never was, seriously doubted; and professed doubters uniformly recognize it in all their actions.

2. It cannot be *denied* without *admitting* it. The denial implies a denier; the denial is the effect of which the denier is the cause.

3. It cannot be *doubted* without assuming its truth, as the doubt is an effect of which the doubter is the cause.

4. The denier knows that he states a falsehood in the denial: for if he did not believe in causality he would not and could not attempt the denial.

5. If he did not believe in causality, he would not attempt to say, do, or think any thing whatever, any more than he would attempt to fly, or make a universe, or create a God.

6. That causality is a matter of universal belief, and every where and necessarily regarded as a first truth, is evident from the fact that nearly every sentence in every language is constructod upon the admission of this truth. What are the nominative case, the verb, and the objective case, but the cause and the effect?

7. No mind can conceive of causality as being *untrue*, and if it could, the very conception itself would be both an instance and a proof of the truth of it; as the conception would be of itself an effect of which the conceiver would be the cause.

8. Theism is based upon this first truth, and is as certain as the foundation upon which it rests. The whole argument for the existence of God is either a single irresistible inference from the existence of the universe, or a series of irresistible inferences standing one upon another, and having for their foundation the certain and immutable truth of causality, or that every event must have a cause. The conclusion is as certain as the premise. The premise every body knows to be true; and if any one denies the truth of the inference, viz., that there is a God, it must be the denial of his heart and not of his intellect. But as Atheism is founded in a denial of this first truth it must be a tissue of absurdity.

II. *Difficulty*. Another difficulty of Atheism is, that it is fundamentally inconsistent with itself. To the doctrine that God created the universe out of nothing, Atheists object, "*ex nihilo nihil fit.*" But in accounting for the *existence* of the universe *as it is*, they ascribe all events to chance. Now chance is either nothing or something. If *nothing*, to ascribe the existence of the universe to it, is to contradict their favorite maxim just quoted. If *something* adequate to the production of such effects, then they admit causality, and chance is only another name for God.

III. *Difficulty*. One of the main pillars of Atheism is the doctrine of an infinite series; and that the present universe is one of an eternal series of changes through which matter has been eternally passing by its own inherent properties, laws, or affinities.

But to this it may be answered:

1. That it both admits and denies causality. It admits it in maintaining that the changes, and even the structure of the universe, are caused by the inherent properties of matter. It denies it by assigning no sufficient or adequate cause. For an inadequate cause is the same as no cause.

2. The properties and laws of matter cannot account for the *existence* of matter.

3. If the self-existence of matter be admitted, the properties and laws of matter cannot account for the *locations* of matter, and consequently for the movements and events of the universe.

4. Were not the locations of matter such as they are, the events of the universe would not be what they are. (See locations of the planetary system.)

5. The structure and location of the organs and parts of the human body, evince incomparably more design and skill, than do the inherent laws and properties of matter.

6. Supposing the universe to have been created out of nothing, the evidence of the divine existence exhibited in the locations of

matter, are to those exhibited in its properties and laws, as myriads to one. For the known properties and laws of matter are but few, while the dispositions or localities of matter are innumerable.

7. The unorganized is the natural state of matter. This is proved by the fact, that in all cases as soon as life is extinct the matter composing organized bodies returns to an unorganized state, by the action of its inherent properties and laws. This fact demonstrates that bodies are not organized, by the action of affinities inherent in matter, but by a principle of vitality or life which modifies and overrules, for the time being, the action of the laws and affinities inherent in matter.

8. If matter were brought into an organized state by the force of its inherent properties and affinities, then all matter would be found in an organized state, and being once in that state, it would for ever remain in it, unless disorganized by some power out of itself.

9. It is plain, then, that the properties and laws inherent in matter, and that power, whatever it is, that organizes matter into living bodies and sustains that organization, are antagonist forces.

10. There are three states in which matter is found—the *unorganized*, as in the clods of earth—that of *vegetable organization*—and that of *animal organization.*

11. We have seen that the first of these states must be *natural,* because all matter, in whatever state of organization, tends, and if left to itself, returns to the unorganized state.

12. The other two states, those of vegetable and animal organization, are the antagonists of the first and differ so widely from each other that by no apparent possibility can these three states be ascribed to the inherent properties of matter.

13. Should it be admitted then, that matter with all its inherent properties and laws, is self-existent, this would not at all account for the dispositions and locations of matter, nor for the existence of living bodies either vegetable or animal.

14. If men, or any race of animals were extinct, no law of matter could restore them.

15. If Geology proves any thing, it proves that the present races of organized beings have not existed always.

16. The universal law that like begets like, proves that the present races of animals did not spring from former races whose remains have been disinterred by the labors of the geologists. This also is proved by geology itself.

17. Therefore the existence of the present organized world demands the interference of a God, to say the least, at the commencement of its being.

But again: This doctrine of an infinite series, the truth of which the Atheist assumes, admits that every event or change is *conditioned* or *dependent* upon its *immediate* cause, that the exis ence of matter in one peculiar form or state of combination is the cause of its passing into another form or state of combination, but a *conditional* event implies and demands an *unconditional cause*, either immediate or remote. Conditional events are like the links of a suspended chain—but a suspended chain, with an infinite number of *dependent* links without some absolute and independent support, is absurd and naturally impossible. An infinite series of dependent events, cannot be, the doctrine then of an infinite series is false and absurd.

But as Atheism assumes its truth as its fundamental support, Atheism is itself false and absurd.

IV. *Difficulty* Atheism attempts to keep itself in countenance by demanding in support of theism, the most unreasonable and impossible kinds and degrees of evidence. For the existence of God, Atheists demand the testimony of sense, and inquire, "Who has seen God"? To this it may be answered:

1. That the objection is founded in a ridiculous ignorance or disregard of the first principles and laws of evidence, one of which is, that a proposition is to be supported by that kind or degree of evidence which the nature of the case admits. But as God is a Spirit it is unreasonable and absurd to demand for his existence the direct testimony of sense.

2. But we have the indirect testimony of sense for the existence of God, just as we have for the existence of men. Who has at any time seen a man? Our senses inform us of the existence of a body, but this which we see is certainly not the man, the thinking agent, but from the phenomena exhibited to our senses by this body, we naturally and necessarily infer the existence of the man or living agent within, for we cannot conceive that these bodily actions and motions should have no cause, and as they are similar to those of which we ourselves are conscious, our reason affirms that the tenant within is a man like ourselves. As we infer the existence of man from the phenomena which he exhibits to our senses, so we infer the existence of God from the phenomena which he exhibits to our senses.

V. *Difficulty*. Atheism as a system, if system it may be called, is founded on, or supported by no self-evident truth, but is merely a system of evasions, which evasions are founded in the denial of first and self-evident truths.

VI. *Difficulty*. Atheism has not a particle of evidence for its support.

VII. *Difficulty*. Atheism is contradicted by a universe of witnesses.

VIII. *Difficulty*. Atheism is a ridiculous system of both *credulity* and *incredulity*. It is ridiculous *credulity* to believe that all things, or any thing comes by chance.

Should a man believe that a watch *chanced* to grow upon a tree, would not this be an evidence and an instance of ridiculous credulity?

But Atheists pretend to believe that all things are by *chance*.

It is ridiculous *incredulity* to doubt what all men know to be true, that every event must have an adequate cause.

IX. *Difficulty*. That modification of Atheism that denies the existence of the material universe is ridiculous incredulity, because it professes to doubt that for which all men have the evidence of all their senses.

X. *Difficulty*. Atheism requires impossible credulity, for its fundamental doctrines never were, nor can be believed by a sane mind. For no human being ever did or can believe that the universe of events exists without a cause.

XI. *Difficulty*. Its tendencies condemn it. These are,

1. To unsettle all belief, for if the evidence in favor of the existence God, be rejected as inconclusive and insufficient to demand belief, it follows that nothing can be proved by evidence, and that universal scepticism on every subject, including our own existence, is the only reasonable state of mind.

2. A second tendency of Atheism is to destroy all science and all knowledge. If no credit is to be given to testimony, if all evidence is to be set aside, then the foundations of knowledge and science are destroyed and no one can reasonably say, that he is certain of any thing, not even of his own existence, or that he has any sufficient ground for believing any thing whatever.

3. Another tendency of Atheism is, to beget universal distrust, and to annihilate that confidence upon which all society is founded. Hence:

4. Another tendency of Atheism is to annihilate all government. Without confidence, certainly no government can exist. If no degree of evidence is to be credited, there is in no case any foundation for confidence, and if no foundation for confidence, government is an impossibility. If then the principles of Atheism were carried out, they must inevitably overthrow all science and all government.

5. Fifth tendency of Atheism is to unbalance mind and to produce universal insanity. What is insanity, but a state of mind that is not influenced by evidence? And Atheism, if real, must to say the least, be a species of moral monomania; as it is, in respect to the existence of God, the setting aside of all evidence and therefore the perfection of irrationality.

6. A sixth tendency of Atheism is to annihilate all restraint upon sin. Remove from the human mind those powerful motives that are connected with a belief in the existence of God, and you unchain the tiger, and burst open the flood-gates of lust and every species of iniquity.

7. Another tendency of Atheism is to confirm selfishness.

That selfishness is the character of unregenerate man is a matter of fact. That selfishness is detestable, is what all men feel. Nothing can annihilate it but faith in the existence, attributes, and character of God. To deny these, is to perfect and perpetuate selfishness forever.

8. Another tendency of Atheism is to annihilate all those motives to virtue which are alone influential in a world like this.

9. Another tendency of Atheism, is to annihilate the domestic virtues and affections. If the existence of God, and that the domestic relations are a divine institution be denied, there can be, in a world like this, no sufficient support and protection of those relations,and consequently universal licentiousness must prevail. Hence,

10. Atheism delivers men over to the gratification of lust as their highest wisdom. Denying as it does the existence of God, of a future state, and all distinction between virtue and vice—all moral accountability and responsibility, the inference of Paul is just, "Let us eat and drink for to morrow we die."

11. Another tendency of Atheism is to lessen infinitely the value of life. Deny the existence of God, the immortality of the soul and adopt the system of Atheism, and of what comparative value is human life? Let the horrors of the French revolution answer.

12. Atheism leaves the mind in universal doubt and distress in regard to all existences and events. Truth is the natural element of the mind. It can by no possibility be at peace without it. To overthrow all evidence—all knowledge—all confidence, is to render the happiness of mind impossible, and to deliver it over to mourning, lamentation, and woe.

13. Atheism renders virtue impossible. It denies the foundation of all virtue. In denying the existence of God and the immortality of the soul, the relation of cause and effect, it completely annihilates the distinction between right and wrong, and renders it impossible that there should be any such thing as holiness, or virtue in the universe.

14. It produces present and insures eternal misery. That Atheists are eminently wretched men, is evident from their history, and from the very nature of mind it must be so. Truth is the element and natural food of mind, and in just as far as it is fed with and conformed to the truth it is happy. But in proportion as it departs from truth it is miserable.

Atheism is the extreme of error, and for this reason it is *necessarily* the extreme of agony.

XII. *Difficulty*. The *spirit* of Atheism condemns it. Atheism manifestly has not its seat in the understanding but in the heart. It is not properly a sentiment, but a temper. This is evident,

1. From the fact that it does not proceed from any want of evidence of the existence of God.

2. Nor is it based on any contrary or opposing evidence. For Atheism has not a particle of evidence for its support.

3. Nor is Atheism an affirmation of reason, but as directly opposed to reason as possible.

4. Nor is Atheism a deduction or a doctrine of science, but, as we have seen, it involves a denial of all science.

5. Nor is it founded in an incapacity to see the bearings of the evidence of Theism. Nothing is more patent, than the everywhere abounding evidence of the Divine existence.

6. Nor does it proceed from a want of time or opportunity to weigh and consider the evidence in favor of Theism.

7. Nor does it proceed from the manifest useful tendency of Atheism, for it were madness to affirm the usefulness of its tendency.

8. Nor has Atheism grown out of any hurtful tendency of Theism.

9. But Atheism is manifestly a spirit of selfishness. It manifests itself, and its own nature in many ways.

(1.) It is a spirit of ingratitude. Should a man on a desolate island, find that every night while he is asleep, his cave was supplied with all the necessaries of life, and should thus continue from month to month and from year to year, without exciting in him the earnest desire to know and thank his benefactor, universal reason would affirm that that was the spirit of ingratitude. And what is Atheism, but ingratitude the most detestable ?

(2.) Atheism is an uncandid spirit. It is the spirit of caviling against stubborn and undeniable facts.

(3.) Atheism is hatred to truth.

(4.) Atheism is a reckless spirit. It strikes with ruthless hand and endeavors to blot out the existence of God and virtue from the universe.

(5.) It is a spirit of prejudice, as is evident from its ex-parte examination of the great question of Theism.

(6.) It carps and cavils at the few apparent, though unreal discrepancies of the word of God.

(7.) It lays great stress upon the absurdities of vulgar prejudice as it profanely styles the sincere though unlearned opinions of believers in a God.

(8.) It triumphs much over the weak and inconclusive arguments of some Theists.

(9.) Atheists are in the habit of ascribing the events of the universe to *nature*, instead of nature's God.

(10.) Atheists cavil, and stumble, and triumph, in view of the physical and moral evils of the world, which could not be, did they possess a considerate and benevolent state of mind.

(11.) Atheists triumph greatly, when in the infancy of any new form of science, any thing is discovered that *appears* to be inconsistent with the doctrine of Theism, but when fuller investigation has corrected their error, and science gives its unqualified testimony in favor of Theism, they are neither convinced nor silenced, but shift their ground and continue their cavils.

(12.) Atheism is the spirit of pedantry. It affects great learning. It professes to be philosophy itself.

(13.) Atheists affect to be independent thinkers, above vulgar prejudice; able to lay aside the shackles of early education and to think for themselves.

(14.) Atheists are impatient of the restraints of religion. They evidently want to be rid of the fear and the knowledge of God, and proudly say to Jehovah, "depart from us for we desire not the knowledge of thy ways."

(15.) Atheists seem determined to rid themselves of the idea of accountability. Theism lays restraints which they abhor upon their lusts. They rave, and madly break away from all reason and truth that they may serve their lusts.

(16.) Atheists reject as unreasonable whatever is *above* reason.

(17.) Atheists demand proof of first, and self-evident truths.

(18.) Atheists deify reason, while at the same time they set at naught its most solemn affirmations.

(19.) Atheists reject as unworthy of credit, whatever they cannot comprehend.

This they do when opposing Theism, but when supporting Atheism, they can swallow a universe of incomprehensibilities and absurdities.

(20.) Atheism is a disputatious spirit.

(21.) It is a spirit of opposition to the providence of God.

(22.) It is uniformly connected with a wicked life.

(23.) It is the spirit of political fanaticism, and always tends, and aims to overthrow all government.

(24.) It is a bloody, cruel, misanthropic spirit. Its history is written in the blood of the French revolution.

LECTURE VI.

DIVINE AUTHORITY OF THE BIBLE.

I will show,

First. That a farther revelation from God, than that which is made in the works of nature and providence is needed.

Second. That such a revelation is possible.

Third. That the partial revelation of God given in the works of creation and providence, renders a still farther revelation of himself probable.

Fourth. That the scriptures of the Old and New Testaments are a direct revelation from God.

Before entering upon the direct discussion of this subject, I will make several remarks upon the nature and degree of evidence to be expected in this case, if the Bible is, as it claims to be, a revelation from God.

1. Such evidence only is to be expected as the nature of the case admits. The divine authority of the Bible is a question of fact. It is a fact of remote antiquity. Facts of antiquity may be proved by contemporaneous history. In case any such history exists oral traditions are not admissible as evidence because they are not the best evidence which the nature of the case admits. Whenever a fact is of such remote antiquity as to have no contemporaneous history, in this case tradition may be received as the best evidence which the nature of the case admits. And when the tradition is manifestly ancient, unbroken, and uncontradicted either by facts or opposing traditions, it is good evidence, and amounts to proof.

2. The burden of proof is always on the affirmative side of the question, or on him who affirms a fact, until the fact is so established in the absence of counter proof, as to demand belief.

3. Where an objection is an affirmation, or consists in an alledged fact, it must be proved, or it is of no weight.. E. g.—If to the fact that the Bible is a revelation from God, it is objected that the Bible is the work of priestcraft, or a fabrication of political men for wicked purposes, this affirmation must be proved, or it can be of no weight.

4. A witness in order to establish a fact must be both competent and credible. Competency relates to the propriety of his being heard at all. A *competent* witness is one against whom there is no such objection as to exclude him altogether from being heard.

Credibility relates to the degree of credit to which the testimony of a witness is entitled. A *credible* witness is one whose testimony ought to be believed.

5. A *record* in order to be proof, must be both authentic and genuine. Its *authenticity* relates to its authorship. Until its authenticity be established, or that it was written by the author to whom it is ascribed, it is incompetent and cannot be received in evidence.

Its *genuineness* relates to its being either the original document, or a true copy, without material alterations or interpolations. The competency or credibility of any written document, depends of course, upon the competency and credibility of its author. If its author be competent and credible, and the authenticity and genuineness of the record be established, the record is then the best evidence which the nature of the case admits.

6. Where a record does not claim to be the original document, but only a genuine copy, an editorial, or explanatory remark, so situated as to be plainly distinguished from the body of the work itself, is not fatal or injurious; but may be rather confirmatory of the truth of the record.

7. If a record be made up of several independent documents, all

relating to the same subject, or compiled and collected and arranged in the order of a book, the credibility of the book is not at all diminished, by such additional remarks of the compiler as, while they can be easily distinguished from the words of the original authors, may yet be important in establishing their connection, and showing their mutual relations or dates.

The credibility of a witness is affected by his interest in the question at issue. If he testifies in favor of his own interest this detracts from his credibility. If he testifies against his own interest, this fact enhances the value of his testimony. This is also true of a letter or any other written document, where an author was interested in the question upon which he was writing. If he wrote on the side of his own interest, the credibility of what he writes, is affected as his oral testimony would be under the same circumstances. So also, if what he wrote was contrary to his interest, it enhances the value of his written as would be the case with his oral testimony.

9. Where there are several witnesses to a fact or collection of facts, there must be a substantial agreement among them, else they will destroy each other's testimony. If they flatly contradict each other in regard to the same facts, their testimony must go for nothing.

10. The same is true of written documents if they are adduced in proof of any fact or collection of facts, there must be a substantial agreement among them, or they do not amount to proof.

11. But such apparent discrepancies as demonstrate the absence of collusion among the witnesses or writers greatly strengthen the proof, if upon close examination it be found that the discrepancies are not real.

12. The proof of any fact or collection of facts is strengthened by the number of competent and credible witnesses testifying to the same fact or facts, or when one witness testifies to one fact, and another to another, if all the facts testified to are consistent with, or dependent upon each other.

13. Proof is greatly strengthened by the testimony of competent and credible witnesses to a great number of independent facts or incidents which, when compared together, are seen to be entirely consistent with each other.

14. The proof is still farther strengthened if these facts have extended through a series of years or centuries, have occurred at different places, and cover in the whole, a large extent of territory. These circumstances strengthen the proof because they forbid the idea of collusion or design on the part of those connected with these circumstances at the times and places when and where they occurred, to impose on the credulity of coming generations.

15. Any thing, and every thing that precludes the idea of collusion among the witnesses or writers, among whose statements or writings there is a substantial coincidence, gives weight to their testimony. Their agreement with each other, and with them-

selves, when they wrote at different places and periods, and under different circumstances, is always to be taken into the account as greatly strengthening the proof.

16. The absence of counter testimony when such testimony might be expected, if the affirmative of the question were not true, is a circumstance that strengthens the proof. E. g.: the utter absence of all counter testimony in regard to the resurrection of Jesus Christ, is a circumstance that greatly confirms the evidence of his resurrection, in as much as, that under the circumstances of the case, it is incredible that no counter testimony should exist, if, as a matter of fact he had not risen from the dead. Also the fact of the entire absence of all counter proof in respect to the authenticity, genuineness, and credibility of any book of the Bible, for it is utterly incredible that all the enemies of Christianity should be, and should always have been unable to disprove either the authenticity or genuineness of a single book of the Bible, if they were not authentic and genuine.

17. Cavils are not to set aside evidence, or even to be noticed, if it is plain that they are nothing but cavils.

18. The power of working miracles confers the highest competency and credibility upon the witness who professes to bring a revelation from God, as a well attested miracle can be nothing else than the seal or testimony of God to the truth of what he asserts.

19. The well attested record of a miracle is as good evidence of the fact of the miracle, as the testimony of eye witnesses would be.

20. The spirit of Prophecy, or the foretelling of future events which actually come to pass, and which none but God could have foreknown, is conclusive evidence, that the prophet bears a revelation from God.

I come now to the direct discussion of the subject.

First. *A farther revelation from God than that made in the works of creation and providence, is needed.*

1. As a matter of fact the true God was known in this world, to a very limited extent. Even the greatest and wisest of men had but very little if any right knowledge of the true God.

2. The way of salvation for sinners, could not be known by the light of nature, and consequently a revelation that would convey this knowledge was imperiously demanded.

3. As a matter of fact, there was no such knowledge among men, as could sanctify them and fit them for heaven.

4. The greatest philosophers on earth felt themselves to be altogether in the dark in regard to that kind of service which God would accept, and altogether doubtful whether God could by any possibility forgive sin.

5. The state of the entire heathen world, even the most learned and polished nations of both ancient and modern times, demonstrates that without the Bible, the light of nature does not as a matter of fact, make men holy.

6. If men never have been, in any nation or generation, made holy without a direct revelation of the will of God to men, it is not at all likely that they ever will be, and therefore certain that a farther revelation from God is needed.

SECOND. *A revelation from God is possible.*

This seems to be true *a priori*, and is therefore to be taken for granted till the contrary be proved. That God, who made mankind, should be able to communicate his will to them, seems to be self-evident, and until the contrary be proved, is to be taken for granted.

THIRD. *The partial revelation made in the works of God, rendered a farther revelation probable.*

1. The benevolence of God as manifested in the works of creation and providence, renders it probable that he would make a farther revelation to mankind.

2. Our moral constitution is such, that we are as a matter of fact, capable of indefinite moral improvement. And as the light of nature does not secure the moral perfection of which our nature is capable, it is unreasonable to suppose that the author of our nature would leave us without higher and more efficient means of improvement. And as these means of improvement could be nothing else than a more perfect knowledge of himself and of his will, such a revelation was highly probable.

3. The great ignorance of mankind, taken in connection with their great necessities and their great desire to know more of the universe and of its author, rendered it highly probable that such a revelation would be given. This was felt, and even predicted by some of the wisest heathen philosophers.

4. The notices in nature both within and without us of moral government—that men are the subjects of moral law, and are going forward to a state of retribution, when properly considered, are calculated to beget the expectation of a farther revelation from God than was contained in the works of creation and providence.

5. The notices within us of our own immortality, being so great as to beget the general conviction that we are immortal, also rendered it highly probable that some more definite revelation in relation to the will of God and the future destiny of man would be given.

6. More especially, the universal consciousness of sin, that has every where manifested itself in all ages and nations, and the great perplexity and ignorance of mankind in regard to its first existence in this world, its desert, and whether it could be forgiven, and on what conditions, and what would be the consequence if unrepented of and unforgiven, not only rendered a further revelation necessary, but highly probable.

FOURTH. *The Scriptures are a Revelation from God.*

Under this head I am to show,

I. The Authenticity of the Bible.

II. Its Genuineness.

III. Its Credibility.

I. *The Authenticity of the Bible.*

I will begin with the authenticity of the New Testament, for if this can be established it will render the proof of the authenticity of the Old Testament more easy and convincing.

1. Here as there is contemporaneous history, that is the best proof which the nature of the case admits, that the several books of the New Testament were written by the authors to whom they are ascribed. It will not be expected that in a mere skeleton, I should give quotations from history. In this skeleton form I can only say, that it is the universal testimony of contemporary historians both Christian and Infidel, that those books were written by the authors to whom they are ascribed. By contemporary historians, I mean those who wrote either at, or immediately subsequent to the time, in which these writings purport to have been written. It is certain from these historians, both infidel and christian, that the several books of the New Testament were then in existence, that they were the reputed writings of the authors whose names they bear, and that these men were universally understood to be their authors.

2. It is agreed by the best judges of the Greek language, that the New Testament must have been written by *native* Jews, at the very time when it purports to have been written. It is written in Hebraistic Greek. None but a Jew who had been brought up in Palestine could have written this dialect, nor could such Jews have written it, before about the time at which it purports to have been written; because, until about that time, the Jews who were natives of Palestine did not understand Greek. Nor could it have been written in Hebraistic Greek, by any generation subsequent to the Apostles, as after the destruction of Jerusalem the Hebraistic Greek ceased to be used.

3. Another consideration that goes to establish the authenticity of the books of the New Testament is, that they are writings of such a nature as would not have been unjustly claimed from ambitious motives by ambitious men. Nor would they have been claimed for ambitious men by their particular friends.

4. The absence of all counter testimony in relation to the authenticity of the New Testament is a strong, and it would seem, conclusive evidence in support of its authenticity, as it would seem utterly incredible that no evidence should exist that these books were written by other than their reputed authors, if that had been in fact the case.

5. Had it been possible the Jews, and jarring Christian sects, would have impeached the authenticity of these books; and the

fact that they have not, and especially that the Jews have not, who were highly interested to do so, and who possessed every possible advantage for doing so, were the thing possible in itself, amounts to a demonstration that these books are authentic.

6. The authenticity of such of them as could be questioned, has been denied, and ample proof has been adduced to substantiate their authenticity.

Particulars respecting the authenticity of each particular book belong more properly to the department of Biblical Literature. What has been said must suffice in respect to the authenticity of the New Testament as a whole.

II. *The Genuineness of the Bible.*

I will next establish the genuineness of the New Testament, after which it may be properly introduced in proof of the authenticity and genuineness of the Old Testament. The credibility of the two Testaments, will be discussed at the same time.

The New Testament which we now have, does not claim to be the original document, but only purports to be a true copy of the original. That it is so, will appear:

1. From the fact, that the various jarring Christian sects which have existed from the time of their publication, would at once have detected any material addition to, subtraction from, or alteration of them.

2. The enemies of Christianity, especially the Jews, and infidels, have always been on the watch, and would have instantly detected any material alterations in those writings.

3. Among thirty thousand manuscript copies of the New Testament, not a single material alteration or omission can be found.

4. Any redundant book or passage would have created confusion. The Apocryphal books are an illustration of this. Those books contain doctrines and state facts, inconsistent with each other, with the rest of the Bible, and with other facts of which we have the most ample proof. This is as might be expected, were any books to set up the claim of a divine revelation, that were not so in fact.

5. The genuineness of the New Testament is established by the fact, that nearly every sentence of it is quoted by one and another of the early friends and enemies of Christianity. And from their quotations it is certain that the text was then just what it is now, as the words as they are found in our Testament exactly correspond with those quotations.

I will now examine the authenticity of the Old Testament.

1. Of the Pentateuch, or of the five books ascribed to Moses. Here I observe, that there is no cotemporaneous history, as these books were in existence long before any written history that has come down to us. Tradition, therefore, previous to all history, is the best evidence the nature of the case admits. And as this tradi-

tion is manifestly as ancient as the writings themselves, and universal among the Jews, and uniform, it amounts to the most convincing proof. For tradition uniformly ascribes the five books of the Pentateuch to Moses as their author.

2. The earliest Jewish writings which we have confirm this tradition. The Prophets are unvarying in their testimony, that Moses was the author of the Pentateuch. Christ also, and all the writers of the New Testament confirm this tradition, and bear an unvarying testimony to this truth.

3. Josephus, and all Jewish historians, as far back as they go, bear their unequivocal testimony to the authenticity of the Pentateuch.

4. There is no counter testimony, either traditionary or historical; which is unaccountable, and it would seem impossible, if Moses were not the real author of these books. What has been adduced then is good proof, and sufficient to establish such a fact in a court of law.

I will examine the authenticity of the other books of the Old Testament.

1. It is not pretended that the authors of every part of the Old Testament were certainly known. Nor is it to be expected, that writings of such very remote antiquity, and in a case in which there is little or no cotemporary history, should all be traced with exact certainty to their real authors. But that these books were all compiled, and of course received by inspired men, is a fact of which there is, to say the least, satisfactory evidence. There are two traditions among the Jews which are easily reconcilable with each other, that seem to set this subject in a satisfactory point of view. One tradition is that the books were compiled by Ezra; and the other tradition is, that they were compiled by Nehemiah. From all the circumstances of the case the probability is, that they were both concerned in their compilation.

2. All Jewish history, so far as I know, accords with these traditions.

3. Josephus mentions all the books of the Old Testament as canonical, and in the order in which they occur in our Bible.

4. Christ and his Apostles confirm their authenticity.

5. The Jews have been and are interested to impeach the authenticity of the books of the Old Testament, as they are appealed to by Christians to establish the Messiahship of Christ. The Jews certainly possessed the most ample opportunities and means of impeaching the authenticity of these books, if such a thing were possible, and in their controversy with Christians, they have been in the highest degree interested to do so; and the fact that they have not done so, amounts almost to a demonstration, that those books are really authentic.

Let me now examine the GENUINENESS of the books of the Old Testament.

1. The jarring sects among the Jews, who held various systems of philosophy, and of course gave a different interpretation of many passages of the sacred oracles, would naturally and certainly have detected any material alteration in them, had any such thing occurred, either by accident or design.

2. The Jews always used extreme caution in preserving their sacred writings from corruption or alteration. They numbered the lines, and words, and letters of every book, and kept such records, as would show the exact middle word or letter of every book. And to many such like devices did they have recourse, to prevent the possibility of alteration by any transcriber, either by accident or design.

3. The New Testament abundantly establishes the genuineness of the Old. Christ repeatedly rebuked the Jews, for their unwritten traditions, many of which were inconsistent with the letter and spirit of their sacred writings; but in no case did he complain of them for having adulterated the scriptures themselves, He uniformly speaks of the writings of the Old Testament as they existed in his day, as being genuine. The Apostles follow his example, and confirm abundantly the genuineness of the different books of the Old Testament.

III. *The Credibility of the Bible.*

I will now establish the credibility of both Testaments. This may be done by evidence both external and internal.

1. That the writers were competent witnesses, or so circumstanced as that nothing can be alledged as a reason why their testimony should not be received, is beyond dispute.

2. The credibility of the writers, or that they were men of good character, is not that I know of called in question.

3. The authenticity then of these books is presumptive evidence of their credibility.

4. Their genuineness is also presumptive evidence of their credibility, as it shows:

(1.) The high and sacred regard in which they were held by those who possessed them, and who possessed the highest means of judging, whether they were or were not a revelation from God.

(2.) Their genuineness is evidence of their credibility, inasmuch as it manifests a direct providence in preserving them from loss and interpolations.

5. Universal tradition anterior to history, of such events as might be expected to be thus preserved; e. g. the deluge, and the preservation of one family, in a vessel or ark. It is found to be true, that in every part of the world traditionary accounts of this event are preserved.

6. Geology confirms the Mosaic account of creation, when that account is rightly understood.

7. The credibilty of the scriptures is confirmed, by the advance of various sciences, and by those sciences too, which in the infancy

of their existence threatened to develop facts, inconsistent with the credibility of the Bible. But the greater maturity of those sciences shows that they are all confirmatory of the truth of the sacred writings.

8. There are no opposing facts; i. e. there is no established fact of history or science, that militates against any fact or doctrine of the Bible. And that this should be so is wholly incredible, were not the Bible true.

9. History by both friends and enemies, as far back as it goes, confirms the credibility of the Bible.

10. It is said that the records of the Roman Empire confirm the principal facts in relation to the death and resurrection of Christ, and many other things recorded in the Bible.

11. The *existence* of the ordinances of both Testaments, is evidence that they must have been instituted at the time, and for the purposes at which and for which the Bible asserts them to have been instituted.

Almost innumerable other external evidences might be adduced; but—

I pass to examine some of the internal evidences of their credibility.

1. Prophecy. The agreement of prophecy with the facts of history is admitted. But it is said that the prophecies were written after the facts occurred. To this I answer:

(1.) That there is abundant proof to the contrary.

(2.) Many of the most important prophecies are now fulfilling and to be fulfilled. These prophecies were written many hundred, and some of them many thousand years since, and cannot therefore, by any possibility, have been written after the occurrence of the facts which they predicted.

(3.) Many of these prophecies were of such a nature as to render it utterly impossible for any one but God to foresee and foretell them. Prophecy, then, with its fulfillment, is conclusive evidence of the credibility of the Bible.

2 Miracles. The miracles recorded in the Bible are admitted as facts; but, by the enemies of revelation are ascribed to delusion, or to infernal agency. It is said that Roman Catholics and the heathen have recorded miracles, in attestation of the truths of their religion. I answer:

(1.) These pretended miracles are all widely different, in kind and circumstances, from those recorded in the Bible. They are not well established by proof. They were not wrought under such circumstances as to render delusion and deception impossible. There is not one of them that can compare with the miracles of Christ and his Apostles, or with the fact of the resurrection of Christ from the dead.

(2.) The gift of languages is another miracle, between which and the pretended miracles in support of other religions, there is no analogy. Miracles are nothing else than the seal of God to that truth, in confirmation of which they are wrought. See Heb. 2:4: "God also *bearing them witness*, both with signs and wonders, and divers miracles, and gifts of the Holy Ghost, according to his own will."

3. There is a substantial and marvelous agreement among a great number of writers, recording a great number of facts, extended through a great number of years and spread over a great extent of territory.

4. There are such apparent, and yet not real discrepancies, among them, as to forbid the supposition of any collusion or common design among them to deceive their readers.

5. The integrity and manifest disinterestedness of the writers, in recording their own faults, are evidence of their credibility.

6. They could have no conceivable motive to impose upon mankind. They certainly could gain nothing earthly by it. And it is absurd to suppose that they could hope to gain a heavenly inheritance, by inducing mankind to believe a lie.

7. They were not only not interested to impose upon mankind, but were in the highest degree interested not to publish those writings especially, if they were untrue. Their publishing those doctrines was certain to make them great trouble in this world, and, if untrue, to bring down the wrath of God upon them in the next.

8. Their circumstances, their lives, and death, attest the sincerity of the writers, and that they really believed what they wrote to be true.

9. The facts were of such a nature, as that they could not be deceived in respect to their truth. They could be inspected by all their senses. The miracles which they recorded were not wrought in darkness, nor in secret, nor in the presence of only a few friends. They were performed in the most public manner and in the presence of all classes of persons. They were so various and of such a nature as to preclude the possibility of deception.

10. There is a marvelous internal correspondence, between these writings and all known facts of history, and philosophy, natural, mental, and moral.

11. The recorded facts are many of them confirmed by various and wide spread traditions, ancient medals, and inscriptions, confirmatory of their truth.

12. Another internal evidence of the truth of the Bible is its agreement with our moral nature and consciousness. Did it contradict our consciousness, or the express affirmations of our reason, we could not believe it. But it most perfectly accords with both; which is a most unaccountable circumstance, upon any other supposition than that the Bible is a revelation from God.

13. The Bible exactly describes the character of man, as established by the history of the world, and explains the otherwise inexplicable mystery of his present condition.

14. Another evidence of the credibility of the Bible is found in the fact, that it is exactly suited to the character and wants of mankind.

15. The Bible places the salvation of men upon a rational and practicable foundation, by rendering forgiveness consistent with a due administration of justice, and at the same time providing adequate means for the reformation of men.

16. The exact accordance between the facts and doctrines of the Bible and the works of creation, is a strong evidence that they both have the same Author.

17. The system of moral government revealed in the Bible, ought to be, and must be the law and government of God.

18. It explains and reconciles the providence of God, and the moral condition of this world, with his character and attributes as manifested in creation.

19. Its tendency to promote good morals, to support good and overthrow evil governments, are facts which strongly confirm its truth.

20. The tendency of the doctrines of the Bible to beget a happy life and a peaceful death, is felt and acknowledged by infidels themselves. It is a contradiction to say that falsehood could produce these effects. Falsehood is what is contrary to the nature and reality of things. But such effects can be ascribed only to what is according to the nature and reality of things, and therefore the Bible must be true.

21. The exact accordance of the Bible with the doctrines of natural religion when properly understood, is demonstration of its credibility.

22. The success of the gospel demonstrates its adaptedness to overthrow whatever is false, and contrary to nature and reality, and this is demonstration of its truth.

23. It challenges investigation, and triumphs in proportion to the scrutiny it receives.

24. The Bible was written by good men or bad men. If by good men, it is what it professes to be; for good men would not lie. If by bad men, then wicked men understood spiritual subjects, devised a system of religion sufficiently spiritual and powerful, and in such exact accordance with the nature and relations of things, as to overthrow all error and sin, and were the perfection of reformers and benefactors of mankind.

25. Many facts were published which might have been and certainly would have been disproved, if untrue, by both Jews and Gentiles. The miracles and resurrection of Christ, and the miracles of the Apostles, among the Gentiles, could have been and would have been disproved if untrue.

26. The writers of the Bible mention many facts as having occurred among those to whom they wrote, of which facts they must have had knowledge, or have known that the writers' statements were false.

27. The Acts of the Apostles is or was perhaps the most easily disproved, if untrue, of any book in the world. Yet no one fact, among the great number recorded in that book, has been disproved.

28. The numerous and manifestly undesigned coincidences of the Epistles and the Acts of the Apostles, strongly corroborate the truth of both.

29. The entire agreement of the two Testaments with each other, considering the circumstances of the case, is strongly confirmatory of their credibility.

30. The standing and increasing evidence from the fulfillment of prophecy, seems to put the credibility of the Bible beyond dispute.

REMARKS:

1. If this testimony does not establish the truth and divine authority of the Bible, there is an end of attempting to establish any thing by evidence.

2. If all this testimony can exist and yet the Bible fail to be true, it is the greatest miracle in the universe.

3. If the Bible be true, every thing is plain, and the whole mystery of our existence and circumstances is explained. If the Bible is untrue we are all afloat. The existence of the universe, the existence, and character, and destiny of man, are highly enigmatical, and we are left in the most distressing darkness and uncertainty, in regard to every thing which we need to know.

LECTURE VII.

INSPIRATION OF THE BIBLE.

FIRST. What is not implied in the inspiration of the Bible.
SECOND. What is implied in it.
THIRD. How a question of this kind cannot be proved.
FOURTH. How it can be proved.
FIFTH. Prove that the Bible is an inspired book.
SIXTH. Answer objections.

FIRST. *What is not implied in the inspiration of the Bible.*

1. It is not implied in the inspiration of the Bible, that the several writers received every thing which they recorded by direct revelation from God. Many things which they recorded may have been known by them, irrespective of divine inspiration. In these cases inspiration was concerned only in directing them what to write and how to write.

2. The inspiration of the scriptures does not imply that the writers were passive instruments, without using their own powers of moral agency in writing.

3. It does not imply that the sacred writers did not preserve their own style and peculiar manner of writing and expressing their thoughts, for this would naturally be true under the direction of the omniscient Spirit of God, whether he merely suggested the thoughts, and left them to the selection of their own words, or whether he suggested the words as well as the thoughts. For in employing human agency, it is as easy for the Spirit of God to conform himself entirely to the habits, education, and natural style of the writer, as to dictate in any other manner. And this would be just what we should expect him to do, to accommodate himself to the habits of that mind which he employed, rather than to set aside those habits.

4. Nor does the inspiration of the sacred writers imply, that they recorded no circumstance of comparatively little importance; for if they were really inspired by the omniscient God, it might be expected that they would write in a very natural and easy manner. And if the connection or circumstances demanded it, that they would mention some things which in themselves are of comparatively little importance.

5. Nor does the inspiration of the Bible imply that no various readings have crept into the text through the carelessness of transcribers.

6. Nor does it imply, that every part of the Bible is equally intelligible to beings in our circumstances.

7. Nor does it imply, that we shall be able infallibly to understand in this age of the world, every thing which they wrote.

8. Nor does it imply, that the writers themselves understood, in all cases, the import of what they wrote.

9. Nor that the different writers would of course notice the same particulars in recording the same transaction. For in relating the same occurrence, some might naturally notice some particulars of the transaction and others other particulars.

10. Nor that we may not, in our circumstances, find some difficulty in some instances in reconciling the different writers with each other. But—

SECOND. *The inspiration of the Bible does imply:*

1. That there is a real substantial agreement among all the writers, and that when rightly understood, they do not in any thing contradict each other.

2. It implies, that the several writers always wrote under such a degree of divine illumination and guidance, whether of suggestion, elevation, or superintendence as to be infallibly secured from all error.

3. That they not only wrote nothing false, but that they communicated authoritatively the mind and will of God.

THIRD. *How not proved.*

1. A question of this kind cannot be settled by an appeal to tradition.

2. Nor by an appeal to history.

3. Nor by an appeal to the miraculous power of the writers, independently of their own assertions in respect to their inspiration. Miracles are God's testimony that what they say is true. But the question is, what do they say?

4. Nor can this question be settled by the assertion of the several writers, unless they were endued with miraculous powers. It has been common in every age of the world, for men to be deceived in regard to their own inspiration. Should those writers therefore insist upon their own inspiration, and should their perfect honesty be admitted, it would not conclusively prove their inspiration of God, without the power of miracles, for they might be deceived.

5. The inspiration of the Bible cannot be proved by any appeal to the elevated and what might seem to us super-human style, in which different parts of it may be written; for that might seem super-human to us, which after all was only the effect of a highly excited though natural state of mind.

6. Nor can the inspiration of the Bible be proved by an appeal to the doctrines it contains.

7. Nor can it be proved, independently of the style and doctrines. Both the style of the sacred writers, and their doctrines, may be and ought to be taken into the account, in the discussion and decision of this question. But neither of them by itself would amount to proof. For if the dotrines were true, and it were admitted that they are the truths of God, it would no more prove the inspiration of the writers of the Bible, than the fact that thousands of other men have written the truths of God, would prove that they were inspired.

FOURTH. *How this question can be proved.*

1. The question in respect to the inspiration of the Bible is not a controversy with professed infidels, but with Unitarians, and those who profess to believe the truth of the Bible.

2. In discussing this subject with them, the authenticity, genuineness, and credibility of the Bible may be taken for granted.

3. The integrity of the several writers may also be taken for granted.

4. Not only may these things be taken for granted, but let it be remembered, that in the preceding lecture, on the divine authority of the Bible, these points have also been proved.

I will now remark, that the proof of this question may be made out with entire satisfaction, by showing:

1. That Christ promised his Apostles both the gift of miracles and of inspiration.

2. They actually possessed miraculous power.

3. They affirm their own inspiration.

4. Their admitted honesty.

5. Their style.

6. Their doctrines.

7. The prophecies which they uttered.

8. Their substantial agreement with each other and with all known facts in history and science.

9. The purity, power, and success of their writings. These, when put and viewed together, will amount to a conclusive argument in favor of the inspiration of the scriptures.

FIFTH. *Prove that the Bible is an inspired book.*

1. By referring to the promises of Christ, when He first sent the Apostles forth to publish his religion. Mat. 10: 19, 20: "But when they deliver you up, take no thought how or what ye shall speak; for it shall be given you in that same hour what ye shall speak. For it is not ye that speak, but the Spirit of your Father which speaketh in you."

2. When he gave them their commission. Luke 12: 11, 12.

3. When he predicted the destruction of Jerusalem. Mark 13: 1. Luke 21: 14–15.

4. In his last address to his disciples, in the 14th and 16th chapters of John.

5. Christ promised that the Spirit should reveal to them many things which he had not taught them. John 16: 12–15.

6. He promised that the Holy Spirit should instruct them in every thing. John 18: 26.

7. That he should reveal to them future events. John 16: 13.

8. That he would give them all the instruction they should need as Apostles and publishers of his religion. John 16: 12, & 14: 26, & 14: 17, & 15: 26, 27, & 16: 13.

9. Christ endued the Apostles with miraculous powers. Mat. 10: 1. Mark 16: 15, 17, 18. Luke 9: 1.

II. By the Apostles and writers of the New Testament.

1. The writers of the New Testament unqualifiedly assert their own inspiration, and God confirms their testimony by miracles. Gal. 1: 11, 12. 1 Cor. 2: 10, 12, 13, & 14: 37. 2 Cor. 2: 17. 1 Thess. 2: 13, & 4: 8. 1 John 4: 6.

2. The writers of the New Testament put their own writings upon a level with those of the prophets and Old Testament writers. Eph. 2: 20. 2 Pet. 3: 15, 16.

3. It has been generally admitted, that the oral instructions of the Apostles were inspired. But they considered their writings as of the same authority with their oral instructions John 20: 31. 1 John 1: 1–4. 2 Thess. 2: 15. 1 Cor. 15: 1. Eph. 3: 3. Acts 15: 28.

4. They consider their own writings as of such high authority that an unqualified reception of them and obedience to them, is every where made by them an indispensable condition of salvation.

5. The belief that the Old Testament was given by inspiration

of God was universal among the Jews, and Christ and the Apostles invariably confirm this opinion. Luke 24 : 27, 44. 2 Pet. 1 : 21. 2 Tim. 3 : 16.

6. They speak of the Old Testament as the word of God. This is so common with them that I need not cite instances.

7. Christ and the Apostles speak of the entire Old Testament as of equal authority ; quoting from all parts of the Old Testament, as from the word of God.

8. The Old Testament writings are called the commandments, testimonies, and ordinances of the Lord.

9. Every act of obedience or disobedience to the Old Testament writers, is considered by Christ and the Apostles as obedience or disobedience to God.

10. There is not an instance in which Christ or the Apostles intimate that a single sentence of the Old Testament is either spurious or uninspired.

11. This is incredible if both Christ and his Apostles did not regard the Old Testament as given by the inspiration of God.

12. It was also dishonest in them thus to treat those writings, if they were not what they were supposed by the Jews to be.

13. In addition to what has been said, let it be remembered that the strict integrity of the writers of the New Testament is admitted and if it were not, it is so apparent on the very face of their writings that it could not reasonably be questioned.

14. Add to this the fact that the style in which the scriptures are written, entirely favors the idea of their inspiration.

15. The doctrines contained in the Bible, must, to say the least, many of them have been given by inspiration, either to the Apostles, or to those from whom they received them, as without a direct revelation from God they could not have been known to men.

16. The prophecies both of the Old and New Testaments are a demonstration of the inspiration of the writers so far as those parts of scripture are concerned.

17. There is beyond all contradiction a substantial agreement among all the writers of the Bible with each other, and with all known facts.

18. The purity, power, and success of the gospel, is corroborative of their claim to inspiration.

These facts when taken together seem to establish the inspiration of the scriptures, beyond doubt.

SIXTH. *Answer objections.*

I. *Objection.* It is objected that Mark and Luke were not Apostles, and therefore the promises of inspiration and of miraculous power, did not extend to them.

Answer.

1. That these promises of miraculous power, and of inspiration were not confined to the Apostles, is evident from the fact that

multitudes besides the Apostles, actually possessed the power of working miracles, and doubtless the gift of inspiration.

2. The gospels of Mark and Luke must have been written under the eye of the Apostles. Or at least the Apostles must have been familiar with them, as Luke was the companion of Paul, and I believe it is generally conceded that Mark was the companion of Peter.

3. If the Apostles had not approved and confirmed these gospels, they could not have been so universally received by the Church as of divine authority from the very first. This seems to be evident from the fact that so many gospels or histories of Christ were at that time rejected by the Church as not inspired.

These considerations are to my own mind satisfactory in regard to these gospels.

II. *Objection.* It is objected, that the Apostles seldom make any direct claim to inspiration.

Answer.

This is easily accounted for by the fact that their claims were already so abundantly established as to render the frequent assertion of their inspiration, not only unnecessary, but improper, inasmuch as it would have had the appearance, either of ostentation or of suspicion that their claim to inspiration was doubtful.

III. *Objection.* It is objected, that Paul, in some instances, seems to declare that he was not inspired.

1 Cor. 7: 10, 12, 25, 40.—"And unto the married I command, yet not I, but the Lord."—"But to the rest speak I, not the Lord." —"Now concerning virgins, I have no commandment of the Lord: yet I give my judgment, as one that hath obtained mercy of the Lord to be faithful."—"And I think also that I have the Spirit of God." 2 Cor. 8: 8, 10, 11, 17.—"I speak not by commandment, but by occasion of the forwardness of others, and to prove the sincerity of your love."—"And herein I give my advice."—

Upon these passages I remark,

1. If Paul really intended to notify his readers that in these instances, he did not write under the influence of a divine inspiration, it greatly confirms the fact of his actual inspiration in all other cases. For why should he be so careful in these particular instances, to guard his readers against the supposition that he spoke by divine authority, if in other cases, he did not in fact do so.

2. But Paul might, and probably did mean nothing more in these instances than that the Lord had given no express command in respect to these particulars, as no universal rule in relation to such matters could be adopted in the then circumstances of the Church, and that he therefore, as an inspired Apostle, did not mean to give a command in the name of the Lord, but simply give his inspired advice as one who had the Spirit of the Lord.

3. In 2 Cor. 11: 17, he says, "That which I speak, I speak it

not after the Lord, but as it were foolishly, in this confidence of boasting."

The Apostle seems here to have meant that he felt embarrassed by the circumstances under which they had placed him, and was constrained therefore to speak not after the example of the Lord, in respect to speaking in his own defence, but was obliged to speak as it were foolishly, as if he were a confident boaster. This does not imply that he did not consider himself inspired, but that his inspiration made it necessary under the circumstances, for him to say what might appear immodest, and as inconsistent with christian humility.

REMARKS.

1. The question of the inspiration of the Bible, is one of the highest importance to the Church and to the world.

2. The necessities of the Church plainly demand an authoritative, and unerring standard, to which they can appeal in all matters of faith and practice.

3. Those who have called in question the plenary inspiration of the Bible, have, sooner or later, frittered away nearly all that is essential to the christian religion.

4. Our faith in the divine inspiration of the Bible is so abundantly supported by evidence, that every christian should be able to give a reason for his confidence in its inspiration.

LECTURE VIII.

DEISM.

FIRST. Define Deism.
SECOND. Notice the different classes of Deists.
THIRD. Notice their principal objections to Christianity.
FOURTH. Consider some of the difficulties of Deism.

FIRST. *Define Deism.*

Deism is Godism, in opposition to no God or Atheism. The name Deist originated in France and was assumed by a class of infidels to avoid the stigma of Atheism.

SECOND. *Different classes of Deists.*

Although there are several modifications of Deism, they are, by their own writers, divided into two classes, and called mortal and immortal Deists. The mortal Deists admit the existence of God, but deny his providential and moral government, the immortality of the soul,the distinction between virtue and vice, and of course future rewards and punishments, and, for the most part, nearly all the doctrines of natural religion. The immortal Deists profess a belief in all these. The peculiarity of all Deists is their rejection of Christianity and of the Bible as a revelation from God. They agree in discarding all pretences to divine revelation as either imposture or enthusiasm.

THIRD. *Their principal Objections to Christianity.*

Obj. I. They object that a revelation is unnecessary; that the powers of the human mind are such, and the light of nature so abundant, as to render any farther revelation of the character and will of God wholly unnecessary. This objection has been sufficiently answered in the preceding lecture. I will only add here, that the true question is not what the human mind, aided by the light of nature, is capable of doing, but what it really has done. Not what men might do were they disposed, but what they really have done in searching out the character and will of God, and in conforming themselves to it.

Obj. II. Another objection is, that a direct revelation from God, is highly improbable. To this I have already sufficiently replied in the preceding lecture.

Obj. III. Another objection is that a direct revelation is impossible—that God is a Spirit, and that man is either wholly material or, at least shut up to the necessity of receiving all his ideas from sensation, and that as God is neither visible nor tangible—as he cannot approach our minds through the medium of our senses, he has no means of communicating directly with our minds, and that therefore a direct revelation, were it necessary, is impossible. To this I reply,

1. It is mere assumption. It is true that we receive our ideas of sensible objects from sensation, but it is not true that we can have no idea of spiritual beings except through sensation.

2. It is not only a gratuitous assumption, that God cannot communicate with minds because he is not a material being, but it is highly absurd. The very fact that he is a spirit, and not a material being, gives him direct access to our minds without either the formality or the difficulty of approaching our minds through our senses.

Obj. IV. Another objection is that there are so many pretended revelations from God, and they differ so fundamentally in their character, that it is the safest and most reasonable course to reject them all as unworthy of credit. To this I reply,

1. That counterfeits imply true coin.

2. That among all the pretended revelations from God, there is not one except our Bible whose claims are of any serious consider-

ation—whose external or internal evidences are of any serious weight.

3. The very fact that so many pretended revelations have been made and received by great portions of mankind, shows how universally mankind have felt the necessity of a divine revelation, and how important it is that a true one should be made.

4. Any thing like a diligent inquiry, would satisfy Deists themselves that there is no analogy between the other professed revelations from God with which the world has abounded, and that contained in the Bible.

5. I believe it is now generally admitted by Deists themselves, that the claims of all other books as pretended revelations from God, are frivolous, and of no account, when compared with the claims and evidences of the christian Bible, as a divine revelation.

6. Hence, their efforts are aimed to overthrow the Bible, and not to discredit other pretended revelations from God.

To the Bible they object,

(1.) That the different books, especially of the Old Testament, are not well authenticated. To this I reply, that it is not pretended that we are acquainted with the name of the particular writer of every book of the Old Testament. Nor is this to be expected. As there is no contemporaneous history, it is not at all wonderful that we should not be certain of the names of the writers or compilers of all these books. The same objection would lie with equal force, against the poems of Homer or the history of Herodotus.

Again, so far as history and tradition go, they are uniform in their testimony in respect to the authenticity and genuineness of those books, the names of whose authors Christians pretend to know.

These books often refer to each other, and to the names of their authors.

Christ and his Apostles uniformly acknowledged them both as authentic and genuine, i. e.: they quoted the Pentateuch as the writings of Moses, the Prophets, the Psalms, &c. as so many parts of divine revelation, thus leaving their impressive testimony to the genuineness of the books of the Old Testament.

(2.) They object to the Bible, that if these books were originally written by the authors to whom they were ascribed, they have become so mutilated by transcribers, so many interpolations and various readings have been introduced as to destroy their credibility.

This has been sufficiently answered in the preceding lecture, but I would here just add, that as a matter of fact, the preservation of the integrity of the text of our Bible, may, when all the circumstances are taken into the account, be justly considered as one of the wonders of the world. That in thirty thousand manuscript copies which have been collected and collated, there should not be one material omission, interpolation, or alteration, is certainly matter of astonishment, and gratitude.

(3.) They object that the different books which compose the

Bible contradict each other. This objection is founded in a very superficial view and consideration of the contents of the Bible. It has been so often and so ably considered, that I need not in this place enter into a critical examination of those particular parts and passages that have been objected to as inconsistent with each other.

(4.) They object to the Bible, that the writers give names to places by which they were not called until after the time when they purport to have been written.

To this I reply, that there are a few instances, in the Old Testament, in which places are called by names by which they were not called at the time when those parts of the Bible purport to have been written. But when this matter is well considered, it does not in the least degree detract from the credibility of these writings. They were written for the benefit of the Jews, and of the world. And passed from time to time under the review of succeeding inspired writers. When therefore, the name of any place was changed, either an inspired or an uninspired transcriber might insert the more modern name of the place alluded to for the benefit of the reader without at all impairing the integrity of the text. Indeed, this is just what might be expected, and what might have been, and plainly must have been of great importance.

(5.) They object, that there are passages found in it which could not have been written by the reputed authors of those books in which they are found. In the Pentateuch, e. g., the death of Moses is recorded, which plainly could not have been written by Moses himself. To this it may be replied, that such passages are so plainly the work of a compiler, as not at all to impair the integrity of the text, any more than if the compiler had said: "Now this passage was written by me, and not by Moses." It was never pretended that every word found in the Bible, was written by the authors to whom the various books were ascribed. It is cheerfully admitted that a few such interpolations as the one above alluded to, are found in different parts of the Bible, and are plainly the notes of a compiler. But still it is reasonably insisted that as these interpolations are easily distinguished from the original text, they in no degree, detract from the credibility of the original text.

(6.) They object that Geology and several other sciences demonstrate that the books of Moses cannot be true. They array Geology against the Mosaic account of the creation. And to the fact that the whole human race sprung from one pair as is recorded by Moses, they object that the great diversity of human languages and complexions, demonstrates that the human race could not have descended from one pair. To their objection on the ground of Geology it is replied; that if Geology really deserves the name of a science, and can really be depended upon as truth, its developments rather confirm than discredit the Mosaic account of creation, when that account is properly understood. And with respect to the objection founded in the diversity of complexions and languages, it may be replied, That the Bible itself gives an account of the confusion and division of the languages of the earth.

That a more extended and recent examination and classification of the languages of the earth, have already rendered it almost certain as a matter of fact, that the languages of the earth were originally one.

And as to the diversity of complexions among mankind, they can be accounted for in the most philosophical manner, by the different habits of mankind, in connection with the different climates in which they reside. These truths have been shown most satisfactorily.

(7.) They object that the Bible contains precepts unjust and unworthy of God, e. g.: Such as the command to the Israelites utterly to exterminate their enemies, men, women, and children. To this it may be replied,

a. That as to the adults of those nations thus devoted to destruction, God had a right to destroy them for their sins by whatever instrumentality he pleased.

b. If all those were to be destroyed whose sins deserved destruction, it was rather an act of kindness than otherwise to destroy with them the infants, inasmuch as they would be left entirely without protection or support.

c. It cannot be shown, nor is it probable that the infant children were sent to hell, but from the known character of God it is highly probable that their being cut off was a great mercy to them, and the means of their eternal salvation. If so God did them no injustice, but showed them an infinite kindness.

d. It may be observed that in giving the commandment to destroy their enemies, He made the Israelites the instruments of executing his own justice upon his enemies. But he gave them no liberty to do this in a wrong spirit, or in any other temper than that of entire benevolence. And it is as certain, and as reasonable to suppose that they might do this in a good spirit, as that any executioner might take the life of any victim of justice without ill-will or malicious feeling.

(8.) They object that the Bible contains doctrines contrary to reason. To this it may be answered, that the Bible contains no doctrine *contrary* to reason. But only, as might reasonably be expected, above reason. And certainly this is no objection to the Bible as a revelation from God, but rather a confirmation of its claims to divine origin. For in this, it is in entire keeping with his works and providence which every where abound, with things too high, and too deep for the human reason to grasp and comprehend.

(9.) They object to the Bible, that it is mystical and unintelligible. I reply,

It is admitted that the more spiritual doctrines of the Bible will of course appear mystical and unintelligible to a *carnal* mind. But it is insisted that, as a whole, the Bible is one of the plainest and most intelligible books in the world.

To this it is objected that there are innumerable christian sects, all claiming to receive their peculiar tenets from the Bible, which, they say, demonstrates its mysticism and unintelligibleness.

To this it may be again replied, that the different christian sects do not differ so much in their fundamental views as is generally supposed, that on the contrary, all that have any reasonable claims to the name of christian are agreed in respect to every doctrine and fact that is fundamental to the Christian system.

There is no more difficulty in understanding the Bible, than in interpreting any other book that claims to lay down rules of human conduct. There has been, for example, much more discrepancy of opinion in respect to the meaning of legislative acts, and much more difficulty in coming at the real meaning of those who have enacted laws, more litigation, expense, and ultimate uncertainty in respect to their interpretation, than there has been in respect to the interpretation of the Bible. And this, to say the least, is not a little wonderful when we consider that human statutes are written with the utmost caution and the utmost precision of human language which the nature of the case will admit. There is perhaps no book in the world of the same size against which the objection of unintelligibleness might not more reasonably be made than against the Bible.

(10.) Deists affirm that the Bible is the work of priest-craft and imposition. To this I reply,

a. That it is bare assertion.

b. That it is utterly uncandid in view of all the testimony in favor of the Bible.

c. They are bound to prove this assertion.

d. They cannot prove it.

e. The utter absence of proof is wholly incredible if in fact the Bible is the production of priest-craft. By what priest or priests was it written? At what time? In what country? In what language? For what purpose? It is next to impossible that there should be no evidence, either historical or traditional of such a fact, if indeed such a fact ever existed.

(11.) They insist that the Bible is the fabrication of political demagogues for political purposes. To this objection the very same answers may be given as above.

(12.) It is objected that the doctrine of Atonement contained in the Bible beggars all credibility—that it is utterly incredible, and morally impossible that God should condescend to do for mankind what the Scriptures represent him as doing in the work of the Atonement. To this I reply,

That this would be a conclusive objection upon any other supposition than that God is *love*. If God is not *love* it is freely admitted that the doctrine of the Atonement is utterly incredible. But if he is love, as the Bible and all his works affirm, the doctrine of Atonement is just what might be expected of such a being under the circumstances, and therefore one of the most reasonable doctrines in the world.

(13.) They object to the general spirit of Christianity as exhibited by its professors. To this I answer,

a. That some of them have objected to the meekness, humility, and excellencies of the christian character, as being unworthy of men, and have recommended the exact opposite spirit and traits of character. To this class of objectors no other answer need to be given than that they are mad, and know not what they say, nor whereof they affirm.

Another class have objected, not to the spirit of Christianity itself, as exhibited and required by its founder, but to an anti-christian spirit every where condemned and denounced in the Bible. If the Bible approved of their wicked conduct and spirit, the objection would be fatal. But as it is, it is of no weight, as it is not of the spirit of Christianity, but of Anti-Christianity of which they complain.

(14.) They object that revealed religion is inconsistent with liberty of inquiry and of opinion. If by liberty of inquiry and opinion they mean that men are, or ought to be at liberty to hold and inculcate any opinion whatever without being morally responsible for their opinions, the objection is absurd and ridiculous. But if they mean that the Bible or the Christian religion does not allow and invite, and even challenge and demand the most solemn and thorough investigation, and the formation of the most solid and well founded opinions on all religious subjects, their objection is false, for this is precisely what the Bible and the Christian religion do demand of every man, that he shall "Prove all things and hold fast that (and that only) which is good."

FOURTH *Consider some of the Difficulties of Deism.*

I. *Difficulty.* The first difficulty that I shall notice, is, that their objections to christianity are almost without an exception, either cavils, or alledged facts, but wholly unsupported by evidence. Most of them are mere cavils, unworthy of serious notice. Some of them might appear reasonable if supported by evidence, and others might be conclusive, were they not manifestly untrue. But as they are, taken together, they are of "no value, and a thing of naught."

II. *Difficulty.* To the doctrine of the mortal Deists, it may be reasonably objected that it is disguised Atheism. For while they profess to believe in the existence of God, their doctrines, or rather denials, blot out in the detail, his natural, and moral attributes

1. They deny his wisdom. Wisdom consists in the choice of the best ends, and of the most suitable means for the obtaining of those ends. But the mortal Deists represent God as having created the universe without any end, and as using no means to bring about any beneficial result. This is certainly involved in their denial of the divine providence.

2. They deny his intelligence, as they represent him as having

acted in creation without any reasonable motive. For certainly, if the universe was not worth governing, it was not worth creating.

3. They deny all his moral attributes, benevolence, justice, mercy, truth, holiness, for which of these is consistent with the creation of such a universe as this, and afterwards refusing to care for it, or exercise a providential government over it.

To mortal Deism I object again, that it is contrary to the belief of all nations in all ages. It has been shown in a former lecture, that all nations of men in all ages, have believed in and acknowledged the grand and peculiar doctrines which mortal Deists deny, such as the immortality of the soul, the distinction between virtue and vice, the doctrine of a divine providence, and a future state of more perfect rewards and punishments.

To their denial of the distinction between virtue and vice, I object,

1. That it is contrary to consciousness. We certainly know that there is such a distinction. It is the dictate of our own moral nature. It is forced upon us by testimony that we cannot resist. And they themselves often manifest a conviction of its truth in awarding praise and blame to those around them.

2. If there is, in fact, no such distinction, our nature is such as to render it impossible for us to believe that there is none. Our moral nature demands such a distinction. And with respect to ourselves we should be morally praise or blame worthy, were there no law except that which is founded in our own nature. But the fact that our nature is what it is, affords the most unanswerable evidence, that a broad and important distinction actually exists between virtue and vice.

3. As our nature demands such a distinction, and as we are capable of perceiving clearly that there is a moral quality in actions, such a distinction must in fact be recognized in the government of God, or God is unjust.

To the doctrine of human annihilation, I object that this also is virtual Atheism, as it denies the essential attributes of God, for which of his attributes is consistent with the annihilation of beings capable of endless improvement, and who need an eternity to develope their faculties, and answer the highest ends of their being.

To the doctrines of immortal Deists, I object,

1. They are inconsistent in holding the doctrines of natural, and rejecting those of revealed religion. For they inculcate precisely the same lessons, so far as natural religion goes, and revealed religion only supplies what is manifestly wanting in the truths of natural religion.

2. The immortal Deists are inconsistent in believing in the moral attributes of God. For a denial of several of these attributes is in fact involved, in rejecting a revelation. E. g.—It involves the denial of his wisdom. Wisdom, I have said, is the choice of the best ends, and the best means for the accomplishment of these ends. Now that revelation as a matter of fact, is the necessary means of attaining the highest perfection of human nature, cannot, with any

show of reason, be denied. With what consistency then do they hold to the wisdom of God, and deny that he has provided the necessary and indispensable means of effecting the holiness and happiness of his kingdom.

3. The immortal Deists, are inconsistent in maintaining the *justice* of God. It cannot, with any show of reason, be maintained that God deals with all men, in this state of existence, precisely according to their character. And without a divine revelation, how could it be positively shown that he would deal upon the principles of exact justice in a future life.

4. They are inconsistent in maintaining the mercy of God. To pardon sin, is the appropriate exercise of mercy. But without a divine revelation, how could it be known that God will pardon sin? How could it be ascertained that he could with any consistency, and safety, dispense with the execution of his law, in the pardon of sin? Some of the wisest men that have ever lived, who were ignorant of the Bible, have maintained that God could not forgive sin, and this conclusion seems to be the perfection of human reason, without a knowledge of the Atonement.

5. They are inconsistent in maintaining the infinite benevolence of God. Infinite benevolence would doubtless do all for man that the nature of the case admits. And the nature of the case certainly admits and demands a revelation.

6. They are inconsistent in holding the power, omniscience, and goodness of God, inasmuch as they deny and set aside the only explanation that reconciles the existence of these attributes in God, with the facts of the universe.

7. To the doctrine that nothing is to be received as an article of faith that is incomprehensible, I object; that this doctrine is destructive of their own system, and quite as inconsistent with it as with the system of christianity. It is also inconsistent with the belief of almost every thing else, as almost every thing, contains something in or about it that is incomprehensible.

8. If they reject revelation, they are bound to maintain the doctrine of universal damnation.

(1.) Because all men deserve it.

(2.) Without the Bible we cannot see how they can consistently be forgiven, should they repent.

(3.) Without the motives presented in the Bible, it is a fact, that mankind never would repent. Without a knowledge of the Atonement, men know not that the goodness of God leadeth them to repentance; but after their hardness and impenitent heart treasure up unto themselves wrath against the day of wrath, and revelation of the righteous judgments of God.

9. Every evidence in favor of the Bible, as a revelation from God, is a difficulty of Deism, with which it must grapple, and to which it is bound to give some reasonable answer.

10. To admit Deism to be true, we must admit that all the evidence in favor of the divine authority of the Bible is false, and that

too without a particle of opposing evidence. This is to set aside all evidence, and consequently all science, and all knowledge, and all belief on every subject.

11. To admit the falsity of all the evidence in favor of a divine revelation, is to swallow the grossest absurdity, and to attempt to sustain Deism by a miracle, more stupendous than all the miracles recorded in the Bible. For certainly, that all this evidence should be false, were the greatest wonder and the greatest miracle in the universe.

12. Therefore Deism requires ridiculous credulity, and almost infinitely more faith, to believe that the Bible is an imposture, in view of all the evidence that exists, than to believe it is what it professes to be.

13. Deism is indebted to Christianity for nearly all the truth that it contains. It is true, that the doctrines of natural religion might be discovered by unaided reason; but as a matter of fact, they never have been to any considerable extent. And none but those Deists who have had access to the Bible have ever given any thing like a consistent account of the doctrines of natural religion.

14. Deists are bound to account for the fact that the most enlightened and virtuous men have believed, that the Bible was a revelation from God. Sir Isaac Newton, than whom a greater philosopher never blessed the earth, was a firm believer in, and defender of the Bible, as a revelation from God.

15. Deists are bound to account for the fact that no one ever renounced the Christian religion upon a death bed, while nothing has been more common than for Deists to renounce their Deism in a dying hour.

16. The lives and deaths of Deists prove the inefficacy of their system to sustain them in virtue while alive, and in peace when they die.

17. Deism is, on many accounts, highly dishonorable to God.

18. It is also ruinous to man.

19. Its spirit condemns it.

20. Its tendencies, when well considered, are a complete refutation of it.

21. Upon the supposition that Christianity is not true, infidels are bound to account for the astonishing change in the conduct of the Apostles, after Christ's resurrection—how it came to pass, that instead of their former timidity, they were so fearless, so persevering, so willing to sacrifice every worldly interest, in defence of the truth that Christ had risen from the dead. If they were not honest and sincere, infidels are bound to show upon what principle of human nature such lives as they lived, and such deaths as they died, can be accounted for. With respect to the resurrection of Jesus Christ, it was a matter about which they could not be deceived. If they had stolen him from the sepulchre, as the Jews foolishly pretended, they knew it, and were certain that he had not risen

from the dead. The certain knowledge that he had risen from the dead, would naturally result in that change which was witnessed in them. But upon no other conceivable supposition can their conduct be accounted for.

22. Again. Upon the supposition that Christianity is not true, Deists are bound to account for the fact, of the exact fulfillment of such great multitudes of prophecies, extending in an unbroken chain, from the present time back through hundreds and thousands of years. These prophecies have been so literally fulfilled, that some opposers of Christianity have insisted upon the great particularity with which they were fulfilled to the very letter, and have consequently inferred, that they were histories written after the occurrence of the facts which they describe.

23. Upon the supposition that Christianity is not true, Deists are bound to disprove or account for the miracles wrought in confirmation of the truth of the scriptures. That these were real and not pretended miracles, there can be no doubt.

24. If Christianity is not true, Deists are bound to account for the fact, that the Apostles so repeatedly appealed to the Jews themselves, and to all classes of persons, before whom and among whom those miracles were wrought, and referred to those miracles as facts, which were universally admitted, and could not be denied. They are bound also to show why it was, that neither the friends nor enemies of Christianity, during the first centuries, ever pretended to call in question the reality of those miracles.

LECTURE IX.

NATURAL ATTRIBUTES OF GOD.

I am to show:

FIRST. What is meant by a natural attribute.
SECOND. What are some of the natural attributes of God.

FIRST. *What is meant by a natural attribute.*

A natural attribute is that which pertains to a thing by a natural necessity, or whatever is attributable to it, as essential to its existence and nature. The natural attributes of God are those qualities, capacities, elements, susceptibilities, and natural perfections that constitute whatever we know of his nature and essence.

SECOND. *Some of the natural attributes of God, &c.*

I. Eternity.
II. Omniscience.
III. Omnipresence.
IV. Omnipotence.
V. Spirituality.
VI. Immutability.

Having established the divine authority of the Bible, we are, from this point in our inquiries, at liberty to quote it freely as a matter of record, and as conclusive evidence of what it plainly and unequivocally asserts. The natural attributes of God may be discovered, and their existence proved by the light of nature. But the infinity of these attributes, at least some of them, can only be fully and unanswerably proven from the Bible.

I. *The Eternity of God.*

1. I will show what is meant by the eternity of God, and also prove that eternity is an attribute of God.

By the eternity of God is meant:

(1.) That he is without beginning.
(2.) That he will never cease to be.
(3.) That he is eternal in such a sense as to grow no older.
(4.) That eternity is to God what present time is to us.

(1.) That he is without beginning, has been already established in the proof of his existence as a first cause of all things.

(2.) That he can never cease to be is certain:

a. Because he is self-existent. Self-existence is necessary existence. But necessary existence cannot cease to be. He cannot destroy himself. No created power can destroy him. He cannot fail or die with age, as he grows no older. If he did, there is no proof that a mere spirit can fail with age. As he exists independently of any cause, it is naturally impossible that he should cease to exist; for there can be no cause of his non-existence or ceasing to exist. His ceasing to exist, then, would be an event without a cause, which is absurd and naturally impossible.

b. The Bible fully declares, that God is without beginning or end; i. e. that he is absolutely eternal. He is spoken of as the "eternal God." And the Bible fully and unequivocally, in many ways, declares his eternity.

(3.) He is eternal in such a sense as to grow no older. If he grows older, it is intuitively certain that he had a beginning:

a. Because, if his age can be at all reduced, by subtracting years or ages, it can be exhausted.

b. If he grows older, his age can be reduced as certainly as ours can.

c. If any thing can be added to his age, then something can be subtracted from it; and it can be reduced to nothing. If any thing could be added to or subtracted from space, so as to make more or less of the aggregate, it could be reduced to nothing.

d. If God grows older, he was once comparatively young. If comparatively young, he was once really young. And if once young, he began to be.

e. If he grows older, he has had new thoughts, exercises, and experiences, in the same sense that we have. In this case it is intuitively certain, that his knowledge commenced, and has increased with his age.

f. If his exercises and experiences are progressive, or if succession can be predicated of them, it is intuitively certain, that not only his knowledge has increased, but his holiness has increased, and both of them must for ever increase.

g. If there is succession in God's existence and exercises, it is intuitively certain that he never was, never will be, never can be, infinite in age, knowledge, experience, holiness, or happiness.

h. If succession can be predicated of God's existence and mental states, it is intuitively certain, that he is not only not infinite, but that he is infinitely less than infinite—that when compared with eternity, he is but a babe, or infinitely young—when compared with omniscience, he is infinitely ignorant—and when compared with infinite blessedness, his happiness falls infinitely short of it. And that in all these particulars, he will for ever remain as far from infinite as he now is, or ever has been.

i. If succession can be predicated of his existence, the existence of every moment must be dependent upon the existence of the preceding moment. He exists this moment, because he existed the moment previous. This involves the absurdity of an infinite series of dependencies. If succession can be predicated of his mental states or exercises, this would involve the same absurdity.

k. There is no need of supposing God's existence to be successive like ours; because, eternity past and future to us, all that we call duration, really exists at present, as much and in the same sense as all space exists. In respect to space, the terms before, behind, and the ideas represented by the words above, below, right, left, there, &c., are only relative; and apart from finite existences, these words have no meaning. Remove all finite existences, and there could be no room for any such language.

With respect to the existence of God, there is no right, left, up, down, there, behind, before, &c. There is here and there to all finite existences; but to God every thing is *here*. So in respect to what we call duration. Times past and future are relative, and respect only finite existences, or such existences as began to be. They cannot possibly respect a being who never began to be, and who grows no older. He can no more pass on through duration, than through space. Neither space nor duration can have any meaning with him, except as it respects finite existence. All space is to him here, a single point where he exists. All eternity is to him now, or that point which is filled up by his present experience. With respect to his existence, he cannot say, yesterday—to-morrow—when I was young—when I am older. And when he speaks of his acts or existence, with respect to duration, as being past or future, he must mean by it just what he would mean, should he speak of his existence or acts in respect to place. If he speaks of working here or there, in this or that place, it does not imply that God is confined to place, or has locality. Nor when he speaks of things as past or future, ought we to understand him as speaking thus in respect to himself. In respect to all finite existences, there is in fact locality, time, and place, past and future. But to affirm these things as true of God, is to suppose him finite instead of infinite.

(4.) Eternity is to God as present time is to us.

a. By time, as it respects ourselves, we mean that portion of duration which commences with our birth and ends with our death.

b. By past time, we mean that portion of this period, through which we have passed and of which nothing remains to us but the remembrance.

c. By present time, we mean that point indicated by present consciousness; the point at which that mental state of which we are conscious is in exercise.

d. Our mental states or exercises are single, and successive. And by past, present, future, we refer to the order in which they or the occasions of them occur.

e. Time to us is the progression of existence and experience. Present time is that which is filled up by our present experience and consciousness. Successive exercises are successive experience. Successive experience is increasing knowledge. Succession, therefore, belongs to a finite being.

f. But God is not a finite being. He cannot be omniscient, and yet obtain knowledge from experience. Succession cannot therefore be predicated of him, either in relation to his existence or mental states. He always has the same mental state or consciousness. He can have no new thoughts, as there is no possible source from which to derive them. He can have no new affections or emotions, as he can have no new ideas or knowledge. Therefore, his present consciousness is his eternal consciousness, and eternity is to him what present time is to us. God's existence is infinite, both in respect to duration and space. This is expressly declared in the Bible; and if it were not true he is infinitely less than infinite. As it respects God's existence then, space has no other idea than *here.* And eternity has no other idea than *now.* All here and there must respect such existences as are not omniscient. All past and future must respect such existences as are not eternally self-existent, and always equally and eternally old.

Omnipresence, to us, means both here, there, any where, and every where. But to God, it means only here. So eternity to us, means all past, present and future duration. But to God it means only *now*. Duration and space, as they respect his existence, mean infinitely different things from what they do when they respect our existence. God's existence and his acts, as they respect finite existence, have relation to time and place. But as they respect his own existence, every thing is *here* and *now*. With respect to all finite existences, God can say I was, I am, I shall be, do, will do; but with respect to his own existence, all that he can say is, I *am*, I *do*.

g. The Bible seems to favor this view of the subject, although it would guard against pressing our minds with such a metaphysical nicety. Thus God calls himself "I AM." Christ says, "Before Abraham was, I AM." To him a thousand years are as one day, and one day as a thousand years. A thousand years here is a definite for an indefinite period. As when God says the cattle on a thousand hills are his, he means the cattle on all hills are his. This I understand to be an expression of the same kind. Its connection plainly leads us to this inference, that by a thousand years we are to understand all time, of which it is said, that it is as one day, or as present time to God.

2. I will now notice some objections to this view.

Obj. I. We can form no conception of an existence, to which there is no succession.

Ans. 1. The difficulty of this conception lies in our finite and progressive existence. All our thoughts, exercises, and experience, and knowledge, are progressive. Consequently we can form no positive conception of the *modus existendi* of a being, to whom succession does not appertain. Nor is this difficulty attributable to any want of perfection in our creation. As we are finite and began to be, it was impossible that God should create us in a manner that would obviate this difficulty. We once had no existence. We must therefore begin to be. Every thing, therefore, with respect to us must be successive. Nor is this a difficulty that need be injurious to us. For we conceive of God with sufficient accuracy for all practical purposes, when we conceive of his existence as coeval with all other existences and events.

2. We can form no other conception of infinity, than that it exists and is that which is unlimited; and of course, that a positive conception of it is inconceivable by finite minds. To say that we have a positive conception or idea of infinity is a contradiction, as it supposes there is a whole of infinity, which implies a bound or limit; which contradicts the true meaning of infinity.

3. Although we can form no positive idea or conception of infinity; yet we can see that to speak of it as incapable either of increase or diminution, is a contradiction. So, although we can have no positive idea of the eternal, self-existence of God; yet we can see, that to say he began to be, is absurd and contradicts his eternity. So, although we can have no positive idea of his existence and mental states, as not successive; yet we can see that suc-

cession in his existence and mental states, involves the absurdity, that he grows older—that he was once young—that he began to be—that he never was and never will be an eternal being—that he never was and never can be an infinite being—that he never can, in the least degree, approach towards being eternal in his duration, or infinite in his knowledge or happiness.

Obj. II. God always speaks just as if his existence and acts were successive.

Ans. He must of course speak of them as they appear and really are to us, or we should receive no ideas from what he says.

Obj. III. God sees things as they are or as they are not. Now as events do really occur in succession, they must appear so to him.

Ans. To us they occur in succession, but not to him. To us they have relation to place, but not to him. To us they occur before, behind, in time past, present, or future; but to him they occur *here*, and they occur *now*.

Obj. IV. It confounds and overturns all our methods of reasoning, with respect to the reality of events.

Ans. Events really are, with respect to us, what they appear to be. Our reasonings concerning the reality and existence of things, may be just as it respects ourselves and as it respects God. And yet, as it regards time and place, every thing may be here and now to him, while to us they are spread through immensity and eternity. In other words, God is infinite and we are finite. We must always conceive of things, and reason as finite beings. He will always conceive of things, and reason as an infinite being, apprehending realities as they are to us, and in the relation they sustain to us in regard to time and place, and also having that infinitely different view of them that respects his own infinite existence.

II. *God's omniscience.*

By the omniscience of God is not meant, merely the capacity of knowing all things. A distinguished commentator has defined omniscience to be a capacity to know whatever is wise to be known. This definition was resorted to, to avoid the inference of personal election from the fore-knowledge of God. Omnipotence, says this commentator, (not to use his words, but his idea,) is not the absolute doing of all that is do-able; but ability to do whatever is wise to be done. Omnipotence, therefore, in its exercises, is directed by wisdom. So omniscience, he says, is under the direction of wisdom. And while God's omnipotence does not do what is unwise to be done, just so omniscience does not know what is unwise to be known. To this statement it is sufficient to reply, that the thing must be previously known, before wisdom could decide whether the knowledge of it would be wise or unwise.

But omniscience is the absolute knowledge of all existences, events, and things, actual or possible.

PROOF.

1. His works afford the most convincing evidence of a degree of knowledge, to which certainly a finite being can fix no bounds.

2. His providential government of the universe, strengthens and confirms this proof.

3. Prophecy would seem to prove that God must really be omniscient. Multitudes of the prophecies respect the future exercises and conduct of free moral agents. And a being who can with certainty predict the events of all time and eternity, foreseeing the end from the beginning, in respect to the exercises, and character, and destiny of moral agents, must be omniscient.

4. The administration of moral government, depends upon the exact knowledge which he possesses of the state of mind of every moral being in the universe, and of the exact result in which every movement of his government and providence will terminate.

5. His works of grace, in searching the heart, and bringing about the conviction, conversion, and salvation of sinners, must prove him omniscient.

6. The Bible expressly ascribes omniscience to him:

John 21: 17: "Thou knowest all things."

John 2: 24, 25: "But Jesus did not commit himself unto them, because he knew all men, and needed not that any should testify of man: for he knew what was in man."

John 16: 30: "Now are we sure that thou knowest all things, and needest not that any man should ask thee: by this we believe that thou camest forth from God."

Ps. 139: 1–6: "O Lord, thou hast searched me, and known me. Thou knowest my down-sitting and mine up-rising; thou understandest my thought afar off. Thou compassest my path, and my lying down, and art acquainted with all my ways. For there is not a word in my tongue, but, lo, O Lord, thou knowest it altogether. Thou hast beset me behind and before, and laid thy hand upon me. Such knowledge is too wonderful for me; it is high, I cannot attain unto it."

1 Chron. 28: 9: "And thou, Solomon my son, know thou the God of thy father, and serve him with a perfect heart, and with a willing mind; for the Lord searcheth all hearts, and understandeth all the imaginations of the thoughts: if thou seek him, he will be found of thee; but if thou forsake him, he will cast thee off for ever."

Rom. 8: 27: "And he that searcheth the hearts knoweth what is the mind of the Spirit, because he maketh intercession for the saints according to the will of God."

1 Cor. 2: 10: "But God hath revealed them unto us by his Spirit: for the Spirit searcheth all things, yea, the deep things of God."

Rev. 2: 23: "And I will kill her children with death; and all the churches shall know that I am he which searcheth the reins and hearts: and I will give unto every one of you according to your works."

III. *The omnipresence of God.*

By omnipresence is meant essential ubiquity. Some understand by the omnipresence of God, not essential ubiquity, but that he merely knows all things. They object to the idea of his essential ubiquity, that it predicates extensibility of God. And that to say that God is every where essentially present, is to maintain that only a part of God is in any one place.

Again, they object, that mind has no relation to place, any more than an hour has. To these objections I answer:

1. They confound mind with matter. God is a real existence; an hour is not. Existence must certainly and necessarily sustain relation to space or place. An hour does not, cannot. God must sustain relation to place, but not the same relation that matter does. Matter fills that portion of space occupied by it, to the exclusion of other material substances. God occupies all space, but not in such a sense as matter occupies space.

2. These objections exclude the idea of God's being any where. Whereness is a necessary idea suggested by the idea of existence, or substance. With respect to the first objection, that essential ubiquity implies that only a part of God is in any one place, it is nonsensical, when applied to mind. The fact is, that wherever mind is, there all the attributes of mind are, and may be exercised, whether in any one point of space or occupying all space.

The proof of the essential ubiquity of God is:

(1.) His works of creation and providence. It is certain, that he must exist wherever he works or exercises any personal agency. It is not supposed that the universe is infinite. Therefore his presence throughout the universe would not prove him absolutely omnipresent. But if he can exist in more places than one at the same time; if he can and does exist in every part of the universe at the same time, the inference is fair, that he may be and is omnipresent.

(2.) The Bible speaks of God as being present in every part of the universe. Ps. 139: 7–10: "Whither shall I go from thy Spirit? or whither shall I flee from thy presence? If I ascend up into heaven, thou art there; if I make my bed in hell, behold, thou art there. If I take the wings of the morning, and dwell in the uttermost parts of the sea; even there shall thy hand lead me, and thy right hand shall hold me."

It is impossible for us to know how extensive the universe is. But, as has been said, absolute omnipresence is a legitimate inference, from creation, providence, and the Bible.

IV. *The omnipotence of God.*

By the omnipotence of God is meant:

1. Not an ability to perform contradictions.

2. But an ability to accomplish whatever is an object of physical power.

The proof of God's omnipotence is:

1. The works of creation.

2. Sustaining and governing the physical universe.

3. The Bible ascribes omnipotence to God. Job 42: 2: "I know that thou canst do every thing." He is frequently called the Almighty.

V. *The Spirituality of God.*

By the spirituality of God, we understand that his existence or substance is immaterial—a substance or existence possessing properties essentially different from those of matter.

The proof of the spirituality of God is:

1. One of the properties of matter is solidity. If God were material, no other material being could exist. As he is omnipresent he would of course, if he were material, exclude all other material existences.

2. If God is material, it is impossible that he should not exhibit any one property of matter.

3. The Bible expressly affirms that "God is a Spirit."

VI. *Immutability of God.*

By immutability is meant the unchangeableness of the nature of God. That he is naturally unchangeable, is evident, because:

1. His existence is necessary, and necessarily just what it is.

2. He did not create and cannot change his own nature.

3. As his existence, as it is, depends on no cause, change in his nature is naturally impossible, as a change in his nature would be an event without a cause.

REMARKS:

1. God's natural attributes are just such as perfectly qualify him to sustain the office of Universal Ruler of the universe.

2. His moral character must be a matter of infinite interest and importance to the universe.

3. His praise-worthiness does not depend upon the existence of his natural attributes, but upon the use he makes of them.

4. Omniscience does not render the existence of events necessary.

5. Omnipotence does not render universal salvation certain nor probable.

6. Natural omnipotence affords no proof that sin could have been prevented under a moral government.

LECTURE X.

MORAL ATTRIBUTES OF GOD.

First. Show what is meant by a moral attribute.
Second. What are some of the moral attributes of God.
Third. Prove that he possesses such attributes.

First. *Show what is meant by a moral attribute.*

A *natural* attribute is that which belongs to the nature of a being. A *moral* attribute is a disposition or state of the will. It is a permanent choice or preference of the mind, in opposition to a constitutional or natural attribute, on the one hand, and to individual exercises, on the other.

Second. *What are some of the moral attributes of God.*

Benevolence may be considered either as an attribute of God, or as the sum of all his moral attributes. It seems to be convenient sometimes to speak of his benevolence as an attribute, and at other times as the sum of them all. It should however, always be understood, that God's entire character, and every moral exercise of his infinite mind, is only some modification of his benevolence. And that when we speak of benevolence as an attribute we do it merely for convenience sake, and for the purpose of directing the mind particularly to that expression of it, that consists in willing good to *its object*. When we speak of justice, mercy, truth, wisdom, holiness, &c., we also use these terms for convenience sake, for the purpose of confining the attention to those particular modifications or expressions of benevolence. I shall consider these attributes in the order in which I have just named them, viz., Benevolence, Justice, Mercy, Truth, Wisdom, Holiness.

Moral attributes, presuppose moral agency. I will therefore, in this place, premise a few remarks upon the subject of the moral agency of God.

1. A moral agent, as has been remarked in a former lecture, is a being who possesses understanding, reason, conscience, and free-will. Understanding, reason, and conscience are all plainly implied in omniscience, for it is impossible that God should know all things without possessing these faculties.

2. That God has a will, must be certain from the fact that the whole power of mind to produce any effect without itself, lies in the will. This we know from our own consciousness to be true of ourselves, and from the phenomena exhibited to our senses, with respect to the existence and nature of God, we necessarily infer that he is a mind like ourselves, and that his power to produce effects without himself, lies wholly in his will. We are so constitu-

ted that we cannot conceive of any other possible manner in which he should produce effects without himself, any more than we can conceive the existence or nature of a class of objects which would require the addition of another sense to enable us to perceive them.

3. The existence then, and phenomena of the universe afford as high evidence that God possesses a will, as that he exists at all.

4. That the will of God is free, I infer,

(1.) From the fact that we know ourselves to be free, with as much certainty as we know that we exist.

(2.) We can form no conception of a voluntary being that is not free, for volition always implies freedom.

(3.) Volition and necessity are terms of opposition. Volition can no more be produced by force, than material changes can be produced by motives. Volition can be produced in no other way than by motive, and if produced by motive, it is absurd, and a contradiction to say that it is not free.

THIRD. *Prove that God possesses such attributes.*

BENEVOLENCE.

1. God must be *benevolent*, or *malevolent*. It is impossible that he should be indifferent, or have no will at all, in respect to his own good, and the good of the universe. It were absurd, to say that he is omniscient, and yet neither wills the happiness or misery of himself or any other being.

2. God can, by no possibility, be both benevolent and malevolent at the same time. In other words, he cannot will both the happiness and misery of himself, and the universe at the same time. These are opposite states of the will, and it is absurd to suppose that they can both exist at the same time.

3. If God is malevolent at all, he must not only be perfectly, but infinitely and unchangeably malevolent. As God is an infinite being, perfect malevolence in him, is infinite malevolence, and it is absurd to say that what is infinite, can be changed.

4. If God is malevolent, he is immutably so, because he can never have any new thoughts as motives that shall induce any change in him. He cannot, from himself, or from any of his creatures, by any possibility, ever get any new information, or possess any new thoughts, and consequently his moral character, whatever it is, is unchangeable. His mind must be made up. He must have decided his own character and *benevolence*, or *malevolence* must be the unalterable state of his will. That he is benevolent, I argue,

5. From the fact of his omniscience. He could not but know all the reasons in favor of benevolence, and all the reasons against malevolence. He could not by any possibility be ignorant of the reasons on either side, nor so divert his mind from them as that they should not have their full influence in deciding his character, and in confirming it forever. Finite beings are ignorant of many of

the reasons for benevolence, and against malevolence. They may and often do divert their attention from those reasons with which they are really acquainted, and do not act under the influence of what knowledge they have. But God is omniscient. Every motive that exists, lies with all its weight upon his mind, and that constantly. And as there are infinitely higher motives to benevolence than to malevolence, and as these motives are fully known, to and appreciated by God, we reasonably infer from this consideration, that he is benevolent.

6. I infer the benevolence of God, from the fact, that the motives to benevolence are absolutely infinite, just as great as the value of his own eternal happiness, and the happiness of the whole universe.

7. I infer his benevolence from the fact that the motives against malevolence are absolutely infinite. Malevolence naturally and necessarily creates mutiny and war, and misery in the mind of a moral agent, while benevolence just as naturally and necessarily produces harmony, peace, and happiness. The motives against malevolence that must be constantly and fully before the mind of God, that are perfectly comprehended and weighed by him, are just as great as his own eternal and infinite misery with the eternal and perfect misery of the whole universe. For certainly perfect and infinite malevolence in God would make himself and the whole universe as miserable as possible.

8. That God is not malevolent, I infer from the fact that the universe as it actually exists, is not what it certainly would be under the government of an infinitely malevolent being.

9. That he is benevolent, is shown in many ways from the constitution of our own nature.

(1.) He is a moral being, and must therefore deserve the respect and esteem of other moral beings. We are so constituted that we admire and esteem benevolence, but naturally and necessarily abhor malevolence. Now if God is benevolent, we are so constituted that we must respect and approve his character in spite of ourselves. The wickedest moral agent in the universe, must respect and approve his character if it is benevolent. But on the contrary, if it is malevolent, he has so created us that we only need to know him to be under the constitutional necessity of abhorring him. It is absurd therefore to say that God is a moral being, and has so created other moral beings, that they are under a constitutional necessity of abhorring him whenever they know him.

(2.) Another evidence of the benevolence of God, which is to be found in our own constitution is the conscious fact that the sight of misery excites compassion in us. If God were a malevolent being, and willed the misery of his creatures, it is absurd to suppose that he would so have constituted moral agents, as that they would feel naturally prompted by the very laws of their being, to relieve misery, and as far as possible prevent it.

Another fact to be noticed in our own constitution is that compassion or benevolence produces happiness in us, and is both accompanied with and followed by a feeling of complacency and happiness. If benevolence is necessarily attended with and followed by happiness and self-complacency, this must afford almost a demonstration that the author of our nature is benevolent and not malevolent. The conscious fact that benevolence always produces peace and happiness, and malevolence a sense of guilt and misery in us, is most decisive proof that the author of our nature is benevolent, and not malevolent.

(3.) The decisions of conscience are also a striking proof that the author of our nature is benevolent and not malevolent. It unhesitatingly approves of benevolence and condemns malevolence, and would as readily condemn malevolence in God as in any of his creatures.

(4.) The place which conscience holds in our mental constitution, is a striking evidence of the benevolence of God. It is manifestly the supreme moral faculty, i. e., it possesses a rightful supremacy, although it has not always the power to contiol the will. It possesses the right though not always the power of government. Now to suppose that God is malevolent and still the author of our nature is absurd, as it would be equivalent to supposing that his disposition is malevolent, and his works benevolent.

10. If God is not benevolent, he must abhor himself. We naturally and necessarily abhor malevolence, both in ourselves and every body else. And if God is a moral being and malevolent, he must abhor himself from the very constitution of his being.

11. If God is a malevolent being, he is infinitely miserable.

12. If he is a benevolent being, he must be infinitely happy.

13. Benevolence is every where manifest in the works of God. There is not only in every department of nature evidence of design, but of benevolent design. There is not only contrivance manifested, but these contrivances manifestly tend to happiness as their end. The universe not only affords the highest evidence that the whole system of events sustain the relation of means to an end, but that this end is happiness. The adaptation of external nature to our intellectual and moral constitution affords the highest proof that the author of the universe consulted the happiness of sentient and moral beings in its creation.

14. The Bible expressly declares that God is love. And all its representations of his character are in accordance with the assertion that God is benevolence.

(1.) The Bible represents God as exercising a universal providence over the universe, and the history of this world shows that it has not been as miserable as it would have been under the providence of a perfectly and infinitely malevolent being.

(2.) His moral law proves his benevolence. Law is an expression of the will of the law-giver. In other words: it is the law-giver's will expressed. But this law requires universal and perfect benevolence. But God's will and law are the same thing. Therefore God is benevolent.

(3.) The sanction as well as the precept of his law, proves him benevolent. The sanction is in the first place indicated,

a. By the natural and necessary connection of benevolence with happiness, and of malevolence with misery.

b. The Bible informs us that God will award eternal happiness to the benevolent, and eternal misery to the malevolent. These sanctions afford the highest evidence that we are capable of receiving of God's infinite benevolence.

(4.) The *Bible* as a revelation from God, is both an instance and a striking proof of the benevolence of God. Its doctrines are a most stupendous revelation of God's benevolence, and afford the highest evidence of its being infinite, that the mind of man or angel can conceive.

The evidences of God's benevolence are as numerous as all his works and ways. It is unnecessary to proceed any farther in the direct proof of his benevolence. I shall therefore now consider such *objections* to the benevolence of God as seem to require notice.

It is admitted on all hands that God must be in some degree benevolent. But it is contended by some that so far as the light of nature goes, it would appear that he is of a mixed character, and that neither his providence nor his works, indicate unmingled benevolence in him. The mixture of both moral and natural good and evil in this world, has induced many heathen nations to adopt the idea of two Gods of opposite characters, a benevolent and malevolent one. Others have supposed that good and evil were eternally existing principles, forever conflicting with each other, and that the prevalence sometimes of one and sometimes of the other, and the modified influence of both, accounts for the actually existing state of the universe.

Many who have possessed the Bible have felt unable to answer the objections that seem to lie against the perfect benevolence of God in the actually existing state of things in the universe. Before I enter upon the consideration of these objections, I must remind you of the substance of what has been said in a former lecture, in regard to the influence of objections in setting aside evidence.

1. When a proposition is well established by evidence, an objection interposed to overthrow it, must be a matter of fact, and not a mere conjecture or assertion.

2. If a fact, it must be plainly inconsistent with the truth of the proposition against which it is alledged, for if the existence of the fact *may be* consistent with the truth of the proposition which is well established by evidence, it does not by any means invalidate the evidence in favor of the truth of the proposition. The objector is therefore bound to show not only that his objection is a reality and a truth, or a fact, but that it cannot be reconciled with the truth of the proposition. Otherwise, when the proposition is well supported by evidence, his objection will not overthrow it. I come now to notice the objections.

Objection I. It is objected that many animals are furnished with weapons or instruments with which to inflict pain.

To this I reply:

1. These weapons were many of them given for self-defence, which shows God's regard for the happiness and rights of their possessors.

2. Many of them were given as means of securing their prey, or the food on which they are to subsist. In neither of these cases was the infliction of pain the end for which these weapons were given. The end, in both cases, was benevolent, and the infliction of pain is only *incidental* to the securing of these benevolent ends.

Obj. II. It is objected that the fact that different species of animals prey and subsist upon each other, is an evidence that God is not perfectly benevolent. To this I reply :

1. Animal life, while it lasts, is a real blessing, and probably in every instance, more than compensates for the pain of death.

2. From the very constitution of animals, they are necessarily mortal, and it is certainly good economy to make the carcass of one, food for others, as in this case a greater number of animals can subsist upon the earth. E. g. : Let the earth be filled with vegetable-eating animals, as many as could subsist upon that species of diet. Then let us suppose another class of animals to subsist upon the flesh of the vegetable-eating animals, and another class to subsist upon the milk both of the vegetable and flesh-eating animals. It is easy to see that in this way a greater amount of animal life, and consequently of bestial happiness can be secured than would be otherwise possible. The fact that animals do so subsist, is therefore a striking evidence of the economic benevolence of the Creator. Just so in the sea. One species of fish may live on certain marine substances, and when the number is so multiplied as that no more can be supplied with such kinds of aliment other species may exist that will prey upon these, as is actually the fact, and thus a greater number of fishes may exist than were otherwise possible.

3. It is a sufficient answer to this objection to say, that it cannot be shown that the whole amount of animal happiness is not greater than if animals and fishes did not prey upon one another.

Obj. III. It is objected that the pains and evils to which we are naturally and necessarily subjected in this world, are inconsistent with the perfect benevolence of God. To this I reply :

1. It cannot be shown that pain was ever purposed as an end, either in the formation or government of any thing in the universe, and wherever there is pain, it is only incidental to the obtaining some benevolent end. Teeth were not made to ache, but for a benevolent purpose. Yet pain is incidental to their existence, or rather arises out of their abuse.

2. All pain or natural evil is the result of an infraction of laws that were established for the accomplishment of wise and benevo-

lent ends. The pain is incidental to the existence of those laws. Those laws are wise and good and benevolent. But the infraction of them produces pain.

Obj. IV. It is objected that infants and innocent animals are often involved in the calamities and evils which they have not deserved by any violation of law physical or moral. Answer,

1. Infants and innocent animals are parts of a great system, and so connected with holy and sinful beings as to be benefitted by their virtues, and injured by their vices. They receive the benefits on the one hand, and the injuries on the other, not because of their own good or ill desert, but as a necessary consequence of the wise and benevolent arrangement that has so connected them with this system of existences.

2. Notwithstanding all the injuries of which they are sometimes the subjects, in consequence of this connection, their existence as a whole, is nevertheless a blessing.

3. It cannot be shown, that in a world like this, sickness, pain, death, and other apparent ills are, after all, real evils. They certainly are often only blessings in disguise. And it cannot be shown, that upon the whole they are not invariably so.

4. With respect to the death of infants and of animals, their death may be mercifully ordered to prevent still greater calamities befalling them. And in the case of infants, there is no reason to doubt that their natural death is only the entrance upon eternal life.

Obj. V. It is objected, that the existence of sin or moral evil in the universe sets aside the proof of the perfect benevolence of God. It is affirmed by some, that aside from revelation, the perfect benevolence of God cannot be proved, as the existence of sin in the universe must appear to be inconsistent, either with his wisdom, power, or goodness. To this I reply:

1. That to set aside the proof of God's benevolence, it must be made to appear, that the universe, as it is, is not, in itself, a good—that upon the whole it is not better than no universe at all; but this can never be shown; because, even in this world, life is regarded as a blessing and as a real good.

2. To set aside the proof of the *perfect* benevolence of God, it must be shown, that the universe is not as perfect as it might have been—that upon the whole, a better and more desirable universe was possible; but this can never be shown. For,

(1.) The universe is valuable only as it results in happiness; and it cannot be shown, that a greater amount of happiness, upon the whole, could have been procured by any possible arrangement, than will result from the present system.

(2.) Freedom, or liberty, is essential to virtue.

(3.) Virtue is essential to happiness.

(4.) The amount of happiness depends upon the amount and strength of virtue.

(5.) The strength of virtue depends:

a. On the perfection of liberty.

b. On the amount of temptation resisted and overcome. Hence:

(6.) There is the most virtue where there is the highest liberty, and the most temptation overcome. Hence:

(7.) The most happiness will result from that system in which there is the most perfect liberty, with the greatest amount of trial or temptation, resisted and overcome. Hence:

(8.) It cannot be shown that the present system, with all its natural and moral evils, does not, after all, result in a greater amount of virtue and happiness than any other system would or could have done. Had there been more temptation, it might have destroyed all virtue. Had there been less, virtue had certainly been less valuable, and final happiness less complete.

3. The existence of sin is no valid objection to the *perfect* benevolence of God, unless it be shown that sin could have been prevented, under a system of moral government. It is manifest that sin could have been prevented in only one of two ways:

(1.) By a refusal on the part of God, to create a universe of moral beings and administer over them a moral government; or,

(2.) By so modifying the administration of moral government, as to have suffered so much less temptation as should have secured universal obedience.

But to have created no universe of moral beings would not have been benevolent, if their existence is a real blessing.

When they were created, to have so modified the administration of government as to have secured universal obedience, might not, to say the least, have resulted upon the whole, in so great strength of virtue, and so perfect happiness in those who are virtuous as will result from the present form and circumstances of God's government. It cannot be shown, therefore, that it would have been either wise or benevolent, so to have modified the form and administration of moral government, as to have excluded sin entirely from the universe.

4. It cannot be shown that wholly to have excluded sin from the universe was naturally possible. Mind is influenced by motive. Motive implies knowledge. All moral beings, except God, begin to be. They are at first entirely destitute of knowledge. Many things they must learn by experience, and can come to a knowledge of them in no other way. And as there would be in the universe no knowledge, either of the nature or tendencies of sin, without experience, it can never be shown, that the prevention of sin, under a moral government, and among races of beings who commenced their existence in a state of entire ignorance, is naturally possible. But until this is shown, the existence of sin is no valid objection to the perfect benevolence of God.

Let it be remembered, that in view of the abundant proof of God's benevolence that every where exists, *we* are called upon only to show, that natural and moral evil *may* be accounted for in consistency with the supposttion that God is *perfectly* and *infinitely* benevolent. We are not bound to show *how* sin came to exist, or *how* God will dispose of it; but only that its existence *may* be accounted for in consistency with the truth of all the evidence for the benevolence of God. It is doubtless true that all natural evil does at the time, or will ultimately result in salutary restraint upon moral beings. And as all moral evil is increasing the experience and knowledge of the universe in respect to its nature and tendencies, it is certain that its ultimate result will be confirmatory of the divine authority over all virtuous minds. Just as the developments of the nature and tendencies of alcohol, give strength and efficiency to the principles and moral obligations of the temperance reformation.

Obj. VI. If God is benevolent, says the objector, why did he create moral beings, knowing as he must have known, that so many of them would fall into sin and perish.

Ans. 1. If the creation of the universe finally results in greater good than evil, its creation was a dictate of benevolence.

2. That it will finally result in greater good than evil we have every reason to believe, from the fact that all virtuous beings will be happy of course, and abundant means are provided for the reclaiming and saving myriads of sinners.

INFERENCES AND REMARKS.

1. If God is infinitely benevolent, it is said that the salvation of all men is secured.

Ans. This assumes, that God *can* wisely save all men.

2. If God is infinitely benevolent he loves all men alike, and will of course save them all.

Ans. With the love of benevolence God does love all men and devils, irrespective of their character; but with the love of complacency, or delight in their character, upon which kind of love his final treatment of them as judge of the world must be based, he does not and cannot regard all men alike. For as a matter of fact, they are not alike.

3. It is said, that if God does not save all men, his love is partial and not universal.

Ans. This would be true, if he were not alike benevolent to all; but it would be partiality itself for him finally to treat all men alike. This would be partiality to the wicked, or treating them with unreasonable favor, and not according to their real characters.

4. If God is benevolent, then he is not angry with the wicked every day, as the Bible affirms that he is.

Ans. He is angry with the wicked every day, and his anger *against* the wicked is only a modification of his benevolence to the universe. His anger against sinners is equal to and a modification of his love of the order and happiness of the universe.

5. If God's benevolence is infinite, he cannot sin; i. e. he cannot be made willing to sin. There can be no such amount of temptation existing as to overcome the infinite strength of his virtue.

6. If God is love, it is certain that he will employ the whole of his natural attributes in promoting the virtue and happiness of the universe, to the full extent of his power.

7. What an infinite privilege it is to live under the government of such a Being, possessing infinite natural attributes, with a heart to use them all with most divine economy for the promotion of happiness and virtue for ever.

8. What an infinite amount of happiness must finally result to the universe, from the administration of a moral government by such a Ruler:

LECTURE XI.

MORAL ATTRIBUTES.—No. 2.

JUSTICE OF GOD.

FIRST. Define the term Justice.
SECOND. Show the several senses in which it is used.
THIRD. Prove that God is just.
FOURTH. Answer an objection.

FIRST. *Define the term Justice.*

Justice is a hearty and practical regard to the rights of all beings. I say it is hearty and practical. It is an affection of the mind; an efficient affection that results in corresponding action.

SECOND. *Different senses in which the term is used.*

1. *Commercial Justice.* This relates to trade, and is the rendering of exact equivalents in human dealings.

2. *Commutative Justice.* This relates to government, and consists in substitution, or the substituting of one form of punishment, which is preferred by the criminal, and equally advantageous to the government, for another form which he deserves, and to which he has been sentenced. Thus banishment or confinement in the state prison during life is sometimes substituted for the punishment of death.

3. *Remunerative Justice.* This is governmental, and consists in bestowing merited rewards upon virtue.

4. *Retributive or Penal Justice.* This also is governmental, and consists in the infliction of merited punishments.

5. *Public Justice.* This also is governmental, and consists in a due and practical regard to the public rights and interests. It is that which the public have a right to expect and demand for the protection of public morals and the public good, and is that which the law-giver is bound to exercise.

6. *General Justice.* This is synonymous with whatever is upon the whole right, and best to be done. This is righteousness and true holiness, and includes both mercy and grace, when their exercise is consistent with what is upon the whole wise and good. Every form of justice is some modification of benevolence. It is a good will to being in general, carried out in its application to the particular circumstances under which it is manifested. Thus benevolence or good will to the public, leads to the infliction of penal evil upon transgressors. This manifestation of benevolence, we call retributive or penal justice.

Commercial justice does not relate to God. All the other forms which I have mentioned do.

THIRD. *Prove that God is just.*

1. The justice of God is manifested by the fact, that he has subjected the universe to laws, physical and moral, with appropriate sanctions.

2. These sanctions are universally remuneratory and vindicatory, i. e. virtue is rewarded, and vice is punished.

3. The sanctions, so far as we can see, are universally proportioned to the importance of the precept.

4. The remuneratory part of the sanction, that which promises reward to virtue, is in no case set aside when the precept is obeyed.

5. The vindicatory part of the sanction, that which threatens evil to disobedience, is in no case dispensed with, unless full satisfaction be made to public justice.

6. The fact that the penalty attaches, and the work of retribution *commences* instantly on the breach of the precept.

7. The instant and constant bestowment, to some extent, of the rewards of virtue upon obedience. The constitution of moral beings is so framed by their author, that obedience and disobedience to moral law, are instantly followed, the one by the sweets which are naturally and necessarily connected with obedience, and the other with the stings, gnawings, and agonies, that are certainly and necessarily connected with disobedience.

8. Nothing but the Atonement, which is the satisfaction of public justice, ever arrests and sets aside the execution of penal justice in any instance.

9. We reasonably infer the justice of God from the very constitution of our nature. We are so constituted, as from the very laws of our being, to approve, honor, and love justice, and to abhor injustice. If, therefore, God is not just, he has so created us, that we need only to know him to render it impossible for us not to abhor him.

10. If God is not just, he must be unjust; for it is naturally impossible that he should be neither.

11. If God is unjust, he is perfectly so. Justice and injustice are moral opposites, and can never be predicated of the same being at the same time.

12. If God is unjust, he is unchangeably so, as he can never have any new thoughts, purposes, designs, or volitions. Whatever therefore is true of his moral character is immutably and eternally true.

13. If God is unjust, he is infinitely so. Every attribute of God must, like himself, be infinite. Perfect Justice in an infinite being must be Infinite Justice.

14. As a matter of fact, the universe cannot be under the government of a being of infinite injustice.

15. If God is unjust, he must be so, in opposition to absolutely infinite reasons against injustice, and reasons, too, that are for ever present to, and acting with all their weight upon his mind.

16. If God is unjust, he is so in spite of absolutely infinite motives in favor of justice, and with the whole weight of those infinite motives fully before and perfectly apprehended by his infinite mind. The supposition that he is unjust, under these circumstances, is absurd, and the thing morally impossible.

17. Injustice is a form of selfishness. And it has been shown that God is not selfish, but infinitely benevolent.

18. But justice is only a modification of benevolence, therefore, God must be just.

19. If God is unjust, he is infinitely wicked and infinitely miserable. It is impossible that injustice should not make a moral being miserable.

20. If God is not just he must abhor himself.

21. If he is unjust it is our duty to hate him.

22. The Bible every where represents God as just:

Deut. 32: 4: "He is the Rock, his work is perfect; for all his ways are judgment: a God of truth, and without iniquity; just and right is he."

Neh. 9: 33: "Howbeit thou art just in all that is brought upon us; for thou hast done right, but we have done wickedly."

Job 4: 17: "Shall mortal man be more just than God? Shall a man be more pure than his Maker?

Isa. 45: 21: "Tell ye, and bring them near; yea, let them take counsel together: who hath declared this from ancient time? who hath told it from that time? have not I the Lord? And there is no God else besides me, a JUST God and a Savior: there is none besides me.

Zeph. 3: 5: "The JUST Lord is in the midst thereof: he will not do iniquity: every morning doth he bring his judgment to light; he faileth not: but the unjust knoweth no shame."

Zech: 9 : 9 : "Rejoice greatly, O daughter of Zion ; shout, O daughter of Jerusalem : behold, thy King cometh unto thee : he is JUST, and having salvation."

Acts 3 : 14 : "But ye denied the Holy One and the JUST."

Acts 7 : 52 : "And they have slain them which showed before of the coming of the JUST ONE."

Acts 22 : 14 : "And he said, The God of our fathers hath chosen thee, that thou shouldest know his will, and see that JUST ONE."

FOURTH. *Answer an objection.*

Obj. As a matter of fact, moral beings are not dealt with according to their characters in this world.

Ans. 1. There is enough of justice visible here, plainly to intimate that God is just, and yet so much wanting as to create a clear inference, that this is a state of trial and not of rewards.

2. The execution of law, both in its remuneratory and vindicatory clauses, commences and only commences in this life, and the process continues to eternity.

3. Facts as they exist, force the conclusion, that the government of God is moving on as fast as circumstances will allow, to a more perfect and most perfect dispensation of rewards, in a future world.

4. The perfection discoverable in the precept of law, must eventually be carried out, in the final perfection of retributive and remunerative justice, or it will involve the character of God in a manifest contradiction, which cannot be.

5. The Bible fully explains the otherwise, to some extent, mysterious state of things in this world, in respect to the administration of justice, and most perfectly reconciles all that passes here, with the infinite justice of God.

6. Final and perfect justice cannot be consistently dispensed till after the general judgment; for until the history of every being is fully known to the universe of moral beings, they could not possibly understand the reasons for his dealings with his creatures. And the dispensation of perfect justice, previous to the universal development of character, might be and doubtless would be a great stumbling block to the universe.

INFERENCES AND REMARKS:

1. If God is just, the duty of restitution where wrong has been done, must certainly be insisted on by him.
2. If God is just, he is no respecter of persons.
3. If God is just, he abhors injustice in us.
4. If God is just, the finally impenitent must be damned.

LECTURE XII.

MORAL ATTRIBUTES.—No. 3.

MERCY OF GOD.

FIRST. Show what Mercy is not.
SECOND. What it is.
THIRD. In what cases it can be exercised.
FOURTH. To what extent.
FIFTH. On what conditions.
SIXTH. That Mercy is an attribute of God.

FIRST. *Show what Mercy is not.*

1. Not mere goodness. Justice is as much an attribute of goodness as mercy is. A judge is good in proceeding to pass sentence and command the execution of law upon a criminal; but in this there is no mercy.

2. Mercy is not mere grace. Grace is gratuitous favor; something unearned, and of course undeserved.

SECOND. *Show what Mercy is.*

Mercy is a disposition to pardon crime. Its exercise consists in the arresting and setting aside the execution of law, when its penalty has been incurred by disobedience. It is in reference to crime the exact opposite of justice. Justice executes the penalty, and mercy pardons or sets aside the execution.

THIRD. *When it can be exercised.*

It can be exercised only where there is guilt. An innocent being cannot possibly be the subject of mercy. He may be the subject of benevolence, and of justice; but he cannot be forgiven, unless he has incurred guilt. Hence,

FOURTH. *To what extent Mercy can be exercised.*

It can be exercised no farther than desert of punishment goes. If a man deserves to be punished for one year, or for a thousand years, thus far he may be forgiven, but no farther. All beyond his desert of punishment is justice and not mercy. If a man be sentenced to the state prison for three years, for three years he may be pardoned; but for a longer time he cannot. When his three years are expired, it is justice and not mercy that releases him from farther confinement.

FIFTH. *On what conditions.*

I have said that in respect to crime, mercy and justice are, in their exercise, direct opposites. Of course they can be reconciled with each other only upon certain conditions. The conditions of mercy are always two, and if in any case mercy is exercised without regard to these conditions, injustice is done.

1. Satisfaction must he made to public justice. Public justice is that which the public have a right to demand for their own security in case of a violation of law. Something must be done, that will as effectually secure the public interests, and act as efficiently in the prevention of crime, as the execution would do, or the penalty cannot be set aside by an act of mercy. Where this can be done, however, to the full satisfaction of public justice, mercy and justice are at one.

2. The other condition is, that the subject of it must be in a suitable state of mind.

(1.) He must be fully sensible of his great guilt and desert of punishment. And while he justifies himself in whole or in part, he is not a proper subject for the exercise of mercy.

(2.) He must repent. He must deeply abhor his conduct, and fully justify the government. He must love the law and abhor himself, or he ought not to be forgiven.

(3.) He must be willing to make his confession as public as his crime; and while he is too proud to confess, he is in no state of mind to be forgiven. And should he be forgiven without confession, his pardon would be a virtual condemnation of the law.

(4.) He must forsake his crime and all disposition to repeat it. Should a man confess that he had committed murder, and yet plead his blood thirsty disposition as an excuse, and shamelessly avow the continuance of this disposition, this were an infinitely good reason why he should not be forgiven.

(5.) He must make restitution. While a thief has the stolen property in possession and refuses to restore it, he is in no state of mind to be forgiven. Nor is the fraudulent man, the liar, or any sinner, in a suitable state of mind to be forgiven, until he has done, and is willing to do all within his power, to make restitution in every case of wrong.

(6.) He must justify the law, both precept and penalty. While he condemns either, as unnecessarily strict or severe, it is a denial of his desert of the threatened punishment; and his asking for mercy is, under these circumstances, only a demand of justice; praying that the penalty may be set aside, upon the ground that he does not deserve it.

(7.) He must justify all the measures of government by which he has been brought under condemnation. While he has any excuse to make, any quarrel with the government, any caviling at the precept or penalty of the law, or any objections to those governmental measures that have laid him under the sentence of death, to forgive him under these circumstances were but to justify his cavils, to echo his sentiments, to adopt his principles, to turn against the law, and go against the government. This, in any just government cannot be.

SIXTH. *Mercy is an attribute of God.*

1. That God is merciful, or disposed to pardon sin, when it can be consistently done, must be fairly inferred from the divine forbearance, as manifested in this world.

2. The same may be inferred from the manifestly disciplinary nature and design of many of his providences.

3. All nations have believed that God is merciful, which belief must be founded upon proof every where existing of the divine forbearance.

4. We justly infer the mercy of God from the constitution of our own nature. We naturally and necessarily admire and approve of a merciful disposition, while we naturally and necessarily disapprove and abhor an unmerciful disposition. If, therefore, God is not merciful, but unmerciful, we need only to know him to be under the necessity of abhorring him.

5. God must be merciful or unmerciful, and perfectly so; for these being opposite states of mind, can never be exercised by the same being at the same time.

6. If God is merciful or unmerciful he must be infinitely so. As his nature is infinite, so are all his attributes.

7. As a matter of fact, the universe cannot be under the government and providence of an unmerciful being.

8. God's mercy must be unchangeable, as whatever is infinite is unchangeable of course.

9. That God is merciful is an irresistible inference from his benevolence. If God is benevolent, a disposition to forgive, in case the public interests can be made consistent with it, is a thing of course in a benevolent mind.

10. If God is unmerciful, he is so in spite of infinitely and fully perceived motives to the contrary.

11. If God is not merciful, he must abhor himself; as a moral being he cannot help it.

12. If God is unmerciful, it is our duty to abhor him.

13. If he is unmerciful, he must be infinitely miserable; as the feelings of self-reproach and self-condemnation must be infinitely strong in his mind.

The doctrines of Atonement and forgiveness of sin, are but a revelation of the mercy of God. The Bible every where ascribes mercy to God, and speaks of its exercise as that in which he has peculiar delight:

Mich. 7: 18: "Who is a God like unto thee, that pardoneth iniquity, and passeth by the transgression of the remnant of his heritage? He retaineth not his anger for ever, because he delighteth in MERCY."

Ps. 25: 10: "All the paths of the Lord are MERCY and truth unto such as keep his covenant and his testimonies."

Ps. 52: 8: "I trust in the MERCY of God for ever and ever."

Ps. 62: 12: "Also unto thee, O Lord belongeth MERCY."

Ps. 86: 5: "For thou, Lord, art good, and ready to forgive; and plenteous in MERCY unto all them that call upon thee."

Ps. 130: 7: "With the Lord there is MERCY, and with him is plenteous redemption."

Luke 1: 50, 54: "And his MERCY is on them that fear him from generation to generation. He hath holpen his servant Israel, in remembrance of his MERCY."

INFERENCES AND REMARKS.

1. If God is infinitely merciful, no sin is too great for forgiveness, if repented of.
2. If he is infinitely merciful, he is just as ready to forgive the greatest as the least sin.
3. If mercy cannot be exercised, but upon the two conditions already specified, but for the Atonement no sin could have been forgiven.
4. Notwithstanding the Atonement, no sin can be forgiven without repentance, reformation, and restitution.
5. Many are deceived in supposing themselves forgiven, who have not confessed and made restitution.
6. Many are shut up in impenitency, by refusing to confess and make restitution.
7. If God is infinitely merciful, we need not wait in the use of means, to move him to the exercise of mercy; as he is continually using means with us to make us willing to accept, or bring us into a state of mind in which it can be consistent for him to exercise mercy.
8. They deny the mercy of God, who say that men are punished according to their deeds, and then go to heaven. This is justice and not mercy. When sinners have been punished according to their deeds, whether in this or any other world, there is no mercy in exempting them from farther punishment. It is justice that gives them a discharge when their term of punishment is completed.
9. To ask or expect pardon, without repentance, forsaking sin, and making restitution, is an insult to God.
10. The necessity of repentance is as much a doctrine of natural as revealed religion. Both alike declare, that without repentance there is no forgiveness.

LECTURE XIII.

MORAL ATTRIBUTES.—No. 4.

TRUTH OF GOD.

FIRST. Define Truth.
SECOND. Prove that Truth is an attribute of God.

FIRST. *Define Truth.*

Truth, as a moral attribute, is a state of mind. It is a disposition to represent things and facts as they are. There are other definitions of truth. But the inquiry now is, what is truth as an attribute of mind? It is the opposite of falsehood, which, considered as an attribute, is a disposition to misrepresentation.

A distinction is sometimes made between physical and moral truth. But I can see no other meaning to the distinction than that one respects physical, and the other moral objects.

SECOND. *Prove that Truth is an attribute of God.*

1. It may reasonably be inferred from the uniformity and certainty of the operation of the physical laws of the universe.

2. His truth may be inferred from his unbending firmness in the execution of the penalty of physical laws, lest public confidence in the entire certainty of their operation, should be shaken. E. g.—With all his benevolence, and tender love for his creatures, what an amount of suffering and pain does he witness and inflict in consequence of a violation of physical laws, rather than interpose by miracle, and thus beget uncertainty in the minds of men with respect to the results of such violation.

3. His truth is strongly manifested by the sacrifice he made in the Atonement, lest public confidence in his veracity should be shaken.

4. Our constitutional love of truth and abhorrence of falsehood affords the just inference that truth is an attribute of God. If he has so constituted us that we necessarily venerate truth and abhor falsehood, if he is not a God of truth, his works entirely contradict the real state of his mind. But this cannot be, for his works are nothing else than the effects of his volitions. Therefore as his character is, so his works are. If moral beings, the only beings capable of truth or falsehood, are so made as necessarily to abhor lies, and approve of truth, it affords the highest evidence that truth is an attribute of God.

5. God must be either true or false. Truth or falsehood must be an attribute of God. It is impossible that he should be inclined to tell neither truth nor falsehood. But he cannot be both. These

are opposite states of mind, and cannot both possibly exist in the same mind at the same time.

6. If falsehood is an attribute of God, he is infinitely and unchangeably false. The same reasonings that have been suggested in speaking of his Benevolence, Justice and Mercy, are as conclusive in respect to this as any of his other attributes.

7. If God is not a God of truth, no moral being can respect or love him.

8. If not, he deserves to be hated by all moral beings.

9. If not, he can have no complacency in himself.

10. If not, he must infinitely and eternally abhor himself.

11. If not, he must be as much more miserable than Satan is, as he is greater than Satan. Satan is a liar and the father of lies. And as truth is the natural element of mind, it must be certain that an infinite disposition to misrepresentation, would produce infinite misery in the mind of God.

12. If falsehood is an attribute of God, it is so in opposition to the influence of absolutely infinite motives in favor of truth.

13. The entire consistency of his works, providence, and word, evinces his truth.

14. His benevolence, affords an unanswerable argument in favor of his truth.

15. The independence of God is such, as that he can have no conceivable motive to falsehood, or, to say the least, motives to misrepresentation are infinitely outweighed by the inducements to represent things as they are.

16. The moral power of God consists wholly in his truth. The power of any being to influence mind, depends upon the confidence reposed in his veracity.

17. Truth must be believed to be an attribute of God, or moral government could not exist.

18. Universal and hearty confidence in this attribute of God, would give entire efficiency to moral government, and render its influence over the minds of moral beings complete.

19. If truth be not an attribute of God, he must forever deceive the universe, or his moral government over the universe must be entirely destroyed.

20. If falsehood be an attribute of God, his disposition to deceive is infinite. It therefore follows with absolute certainty that he always will so perfectly deceive his creatures, as to render it impossible for them to perceive that truth is not an attribute of his.

21. The Bible proves his truth.

(1.) It requires truth of us.

(2.) It requires us to abhor liars.

(3.) It declares that God abhors liars.

(4.) That he is a God of truth.

(5.) That he cannot lie.

(6.) That he is a God keeping his covenants and promises, fulfilling his threatnings, and many instances are recorded in the Bible of his great faithfulness and truth.

(7.) The fulfillment of prophecy.

(8.) The redeeming his pledge to support his government by the sacrifice of his Son.

(9.) He requires us to believe him upon pain of eternal death.

As the Bible has been shown to be true, its testimony is both admissible and conclusive.

22. Faith or confidence in his veracity is the *sine qua non* of all virtue.

23. Confidence in his truth invariably produces a holy life.

OBJECTION.

To the truth of God it is objected that as a matter of fact, God did not fulfill his threatning denounced against Adam, nor against Nineveh. To this I answer:

1. In Jer. 18: 7, 8, we are informed of the principle in the government of God, involved in all his dealings with his creatures. "At what instant I shall speak concerning a nation, and concerning a kingdom, to pluck up, and to pull down, and to destroy it; If that nation, against whom I have pronounced, turn from their evil, I will repent of the evil that I thought to do unto them."

2. A promise, or threatning, positive in form, may imply a condition, and when the condition is understood, or may and ought to be understood, there is exact truth, if God acts in conformity with the threatning or promise, whenever the condition is fulfilled.

3. It is plain that Jonah and the Ninevites understood that God's threatning was conditional. Jonah expressly informs God that he so understood him. Jonah 4: 2.—"And he prayed unto the Lord, and said, I pray thee, O Lord, was not this my saying when I was yet in my country? Therefore I fled before into Tarshish; for I knew that thou art a gracious God, and merciful, slow to anger, and of great kindness, and repentest thee of the evil." That the Ninevites understood his threatning as conditional, is perfectly plain both from what they said, and what they did. The king proclaimed a fast expressly with the hope and expectation that the city would be spared if the people repented. Jonah, 3: 5—10:—"So the people of Nineveh believed God, and proclaimed a fast, and put on sackcloth, from the greatest of them even to the least of them. For word came unto the king of Nineveh; and he arose from his throne, and he laid his robe from him, and covered him with sackcloth, and sat in ashes. And he caused it to be proclaimed and published through Nineveh, (by the decree of the king and his nobles,) saying, let neither man nor beast, herd nor flock, taste any thing; let them not feed, nor drink water. But let man and beast be covered with sackcloth, and cry mightily unto God: yea, let them turn, every one from his evil way, and from the violence that is in their hands. Who can tell if God will turn and repent, and turn away from his

fierce anger, that we perish not? And God saw their works, that they turned from their evil way; and God repented of the evil that he had said that he would do unto them; and he did it not."

4. The passage already quoted from Jer. shows that all God's promises and threatnings are conditional, whether the condition is expressed or not—that this is a universal principle with him.

5. With respect to Adam it is no doubt true, that death, in the sense intended by God, really began its ravages immediately upon his transgression.

REMARKS.

1. If God is a God of truth, he means as much by what he says, as he appears to mean.

2. If so, he has no secret will contrary to his expressed will.

3. If so, he really deserves universal confidence.

4. If so, how great must be the sin of unbelief.

LECTURE XIV.

MORAL ATTRIBUTES.—No. 5.

WISDOM OF GOD.

First. Define Wisdom.
Second. Prove that Wisdom is an attribute of God.

First. *Define Wisdom.*

1. Wisdom is the most benevolent use of knowledge and power.

2. The attribute of wisdom in God, is his disposition to use his knowledge and power in the most benevolent manner. In other words, to exercise his natural attributes for the promotion of the highest good.

3. It is the choice of the best or most benevolent ends, and of the most suitable means for the accomplishment of those ends.

Second. *Wisdom is an attribute of God.*

1. The benevolence of God has been established. Benevolence is good willing, or the love of being and of happiness. The exercise of benevolence, together with its carrying out, or its gratification, constitutes the happiness of God.

2. God's happiness is infinitely the greatest good in the universe. It is plainly the greatest possible good. To purpose to do what he most loves to do, and thus promote his own happiness by the exer-

cise and gratification of his infinitely benevolent disposition, is certainly the perfection of wisdom. His supreme end must have been the promotion of his own glory and happiness, as this was the highest, most worthy, and desirable end that he could propose to himself. A subordinate end, is the virtue and happiness of his creatures. Their happiness is not regarded as a mere means of promoting his own, but as an end, something chosen for its own sake. Yet an end subordinate to his own glory and happiness, as the virtue, glory, and happiness of all creatures, is infinitely less valuable than the glory and happiness of God.

3. The Bible declares that God made all things for himself.

4. The Bible declares that God governs all things for his own glory. This certainly is wise.

5. The means which he has selected and which he uses for the promotion of these ends declare his wisdom.

(1.) The creation of the material universe must have been a source of enjoyment to him. At the end of every day's labor, he declared his satisfaction by pronouncing it good.

(2.) In the works of creation all his natural attributes were exercised and reflected upon him.

(3.) His providential government is a continued exercise and reflection upon himself of his natural and moral attributes.

(4.) If an artist takes pleasure in imitating the works of God, what must have been God's happiness in creating, and what must now be his happiness in sustaining the universe. Every moral being is in some degree sensible of the pleasures of taste. There is reason to believe that the taste of God is infinitely refined and exquisite. The beautiful and diversified scenery of the world and of the universe—the exquisite and inimitable penciling of the flowers—the colors and sweet sublimity of the rainbow, and a countless number of grand, sublime, beautiful, and exquisite things in the creation of God, render it manifest that he not only possesses taste of a most refined character, but that he has given himself full scope in its exercise and gratification. The great western prairies are his flower-gardens. He has scattered a profusion of beauties, not only wherever there are mortal eyes to behold them, but also where no eye but his own beholds them.

(5.) His happiness must have been still more refined and exquisite in the creation and government of sentient beings, and in the numberless adaptations and contrivances for the promotion of their happiness.

(6.) The providential care of them must also be a source of continual enjoyment to him.

(7.) But most of all, the creation, government, and happiness of moral beings, afforded him exquisite enjoyment. When he had made man, he manifested his supreme pleasure in this work by pronouncing it "*very good.*" Moral beings are capable of sympathizing with him, of being governed by the same motives, of forming the same character, of enjoying the same kind of happiness, capable of understanding his works and word, and of holding communion and fellowship with him. Thus it appears that God has chosen the highest ends, and the best means of accomplishing them, which is the perfection and the whole of wisdom.

6. The Bible every where ascribes wisdom to God, and affirms that all wisdom belongs to him. It speaks of him as "God only wise," and "the only wise God," and affirms that wisdom is an eternal attribute of God.

REMARKS.

1. In the material and moral universe, God has spread out before himself a vast field of usefulness.
2. In the works of creation he has opened to himself an endless source of enjoyment.
3. He takes more pleasure in giving than we do in receiving.
4. All that he has done and is doing for sinners must afford him great satisfaction.
5. The more we depend on him to do for us, the more highly we please him.
6. We can be truly happy only as we imitate God.

LECTURE. XV.

MORAL ATTRIBUTES.—No. 6.

HOLINESS OF GOD.

FIRST. Premise several remarks.
SECOND. Define Holiness.
THIRD. Prove that Holiness is an attribute of God.

FIRST. *Remarks.*

1. The whole of a moral being is his nature and his character.
2. His nature composes his substance and essence, including the whole of his natural attributes.
3. His character consists in the exercise or use he makes of his nature.
4. A natural attribute has no moral character.
5. A moral attribute is a disposition, and as a disposition is a voluntary state of mind. Therefore moral attributes are what principally constitute moral character.

SECOND. *Define Holiness.*

It is a disposition to do universally right in opposition to wrong. It is a disposition to do what is upon the whole best to be done. It is moral purity. It is benevolence, guided by wisdom, justice, and mercy. It includes complacency in right character, and opposition to sinful character. Holiness is moral perfection, and nothing short of moral perfection, or moral rectitude, is holiness. In other words: it is conformity of heart and life to the perceived nature and relation of things. In creatures it may improve in degree, because knowledge may improve. But in kind it can never improve. Holiness is holiness. It is the opposite of all sinfulness, and all improvement in holiness must be in degree and not in kind.

In God holiness can never improve in any sense, because his knowledge is already infinite. Holiness in man expresses the whole of moral excellence. So in God it may express the whole of his moral excellence, and is properly styled an attribute only in the largest sense of that term, or in the same sense in which benevolence may be styled an attribute of God. God is called light. His moral attributes viewed separately are like prismatic colors. When combined they are an ineffable blaze of holiness. In other words, the holiness of God when considered as embracing his whole moral perfection, is a moral light, so ineffably intense as that the highest intelligences in the universe are represented in the Bible as unable to behold it without veiling their faces.

That holiness is purity or moral *perfection*, is proved by the following facts:

1. That the Bible represents holiness as the contrast of defilement or pollution.

2. That whatever was to be set apart, or consecrated to God, and considered as sanctified, must be physically *perfect*. Any blemish or imperfection was inconsistent with its being sanctified.

3. The Bible represents holiness as the opposite of sin.

THIRD. *Holiness is an attribute of God.*

1. God is holy or sinful. As he is a moral being, it is impossible that he should not be one or the other. As was said of his benevolence, so I now say of his holiness, that he cannot possibly be of a mixed character. He must be *perfectly* holy or sinful, because holiness and sin are opposite states of mind, and he cannot by any possibility exercise them both at the same time.

2. His character, whether holy or sinful, must be unchangeable. As he can have no new thoughts, and consequently no motives of any kind whatever to change.

3. His holiness or sinfulness must be infinite, for as his nature is, so are his attributes. But that the universe was not created and is not governed by an infinitely wicked being is most evident.

4. Our own nature is proof of the holiness of God. We constitutionally approve of holiness and disapprove of sin. If God is not holy he has so created us as to lay us under the constitutional necessity of abhorring him whenever we know him.

5. If he is not holy he must abhor himself.

6. If he is infinitely sinful, he must be infinitely miserable.

7. All holy beings know from their own consciousness, that holiness necessarily results in happiness, and that sin necessarily results in misery. If therefore, God is holy, he is infinitely happy: if sinful, he is infinitely miserable.

8. If not holy he must resist absolutely infinite motives to holiness.

9. The physical perfection of his works, declares his moral purity.

10. The Bible every where ascribes holiness to God.

11. His moral law is but an expression, or an embodying and holding forth the holiness of his heart.

12. The work of atonement is an overwhelming proof of the holiness of God.

13. The conditions of the Gospel are such as strongly to manifest the holiness of God.

14. He is worshiped in heaven as a holy God. Isa. 6: 3: "And one cried unto another, and said, holy, holy, holy is the Lord of hosts; the whole earth is full of his glory." Rev. 4: 8: "And the four beasts had each of them six wings about him; and they were full of eyes within; and they rest not day and night, saying, Holy, holy, holy, Lord God Almighty, which was, and is, and is to come."

LECTURE XVI.

UNITY OF GOD.

First. What is intended by the term unity, as applied to God.

Second. Some remarks in respect to the manner in which this subject has been treated in different ages and nations.

Third. Prove the Unity of God.

First. *What is intended by the Unity of God.*

1. It is not intended that he is one in the sense of Unitarians, who deny the proper divinity of the Son and of the Holy Spirit.

2. Nor that he is one in the sense of the Swedenboergens, who hold the Son to be only the human nature of the Father, and the Holy Spirit to be only the divine power, influence, or operation; but,

3. By the unity of God is intended that he is one in opposition to Polytheism, or the doctrine of the existence of many gods.

4. That he is one in opposition to the doctrine of Dualism, or the sentiment that there are two gods, the one good, the other evil.

5. That he is one in opposition to Tritheism, or the doctrine that there are three distinct, separate and independent beings in the god-head, the Father, Son, and Holy Spirit; and that their unity is only a moral one.

6. By the unity of God it is intended that God is one in essence or substance, one substratum of being, yet subsisting in three persons.

SECOND. *Some remarks upon the manner in which this subject has been treated.*

1. It has been supposed by many that the doctrine of the divine unity is exceedingly plain and manifest, and among the most easily discerned truths of natural religion. To this it may and should be answered:

(1.) That if this were true, the fact cannot be accounted for that the most enlightened nations, that have not enjoyed the light of revelation, have believed in the existence of many gods. They have felt the force of the evidence every where abounding in favor of the existence of a God or Gods, but have, almost without exception, settled down upon the conclusion, either of Dualism or Polytheism.

(2.) The wisest philosophers of the most enlightened nations have not, except in a very few instances, arrived even at the conception of the idea of the unity of God, and have felt such great difficulties in the way of demonstrating it, without the aid of revelation, as to leave them, after all, in much doubt.

(3.) The mass of the Jews themselves, previous to the Babylonish captivity, believed in the existence of many gods, and only supposed Jehovah, or their God, to be superior to all other gods. They only claimed the supremacy of their God, at the same time admitting the real existence, and agency, and providence of the gods of other nations. This accounts for their repeated relapses into Polytheism. Their inspired men held more worthy notions in respect to the unity of God. But the great mass of the nation appear to have been in great ignorance upon this subject until after the Babylonish captivity.

Jacob in his early life appears to have admitted the existence of more gods than one, and suffered the existence of idolatry in his family, as appears from the fact that Rachel, his favorite wife, stole her father's gods.

Solomon either admitted the existence of more gods than one, or was guilty of the most criminal neglect in suffering his wives to practice idolatry even in the holy land.

2. Since revelation has poured its clear light upon the subject of the unity of God, it is easy for us to see the consistency of this truth with natural reason. But it is a remarkable fact that no nation that has once lost the true idea of the unity of God, has ever

again arrived at the truth upon this subject without divine revelation. It is often easy when a truth has been suggested, to demonstrate it by the light of nature. But it is a very different thing, as all experience shows, to discover truth before it has been suggested by revelation.

THIRD. *Prove the unity of God.*

There is positive proof of the existence of a first cause at the head of a series of events.

2. It is impossible that there should be more than one first cause of the same series.

3. There is no necessity for supposing the existence of more than one first cause of all events.

4. The supposition of more than one is therefore unphilosohpical.

5. The human mind evidently feels a difficulty in admitting the existence of more than one infinite being. All Polytheistical nations have conceived of their gods as being finite, not infinite. And whenever the idea of the existence of one infinite God has been entertained, he has been regarded as the supreme God, and no nation has admitted the idea of more than one infinite God.

6. There is not a particle of proof that more than one infinite God exists. One of the principal reasons for supposing the existence of many gods, by heathen nations, was the fact that the creation of the universe was regarded as too great a work to have been performed by any one being. This conclusion was just in them, as they regarded their gods as finite, and not infinite. But when the infinity of God is understood, there is no longer any reason for supposing the existence of more gods than one.

The doctrine of Dualism, or that two Gods exist, one the author of good, the other the author of evil, was founded in the fact of the existence of both good and evil in the universe. That a good God could not be the author of the evil, they justly inferred. And taking it for granted that evil must have some other author than its perpetrator, they ascribed it to the existence and agency of a wicked god. But the existence of good and evil affords no evidence, when rightly understood, of the existence of more than one God. It is true that the evil cannot be attributed to a good God as its author; but it is also true that a good God might create moral agents, and place them under moral government, and for wise reasons decline absolutely preventing their falling into sin. This suggestion sufficiently accounts for the existence of sin in the universe, which leaves Polytheism and Dualism destitute of a vestige of proof. Therefore,

7. The belief in more than one God is utterly unreasonable, as it is the belief of that of which there is no evidence.

8. If there is more than one God, it is of the highest importance that we should be acquainted with the fact, and be able to pay that homage and service to each which we must owe to God.

9. If there is more than one God, the total absence of all evidence of this truth seems incredible.

10. The universe as a whole is a unit.

(1.) This is indicated by its name.

(2.) One set of laws every where prevail.

(3.) This is also evident from the mutual dependence of all its parts.

11. There is a manifest unity of design running through all the universe, which affords the strongest presumptive proof of the unity of God.

12. In view of all these considerations, if the doctrine of more than one God is asserted, the *onus probandi* lies on him who asserts it.

13. Tritheists do not pretend to find in the light of nature the proof of the existence of three distinct and infinite beings, united in the office, and called by the official name of God, but base their theory upon scripture testimony, affirming that the Bible teaches that the Father, Son, and Holy Ghost are distinct, separate and infinte beings; and that the unity of God, so largely insisted on in the Bible, is only a moral unity.

14. If the bible does not teach the absolute unity of existence or being in the God-head, it seems impossible that any language should teach this doctrine.

(1.) It is affirmed that God is *one*.

Deut. 6: 4: "Hear O Israel; The Lord our God is ONE GOD."

1 Cor. 8: 4, 6: "There is none other God but one." "There is but one God, the Father, of whom are all things, and we in him, and one Lord Jesus Christ, by whom are all things, and we by him."

Mark 12: 29: "The first of all the commandments is, Hear O Israel; The Lord our God is ONE Lord."

Gal. 3: 20: "Now a mediator is not a mediator of one, but God is ONE."

Eph. 4: 6: "ONE God and Father of all, who is above all, and through all, and in you all."

Mat. 23: 9: "Call no man your father upon the earth: for ONE is your Father, which is in heaven."

John 8: 41: "We have ONE Father, even God."

1 Tim. 2: 5: "For there is ONE God, and one mediator between God and men, the man Christ Jesus."

James 2: 19: "Thou believest that there is one God; thou doest well: the devils believe and tremble."

(2.) He is God and Jehovah *alone*.

2 Kings 19: 15: "And Hezekiah prayed before the Lord, and said, O Lord God of Israel, which dwellest between the cherubim, thou are the God, even thou ALONE, of all the kingdoms of the earth."

Ps. 86: 10: "For thou art great and doest wondrous things, thou art God ALONE."

Isa. 27: 16, 20: "O Lord of hosts, God of Israel, that dwellest between the cherubim, thou art the God, even thou ALONE, of all the kingdoms of the earth." "Now therefore, O Lord our God, save us from his hand, that all the kingdoms of the earth may know that thou art the Lord, even thou ONLY."

Neh. 9: 6: "Thou, even thou art Lord ALONE."

(3.) There is none *else.*

Deut. 4: 39: "Know therefore this day, and consider it in thine heart, that the Lord he is God in heaven above, and upon the earth beneath: there is NONE ELSE."

Isah. 44: 8: "Is there a God beside me? yea, there is no God; I know not any."

Deut. 4: 35: The Lord he is God, there is NONE ELSE besides him."

Isa. 45: 5, 6, 14, 22: "I am the Lord, and there is NONE ELSE." "That they may know from the rising of the sun, and from the west, that there is none beside me: I am the Lord, and there is NONE ELSE." "Surely God is in thee, and there is NONE ELSE; there is no God." "I am the Lord, and there is NONE ELSE." "Look unto me, and be ye saved, all the ends of the earth, for I am God, and there is NONE ELSE."

Isa. 46: 9: "Remember the former things of old; for I am God, and there is NONE ELSE."

(4.) There is none *beside* him.

2 Sam. 7: 22: "Wherefore thou art great, O Lord God: for there is none like thee, neither is there any God BESIDES thee."

2 Sam. 22: 32: "For who is God save the Lord? and who is is a rock, save our God?"

2 Kings 5: 15: "Behold now I know that there is NO God in all the earth, BUT in Israel."

Hosea 13: 4: "Yet I am the Lord thy God from the land of Egypt, and thou shalt know NO God BUT me: for there is no Savior BESIDES me."

(5.) None *with* him.

Deut. 32: 39: "See now that I, even I, am he, and there is no God WITH me."

(6.) None *before* him.

Ex. 20: 3: "Thou shalt have NO other gods BEFORE me."

Isa. 43: 10: "Ye are my witnesses, saith the Lord, and my servants whom I have chosen; that ye may know and believe me, and understand that I am he: BEFORE ME THERE WAS NO GOD FORMED."

(7.) None *like* him.

Ex. 8: 10: "That thou mayest know that there is none LIKE unto the Lord our God."

Ps. 35: 10: "All my bones shall say, Lord, who is LIKE unto thee?"

Micah 7: 18: "Who is a God LIKE unto thee?"

1 Kings 8: 23: "And he said, Lord God of Israel, there is no God LIKE thee, in heaven above, or on earth beneath."

Ex. 9: 14: "For I will at this time send all my plagues upon thine heart, and upon thy servants, and upon thy people; that thou mayest know that there is none LIKE me in all the earth."

Deut. 33: 26: "There is none LIKE unto the God of Jeshurun."

2 Sam. 7: 22: "Wherefore thou art great, O Lord God: for there is none LIKE thee."

1 Chron. 17: 20: "O Lord there is none LIKE thee."

Ps. 86: 8: "Among the gods there is none LIKE unto thee."

Isa. 46: 9: "Remember the former things of old; for I am God, and there is none else; I am God, and there is none LIKE me."

Jer. 10: 6, 7, 10: "Forasmuch as there is none LIKE unto thee, O Lord; thou art great, and thy name is great in might. Who would not fear thee, O King of nations? for to thee doth it appertain: forasmuch as among all the wise men of the nations, and in all their kingdoms, there is none LIKE unto thee." "But the Lord is the true God, he is the living God, and an everlasting King: at his wrath the earth shall tremble, and the nations shall not be able to abide his indignation."

Isa. 40: 18: "To whom then will ye liken God? or what likeness will ye compare unto him?"

Isa. 46: 5: "To whom will ye liken me, and make me equal, and compare me, that we may be like?"

30. These things cannot possibly be true if there is more than

one separate, independent existence, possessing the attribute of God.

31. Natural and revealed theology agree in revealing *but one* God.

32. They agree in rejecting the idea of more than one.

33. Natural religion reveals this with the highest evidence that the nature of the case admits.

34. The Bible reveals it in the most full and unqualified manner conceivable.

LECTURE XVII.

TRINITY OR TRI-UNITY OF GOD.

FIRST. State the doctrine.

SECOND. The point now under consideration.

THIRD. The sources of evidence.

FOURTH. The amount of evidence to be expected, if the doctrine be true.

FIFTH. Adduce the proof.

SIXTH. Answer objections.

FIRST. *State the doctrine.*

1. That there is one only living and true God.

2. That he subsists in three persons, the Father, Son, and Holy Ghost.

3. That there are three divine, distinct, though not separate moral agents, in the Godhead.

4. That they exist in one essence, or substratum of being.

SECOND. *The point now under consideration.*

1. Not the unity of God, or that the Father, Son, and Holy Ghost, are one. The divine unity has been already established. But:

2. The point of inquiry before us respects the distinct personality and divinity of the Father, Son, and Holy Spirit.

THIRD. *The sources of evidence.*

1. We are not to expect to gather clear evidence of the doctrine of the Trinity or Tri-Unity of God, from the works of creation, as the perfect moral and essential unity of the Father, Son, and

Holy Spirit, would preclude all possibility of discrepancy of views or operations in the creation or government of the universe. Every thing, therefore, in the creation and government of the material universe, may be expected to indicate only the existence of one God, without distinct notices of a Trinity of persons.

2. The only source from which we can expect proof, is that of direct revelation, oral or inspired.

FOURTH. *The amount of evidence to be expected, if the doctrine is true.*

1. We are not to expect that the *quo modo*, or mode of the divine existence will be, by revelation, made intelligible to, or brought so within the comprehension of our minds, that we shall be able fully to understand it. All that we can know of infinite is, that it exists; but whether an infinite mind subsists in one or many persons in one substratum of being, we cannot know but by a divine revelation. And by revelation we can only know the fact, without a possibility of comprehending the *quo modo*.

2. We are not to expect such a formal and metaphysical statement of the doctrine as has been common in polemic theology; for this is not the manner in which revelation is given upon any subject.

3. We may reasonably expect evidence, direct, inferential, incidental, full, and conclusive, or otherwise, as the knowledge and belief of it is more or less essential to salvation.

4. If it be a fundamental doctrine, or a doctrine the belief of which is essential to salvation, it is reasonable to expect traditionary notices of it, where there are traditionary notices in heathen nations of other fundamental truths of revelation.

5. We may expect to find the traditionary notices such as we have of other important truths, such as images, medals, oral or written statements, more or less obscure, in proportion as other fundamental truths are known and preserved among men.

6. If the doctrine of the Trinity in the God-head be a fundamental doctrine, we may expect its announcement at the commencement of revelation, to be more or less full, in proportion as other fundamental doctrines are there revealed.

7. We might expect the revelation of this truth in its fuller and fuller development, to keep pace with the fuller revelation of other fundamental doctrines.

8. We might suppose, that before revelation closed, it would be revealed with such fulness, as to satisfy an honest mind, that was disposed to rest in the naked testimony of God.

9. But we should expect this and every other fundamental doctrine, to be so left by revelation as not to preclude all cavil, evasion, or gainsaying. This might be expected, from the nature of probation, moral agency, and the existence and design of moral government.

10. It would not be unreasonable to expect some intimation of the doctrine in the name of God.

11. It would not be unreasonable to suppose, that their common or collective name, should be plural, and when action is ascribed to them, that the verb should be singular.

12. Beside this, it would not be unreasonable to expect each person to have a singular name, or appellation peculiar to himself, as Father, Son or Word, and Holy Ghost.

13. We should expect the unity of God as opposed to Dualism, Tritheism, and Polytheism, to be fully and strongly revealed.

14. We might reasonably expect also, a full revelation of the distinct personality of the Father, Son, and Holy Ghost,; but in such a way as not to contradict the essential unity of God.

15. If the doctrine of the Trinity be a doctrine of revelation, we may expect the absolute Deity of the three persons to be fully revealed.

16. We might expect that the common or collective name, or names of the God-head, would be given to each and either of the three persons indiscriminately.

17. We might expect that divine attributes should be ascribed to each and all of them.

18. We might expect the works of God to be ascribed to either and each of them indiscriminately; for if they subsist in one substratum of being; what one does, they all do by him.

19. It might be expected that what one of the persons did or does, would be represented either as *his* act, or as the act of *the whole God-head.*

20. We might expect a perfect moral unity, to be plainly asserted or implied in revelation.

21. We might expect that each person, would be represented as filling a distinct office, as exercising peculiar functions, and as sustaining peculiar relations to the universe.

22. We might expect that they would speak of each other as distinct persons.

23. It might be expected they would speak of themselves altogether as one.

24. That they would all claim and receive divine honors.

25. We might expect that when any official act or relation demanded it, they would claim superiority, or acknowledge inferiority and dependence, as their official relations and functions might require.

26. If the official work or relations of either person to creatures, were such as might obscure the evidences of his divinity, we might expect a correspondingly full revelation of the divinity of that particular person. See Christ.

27. So if for these or for other reasons, the distinct personality of either required special proof, we might expect to find it in revelation. It is not pretended that the proof would not be sufficient, if in all the above named particulars it was not complete. Yet

when the importance of the doctrine is considered, in connection with the infinite benevolence of God, and his great desire to enlighten and save mankind, it is not unreasonable to expect those intimations of it which have been above noticed.

FIFTH. *Adduce the proof.*

Here I will premise the following remarks:

1. The full proof of this doctrine includes the proof of the Divinity of Christ, and of the personality and Divinity of the Holy Ghost. In the present skeleton I shall not examine those subjects extensively, but defer their proof to a future occasion.

2. I remark, that many seem to have come to the examination of this subject, with a determination not to receive this doctrine, unless it is so unequivocally taught in the Bible as that it can by no possibility be explained away or evaded.

3. Many of the German and other critics have practically adopted this as a sound rule of Biblical interpretation, that every text is to be so explained as to evade this doctrine, if it possibly can be evaded.

4. They have manifestly set aside, in practice, what all Biblical scholars admit in theory—that the Bible is to be received in its plain, natural, and common sense import, unless there be some obvious reasons for resorting to another mode of interpreting a particular passage.

5. The opposers of this doctrine, and not a few of its advocates, have manifestly adopted the principle, that, judging *a priori*, the doctrine of the Trinity or Tri-Unity of God, is highly improbable, and unreasonable, and therefore, that no text is to be received as teaching this doctrine, if it will by any possibility admit of any other construction.

6. I feel bound to protest against this assumption, and the practical adoption of this rule of Biblical interpretation, either by the enemies or friends of this doctrine.

7. I insist that the doctrine of a Trinity in the God-head is so far as we can see, as consistent with reason as any other view of the subject whatever. And that we are to come to the Bible, in examining this question, with this plain and simple rule of interpretation before us—that every passage, as read in the original, is to be taken in its plain and obvious import, entirely irrespective of the difficulty or mysteriousness of the doctrine of the Trinity of God.

8. In referring to the different texts, especially in the Old Testament, I shall follow very much the order in which Knapp has conconsidered them.

9. It will not be expected in this skeleton form, that I should enter into a critical examination of the opinions of learned divines upon them; but leave you to consider them according to their obvious import.

10. It is not generally pretended by the friends of this doctrine, nor do I contend that the doctrine of the Trinity in the God-head is

formally and unequivocally taught in the Old Testament; but it is contended that it is so plainly intimated in different passages, when viewed in their connections and relations to each other, as fully to account for the fact of the extensive understanding and reception of this doctrine by the Jews.

11. I propose now to consider only some of those passages that treat in a more general manner of the doctrine of the Trinity, leaving, as I have already intimated, the particular examination of the personality and divinity of the Father, Son and Holy Spirit, for future occasions.

12. This doctrine, like all other fundamental doctrines of the Bible, is revealed with greater and greater fulness and distinctness as revelation progresses, and is brought out in connection with the Atonement, and by the New Testament writers, as might be expected, in a much fuller and more satisfactory manner than in the Old Testament.

I come now to the examination of scripture testimony.

I. The plural names of God, Eloheim, Adonai, &c. It is said that these forms *may be* regarded as the *pluralis excellentiæ* of the oriental languages. To this I answer,

1. That they *may* be, but that this proves nothing.

2. The plural form of the name of God is, as might be expected, if the doctrine of the Trinity were true.

3. We are to give this circumstance no greater or less weight than belongs to it, and by itself, it would prove nothing satisfactory Yet taken in connection with the other and abundant proofs of this doctrine, the plural forms of the divine name are to be regarded as a circumstance of importance.

II. Those passages that speak of God as more than one.

1. Gen. 1: 26: "And God said, let US make man after OUR image."

Of this passage it has been suggested, that God addressed the angels, when he said, Let us make man. To this I reply:

(1.) It is mere conjecture.

(2.) Those whom he addressed were not mere witnesses, but actually concerned in the creation of man, and must therefore have possessed divine power.

(3.) There is no instance, unless this is one, in which God is represented as consulting creatures in respect to what he should do, not even in cases where they are co-workers with him.

2. Gen. 3: 22: "And the Lord God said, Behold the man is become as one of US."

This passage is remarkable. Here God says of Adam, "Behold the man is become as one of US." This seems as plainly to imply a plurality in the God-head, as any form of expression could.

3. Gen. 11: 7: "Go to, let us go down, and there confound their language, that they may not understand one another's speech."

Here again God is represented as consulting other divine personages, and saying, "Let us go down," &c. To these passages it has also been replied, that they may be only the *pluralis excellentiæ*, such language as kings are in the habit of using when speaking of themselves. To this I reply:

(1.) God is represented as using this language before any kings existed.

(2.) The fact that such language might have been in use when Moses wrote, does not seem sufficiently to account for the plural form of the divine name; and,

(3.) As Polytheism was the great sin of the world, in making a revelation to man, we should expect all such language to be avoided, as might convey the idea of a plurality in the God-head, unless that were really the fact.

III. I refer to those texts in which there seems to be more than one Jehovah, and more than one Eloheim.

1. Gen. 19: 24: "Then the Lord rained upon Sodom and Gomorrah brimstone and fire from the Lord out of heaven."

Here it is said Jehovah rained upon Sodom and upon Gomorrah brimstone and fire from Jehovah out of heaven. The Jehovah here mentioned as raining upon Sodom, appears to be the same person who the day before had visited Abraham, and to whom Abraham had presented several petitions, which were granted. It appears that Lot prayed to him to spare Zoar, which request also was granted. He said to Lot respecting Zoar, "Haste thee, for *I can* do nothing till thou be come hither." This Jehovah, to whom Abraham and Lot prayed, is the identical Jehovah that rained fire and brimstone from Jehovah out of heaven, as if one Jehovah were in heaven and another on earth.

2. Dan. 9: 17: "Now therefore, O God, hear the prayer of thy servant, and his supplications, and cause thy face to shine upon thy sanctuary that is desolate, for the Lord's sake."

Here Daniel is represented as praying to God in the name of the Lord. To this it has been said, that it may mean nothing more than that God would answer his prayer for his own sake. To this I answer:

The inquiry is not what it might by some possibility mean. But what does such language, in its obvious import seem to imply? "Hear, O our God, hear the prayer of thy servant for the Lord's sake." This, taken in connection with the many passages where God is besought to do things for the Lord's and Christ's sake, appears to be a parallel passage and to mean the same thing.

3. Zech. 10: 12: "And I will strengthen them in the Lord and they shall walk up and down in his name saith the Lord."

Here Jehovah speaks of another Jehovah, in whose name they shall walk up and down.

4. Zech. 2: 8, 9: "For thus saith the Lord of hosts, After the glory hath he sent me unto the nations which spoiled you; for he that toucheth you toucheth the apple of his eye. For, behold, I will shake mine hand upon them, and they shall be a spoil to their servants; and ye shall know that the Lord of hosts hath sent me."

Here Jehovah of hosts speaks of a Jehovah of hosts that had sent him, and declares that they that touch Zion touch the apple of that Jehovah's eye who had sent him. Again in the 11th verse, Jehovah of hosts speaks of himself as having been sent by Jehovah of hosts. And continuing to the 13th verse, he speaks of Jehovah as one distinct from himself, and as raised up out of his holy habitation."

5. Ps. 45: 7: "Thou lovest righteousness, and hatest wickedness: therefore God, thy God, hath anointed thee with the oil of gladness above thy fellows."

Here God, or *Eloheim*, addresses another Eloheim.

IV. I refer to those texts where God is spoken of as three.

1. Is. 48: 16: "Come ye near unto me, hear ye this; I have not spoken in secret from the beginning; from the time that it was, there am I: and now the Lord God, and his Spirit hath sent me."

It is contended by some that this passage should be rendered, "The Lord God hath sent me and his Spirit." Which ever rendering is preferred, it cannot reasonably be denied that three distinct persons are recognized in this text as divine. The person spoken of as being sent declares that he had not spoken in secret from the beginning, or from eternity. It is plain beyond all reasonable debate, that in this text the Father, Son and Holy Spirit are spoken of.

2. Num. 6: 24—26: "The Lord bless thee, and keep thee; the Lord make his face shine upon thee, and be gracious unto thee; the Lord lift up his countenance upon thee, and give thee peace."

The repetition of the divine name, Jehovah, three times in this passage is very remarkable, and, as we shall by and by see, was understood by the Jews to intimate the doctrine of a divine Trinity.

3. Mat. 28: 19: "Go ye therefore, and teach all nations, baptizing them in the name of the Father, and of the Son, and of the Holy Ghost."

Here the Father, Son and Holy Ghost are spoken of in connection, and in such a manner as that no one of them is represented as divine any more than the other.

2. Deut. 6: 24: "And the Lord commanded us to do all these statutes, to fear the Lord our God, for our good always, that he might preserve us alive, as it is at this day."

4. John 14: 23: "Jesus answered and said unto him, If a man love me, he will keep my words: and my Father will love him, and we will come unto him, and make our abode with him."

Here Christ promises that himself and his Father will come and make their abode with those who love him. Other passages abundantly teach that they come in the person of the Holy Spirit.

5. 2 Cor. 13: 14: "The grace of our Lord Jesus Christ, and the love of God, and the communion of the Holy Ghost, be with you all. Amen."

This benediction appears to be a prayer addressed to the three persons of the God-hėad.

V. I refer to those passages where the Son of God is spoken of in the Old Testament.

1. Ps. 2: 7: "I will declare the decree: the Lord hath said unto me, Thou art my Son; this day have I begotten thee."

That the Son of God, or the Messiah, is here spoken of, is attested by the Apostles.

Acts 13: 33: "God hath fulfilled the same unto us their children, in that he hath raised up Jesus again: as it is also written in the second psalm, Thou art my Son, this day have I begotten thee."

2. Ps. 72: 1: "Give the king thy judgments, O God, and thy righteousness unto the king's Son," compared with,

Ps. 89: 27: "Also I will make him my first born, higher than the kings of the earth."

These passages have always been understood as relating to the Son of God as Messiah. They do not indeed prove the divinity of the Son; but speak of him as distinct from the Father.

With respect to the Holy Spirit, I observe that he is so often spoken of throughout the Bible as distinct from the Father, that I will not here enter into an examination of any of the texts.

I will now close the examination of scripture testimony upon this question, reminding you that the principal scripture proofs of this doctrine are to be examined in considering the personality and divinity of the Son, and of the Holy Spirit.

I will next refer you:

1. To intimations of this doctrine among ancient heathen nations, which I shall borrow from Dwight's Theology, vol. 2, page 390:

(1.) "*The Hindoos have, from the most remote antiquity, holden a Triad in the Divine nature.*

The name of the Godhead among these people is *Brahme*. The names of the three persons in the Godhead are *Brahma*, *Veeshnu*, and *Seeva*. Brahma they considered as the Father, or Supreme Source; Veeshnu as the Mediator, whom they assert to have been incarnate; and Seeva as the Destroyer, and Regenerator: destruction being in their view nothing but the dissolution of preceding forms, for the purpose of reviving the same being in new ones.

The three faces of Brahma, Veeshnu, and Seeva, they always formed on one body, having six hands; or two to each person. This method of delineating the Godhead is ancient beyond tradition, universal, uncontroverted, and carved every where in their places of worship; particularly in the celebrated cavern in the Island of Elephanta.

(2.) *Equally well known is the Persian Triad; the names of which were* ORMUSD, MITHR, AND AHRIMAN; *called by the Greeks* OROMASDES, MITHRAS, *and* ARIMANIUS. Mithras was commonly styled *Triplasios*. Among *them*, as well as among the Hindoos, the second person in the Triad was called the Mediator, and regarded as the great Agent in the present world.

In the Oracles ascribed to Zerdusht, or Zoroaster, the famous Persian Philosopher, are the following declarations:

'Where the Eternal Monad is, it amplifies itself, and generates a Duality.'

'A Triad of Deity shines forth throughout the whole world, of which a Monad is the head.'

'For the mind of the Father said, that all things should be divided into Three; whose will assented, and all things were divided.'

'And there appeared in this Triad, Virtue, Wisdom, and Truth, who knew all things.'

'The Father performed all things, and delivered them over to the Second mind, whom the nations of men commonly suppose to be the First.'

The third Person, speaking of himself, says, 'I Psyche, or Soul, dwell next to the Paternal mind, animating all things.'

(3.) *The Egyptians, also, acknowledge a Triad, from the earliest antiquity, whom they named originally* OSIRIS, CNEPH, *and* PHTHA; *and afterwards Osiris, Isis, and Typhon.* These Persons they denoted by the symbols Light, Fire, and Spirit. They represented them, also, on the doors, and other parts of their sacred buildings, in the three figures of a Globe, a Wing, and a Serpent. Abenephius, an Arabian writer, says, that 'by these the Egyptians shadowed *Theon trimorphon*, or God in three forms.'

One of the Egyptian fundamental axioms of Theology, as given by Damascius, and cited by Cudworth, is, 'There is one Principle of all things, praised under the name of the Unknown Darkness, and this thrice repeated.'

In the Books, attributed to Hermes Trismegistus, is the following passage:

'There hath ever been one great, intelligent Light, which has always illumined the Mind; and their union is nothing else but the Spirit, which is the Bond of all things.'

Here light and mind are spoken of as two Persons, and the Spirit as the third; all declared to be eternal.

Jamblichus, a Platonic Philosopher, styled by Proclus the Divine, declares, that 'Hermes speaks of Eicton as the first of intelligences, and the first intelligible; and of Cneph, or Emeph, as the Prince of the Celestial Gods; and of the Demiurgic, or creating Mind, as a third to these. Jamblichus calls these the Demiurgic Mind, the Guardian of Truth, and Wisdom.

(4.) *The Orphic Theology, the most ancient recorded in Grecian history, taught the same doctrine.*

In the abridgement of this Theology by Timotheus, the Chronographer, are found its most important and characteristical doctrines. Of these the fundamental one is, that an Eternal, Incomprehensible Being exists, who is the Creator of all things. This supreme and eternal Being is styled in this Theology, *Phos, Boule, Zoe;* Light, Counsel, Life.

Suidas, speaking of these three, says, 'they express only one and the same power.' Timotheus says further, that Orpheus declared, 'All things to have been made by One Godhead in three names; or rather by these names of One Godhead; and that this Godhead is all things.'

Proclus, a Platonic Philosopher, aleady mentioned, says, that Orpheus taught 'the existence of One God, who is the ruler over all things; and that this One God is three Minds, three Kings; He who is; He who has, or possesses; and He who beholds. These three Minds he declares to be the same with the Triad of Orpheus; viz: Phanes, Uranus, and Chronus.

(5.) *The Greek Philosophers, also, extensively acknowledged a Triad.*

Particularly, Pythagoras styled God *to hen*, or the Unity; and *monas*, or that which is alone; and also *to agathon*, or the good.

'From this Eternal Monad,' says Pythagoras, 'there sprang an infinite Duality; that is from Him, who existed alone, two proceeded, who were infinite.'

Plato also held a Triad; and named them *to Agathon*, the Good; *Nous*, or *Logos*, Mind, or Word; and *Psuche kosmou*, the Soul of the World. The *to Agathon* he also calls *protos Theos*, and *megistos Theos.*

Parmenides, the founder of the Eleatic Philosophy, says, The Deity is *hen kai polla;* one and many. Simplicius, commenting on Plato's exhibition of the doctrine of Parmenides, says, that 'these words were a description of the *autou Ontos*,' the true or original existence; and Plotinas says, that Parmenides acknowledged three Divine Unities subordinated. The first Unity he calls the most perfectly and properly One; the scond, One many; and the third, One and many. Plotinus further says, that Parmenides acknowledged a Triad of original Persons. Plotinus speaks of God as being 'the One, the Mind, and the Soul;' which he calls the original or principal persons. Amelius calls these Persons three Kings, and three Creators.

Numenius, a famous Pythagorean, acknowledged a Triad. The second Person he calls the Son of the first; and the third he speaks of, as proceeding also from the first.

(6.) *In the Empires of Thibet and Tangut, a Triune God is constantly acknowledged in the popular religion.* Medals, having the image of such a God stamped on them, are given to the people by the Delai Lama, to be suspended, as holy, around their necks, or otherwise used in their worship. These people also worshipped an idol, which was the representation of a three-fold God.

(7.) A medal, now in the Cabinet of the Emperor of Russia, was found near the River Kemptschyk, a branch of the Jenisea, in Siberia, of the following description:

A human figure is formed on one side, having one body and three heads. This person sits upon the cup of the Lotos; the common accompaniment of the Godhead in various Eastern countries; and on a sofa, in the manner of Eastern Kings. On the other side is the following inscription: 'The bright and sacred image of the Deity, conspicuous in three figures. Gather the holy purpose of God from *them:* love *him.*' A heathen could not more justly or strongly describe a Trinity.

(8.) *The ancient Scandinavians acknowledged a Triad; whom they styled Odin, Frea, and Thor.*

In the Edda, the most remarkable monument of Scandinavian Theology, Gangler, a Prince of Sweden is exhibited as being introduced into the hall or palace, of the gods. Here he saw three thrones raised one above another, and on each throne a sacred person. These persons were thus described to him by his guide: 'He, who sits on the lowest throne, is Har, or the Lofty One. The second is Jafn Har, or Equal to the Lofty One. He, who sits on the highest throne, is Thridi, or the Third.'

(9.) *The Romans, Germans, Gauls, acknowledged a Triad, and worshipped a Triad, in various manners.*

The Romans and Germans worshipped the Mairiæ; three goddesses inseparable, and always united in their worship, temples, and honors.

The Romans also, together with the Greeks and Egyptians, worshipped the Cabiri, or Three Mighty Ones.

The Diana of the Romans is stamped on a medal, as having three faces or three distinct heads, united to one form. On the reverse is the image of a man, holding his hand to his lips; under whom is this inscription: 'Be silent; it is a mystery.'

The German goddess Trygla, was drawn in the same manner.

The Gauls also, united their gods in triple groups, in a manner generally similar, as is evident from sculptures, either now or lately remaining.

(10.) *The Japanese and Chinese anciently acknowledged a Triad.*

The great image of the Japanese is one form, with three heads; generally resembling that of Brahma, Veeshnu, and Seeva, already described as worshipped by the Hindoos. The Chinese worshipped in ancient times one Supreme God, without images, or symbols of any kind. This worship lasted until after the death of Confucius, about 500 years before the birth of Christ.

Lao-Kiun, the celebrated founder of one of the philosophical, or religious sects, in China, delivered this, as the great leading doctrine of his philosophy: 'That the Eternal Reason produced One; One produced Two; Two produced Three; and Three produced All things.'

(11.) *The American Nations also, have in several instances acknowledged a Triad.*

The Iroquois hold, that before the creation, three Spirits existed; all of whom were employed in creating mankind.

The Peruvians adored a Triad, whom they styled the *Father* and *Lord Sun*, the *Son Sun*, and the *Brother Sun*.

In Cuquisaco, a province of Peru, the inhabitants worshipped an image, named *Tangatanga;* which in their language signifies *One in Three, and Three in One.*"

2. I will refer you to the testimony of the ancient Jewish Church, which I shall borrow from the same source: Vol. 2, p. 386:

"Philo, the celebrated Jew of Alexandria, who lived before the birth of our Savior, calls the *Logos* the Eternal *Logos* or Word; and says, that 'he is necessarily eternal, and the image of the invisible God.'

Further, he says, 'He, who *is*, is on each side attended by his nearest Powers; of which one is *Creative*, and the other *Kingly*. The Creative is God, by which he founded and adorned the Universe. The Kingly is Lord. He who is in the middle, being thus attended by both his Powers, exhibits to the discerning mind, the appearance, sometimes of One, and sometimes of Three.'

Of the *Logos* he says, 'He, who is the begotten, imitating the ways of his Father, and observing his archetypal patterns, produces forms; that is, material things. He often calls the *Logos*, the *Divine Logos;* and represents him as the Manager, or Ruler of the world. He further says, that God governs all things according to the strictest justice, having set over them his righteous *Logos*, his first begotten Son.' The duration of created things he ascribes to this cause; that they were framed by Him, who remains; and who is never in any respect changed; the *Divine Logos*.' Finally, he calls the *Logos* an Angel; the name of God; a man; the beginning; the eternal image; the most ancient Angel;

the Archangel, of many names; and the high priest of this world; and says, 'His head is anointed with oil.'

The Chaldee Paraphrasts, and other Jewish commentators, speak of this subject in a similar manner.

They speak of the Mimra, the Hebrew term, rendered in the Greek *Logos*, and in the English *Word*, as 'the Word from before the Lord,' or which is before the Lord; as a Redeemer; as only begotten; as the Creator. They say, 'the Word of the Lord said, 'Behold Adam, whom I have created, is the only begotten in the world; as I am the only begotten in the highest heavens.' They paraphrased the text, Genesis 3: 8: *And they heard the voice of the Lord God, walking in the garden, thus:* '*They heard the Word of the Lord God*,' &c.

Several Jewish commentators say, that 'it was the Voice which was walking.'

One of them says, that 'Our first parents, before their sin, saw the Glory of God speaking to them; but after their sin, they only heard the Voice walking.'

Philo and Jonathan both say, that 'it was the Word of God, which appeared unto Hagar.'

Jonathan says, 'God will receive the prayer of Israel by his Word.' Paraphrasing Jer. 29: 14: he says, 'I will be sought by you in my Word.'

The *Jerusalem Targum*, or Paraphrase, says, 'Abraham prayed in the name of the Word of the Lord, the God of the world.'

Jonathan says also, 'God will atone by his Word for his land, and for his people; even a people saved by the Word of the Lord.'

Psalm 110: 1: They paraphrase, '*The Lord said unto his Word*,' instead of '*My Lord*,' as in the original.

The Jewish commentators say, 'there are *three Degrees* in the Mystery of Aleim, or Elohiem; and these *degrees* they call *persons*. They say, 'They are all one, and cannot be separated.'

Deut. 6: 4: *Hear, O Israel!* JEHOVAH, *our Aleim is one* JEHOVAH, is thus rendered by the author of the Jewish Book *Zohar:* 'The Lord, and our God, and the Lord, are One.' In his comment on this passage the author says, 'the LORD, or JEHOVAH, is the beginning of all things, and the perfection of all things; and he is called the Father. The other, or our God, is the depth or the fountain of sciences; and is called the Son. The other, or Lord, he is the Holy Ghost, who proceeds from them both, &c. Therefore he says, *Hear, O Israel!* that is, join together this Father, the Son, and the Holy Ghost, and make him One Essence; One Substance; for whatever is in the one is in the other. He hath been the whole; he is the whole; and he will be the whole.'

Again: 'What is the name of King Messiah? Rabbi Akiba hath said, JEHOVAH is his name. As it is declared, Jer. 23: 6: *And this is his name, by which they shall call him, Jehovah our Righteousness*.'

These commentators, also, call him the Branch; the Comforter; Gracious; Luminous; &c.

And again: 'The Holy Ghost calls the King Messiah by his name: JEHOVAH is his name: for it is said, Exodus 8: 1: *The Lord is a man of war; Jehovah is his name.*'

3. The testimony of the early Christian fathers. Vol. 2, p. 183:

(1.) "*To the Pre-existence of Christ the following testimonies must, I think, be regarded as complete.*

a. Justin Martyr, who flourished in the year 140, and was born about the close of the first century, declares Christ to have been the person who appeared to Abraham, under the Oak of Mamre; and asserts that the person, here called LORD or JEHOVAH, to whom Abraham prays for Sodom, and who in the next chapter, is said to rain fire and brimstone on the *Cities of the Plain*, was no other than Christ. He also asserts, that Christ appeared to Moses in the bush.

b. Irenæus, who flourished in the year 178, declares, that Christ, as God, was adored by the Prophets; was *the God of the living, and the living God;* that he spoke to Moses in the bush; and that afterwards the same person refuted the doctrine of the Sadducees, concerning the resurrection of the dead. He further says, that Abraham learned divine truth from the *Logos*, or *Word of God.*

c. Theophilus of Antioch, who flourished in the year 181, declares, that Christ, assuming *to prosopon tou patros*, the character of the Father, that is, the Divine character, came to Paradise in the appearance of God, and conversed with Adam.

d. Clemens Alexandrinus, who flourished in the year 194, exhibits Christ as the Author of the former precepts, and of the latter; that is, of the scriptures of the Old Testament, and of the New; deriving both from one fountain.

e. Tertullian declares, that it was the Son of God who spoke to Moses, and who appeared, that is, as God, at all times; that he overthrew the Tower of Babel; confounded the languages of men; and rained fire and brimstone on Sodom and Gomorrah. He calls him *Dominus a Domino;* and says, that he only, and alway, conversed with men, from Adam down to the Patriarchs and Prophets, in visions and dreams; and that no other God conversed with men, beside *the Word who was* afterward *to be made flesh.*

(2.) *That Christ was the Creator of the world, in the view of the ancient Church, the following testimonies satisfactorily prove:*

a. Barnabas, who, as you well know, was a companion of the Apostles, and could not but know their views of this subject, says, in an epistle of his, yet remaining, 'The Sun in the heavens was the work of the Son of God.'

b. Hermas, also a companion of the Apostles, says, that 'the Son of God was more ancient than any creature; seeing he was present with the Father at the creation of the world.'

c. Athenagoras, who flourished in the year 178, says, that 'by Christ, and through Christ, all things were created; since the Father and the Son are *hen;* one thing; one substance.'

d. Justin Martyr declares, that 'more than one Divine person is denoted by the phrase, *The man is become as one of us;* and that one of these is Christ.'

e. Clemens Alexandrinus says, 'The *Logos* is the universal Architect;' that is, the Maker of all things. He further says, 'The *Logos* is the Creator of men and of the world.' He also speaks of the *Logos* as the universal Ruler, and Instructer.

(3.) *That Christ was truly God, in the view of the ancient Church, will fully appear from the following testimonies:*

a. Clement of Rome, who was a companion of the Apostles, calls Christ 'the sceptre of the greatness of God,' and says, 'he had it in his power to have come with pomp and magnificence, but would not.'

b. Polycarp, a disciple of St. John, when at the stake, addressed a prayer to God, which he concluded in this manner: 'For all things I praise thee; I bless thee; I glorify thee; together with the eternal and heavenly Jesus Christ; with whom, unto thee, and the Holy Spirit, be glory, both now and for ever, world without end Amen.'

c. Justin Martyr declares, that 'Christ the *first born Word of God*, existed as God; that he is Lord and God, as being the Son of God; and that he was the *God of Israel.*'

He also says, 'We adore and love the *Word* of the unbegotten and invisible God.' And again: 'Him (the Father of righteousness) and *that* Son who hath proceeded from him, and the Prophetical Spirit, (that is, the Spirit of Inspiration) we worship and adore.'

This doctrine, also, Trypho, his Jewish antagonist, admits as the doctrine of the Gentile Christians, generally.

d. The Church of Smyrna, in their Epistle to the other churches concerning the martyrdom of Polycarp, in which the above mentioned doxology is quoted, says, 'We can never forsake Christ, nor worship any other; for we worship him as being the Son of God.'

e. Athenagoras says, 'The *Nous kai Logos*, Mind and Word of God, is the Son of God;' and, 'We who preach God, preach God the Father, God the Son, and Holy Ghost; and the Father, the Son, and the Holy Ghost are ONE.'

f. Tatian, Bishop of Antioch, who flourished in the year 172, says, 'We declare that God was born in human form.'

g. Melito, Bishop of Sardis, who flourished in the year 177, says, 'We are worshippers of one God, who is before all, and in all, in his Christ, who is truly God the Eternal Word.'

h. Theophilus, Bishop of Antioch, says, 'The three days before the creation of the heavenly luminaries, represent the Trinity; God, and his Word, and his Wisdom.'

i. Clemens Alexandrinus prays to Christ to be propitious, and says, 'Son and Father, both one Lord, grant, that we may praise the Son and the Father, with the Holy Ghost, all in ONE; *in* whom are all things, *through* whom are all things in ONE, through whom is Eternity, of whom we are all members, to him, who is in all things good, in all things beautiful, universally wise and just, to whom be glory, both now and for ever. Amen.' He also says, 'Gather together thy children, to praise in a holy manner, to celebrate without guile, Christ, Eternal *Logos*, infinite age, Eternal Light, Fountain of Mercy.'

k. Tertullian says, 'The name of Christ is every where believed, and every where worshipped, by all the nations mentioned above. He reigns every where, and is every where adored. He is alike to all a King, and to all a Judge, and to all a God and a Lord.'

Again: 'Behold all nations henceforth emerging from the gulf of error, to the Lord God the Creator, and to God his Christ.'

Tertullian also declares, that 'Tiberias received accounts from Palestine, of the things, which manifested the truth of Christ's Divinity.'

To these Christian testimonies, all of the two first centuries, I shall subjoin a few others, out of multitudes, which belong to a later period.

The testimony of Origen, in his comment on the text, has been already seen. He, also, says, 'We (Christians) worship ONE God, the Father and the Son.'

He further says, 'Now, that you may know the omnipotence of the Father and the Son to be one and the same, as He is one and the same God and Lord with the Father; hear what St. John hath said in the Revelation: These things saith the Lord, which is, and which was, and which is to come, the Almighty. For who is the Almighty that is to come, but Christ?'

He, also, mentions the Christians, as saying, 'that the Father, the Son, and the Holy Spirit, are ONE God; and speaks of this as a difficult, and perplexing doctrine, to such as hear not with faith, or are not Christians.'

Again, he says: 'When we come to the grace of Baptism, we acknowledge ONE God only, the Father, the Son, and the Holy Ghost.'

Origen flourished in the year 230.

Cyprian, Bishop of Carthage, who flourished in the year 248, says, 'Christ is our God; that is, not of all, but of the faithful, and believing.'

The Council of Antioch, which sat about the year 264, in their Epistle, say, 'In the whole Church, he is believed to be *God*, who emptied himself, indeed, of a state of equality with God; and *man*, of the seed of David, according to the flesh.'

Eusebius, the celebrated ecclesiastical historian, who flourished in the year 315, declares, that Pilate, in his letter to Tiberias, concerning the miracles of Christ, says, that 'he was raised from the dead; and that he was already believed by the body of the people to be God.'"

4. The representation of heathen nations concerning the Christian doctrine of the Trinity. Same: Vol. 2, p. 336:

"Pliny the Younger, in his letter to the Emperor Trajan, from the province of Bithynia, whither he went with proconsular authority, writes, that 'certain Christians, whom he had examined, affirmed, that they were wont to meet together on a stated day, before it was light, and sing among themselves, alternately, a hymn to Christ, as to some God.' This letter is, with the highest probability, placed in the year 107.

Celsus, an eminent Epicurean Philosopher and adversary of the Christians, charges them with worshipping Christ, 'who,' he says, 'has appeared of late;' and whom he calls, 'The Minister of God.' Celsus flourished in the year 176.

At the same time flourished Lucian, the celebrated writer of Dialogues, and a philosopher of the same sect. In the Philopatris, a dialogue frequently attributed to him, Triphon represents the Christians as 'swearing by the Most High God; the Great, Immortal, Celestial Son of the Father; the Spirit, proceeding from the Father; ONE of three, and three of ONE.'

Hierocles, who flourished about the year 303, a heathen philosopher also, says that 'the Christians, on account of a few miracles, proclaim Christ to be God.'

On these testimonies I shall only ask a single question. Can any person, who has them before him, doubt for a moment, that the Christian Church, in its earliest ages, acknowledged and worshipped, the Father, the Son, and the Holy Ghost, as the only livin and true God?"

SIXTH. *Answer Objections.*

Obj. I. It is objected, that the doctrine of a Trinity in Unity is a contradiction. To this I reply:

It is no contradiction, because it is not affirmed, nor was it ever supposed, that God is three and one, in the same sense.

Obj. II. This doctrine is said to be unreasonable.

Ans. It is only *above* reason.

Obj. III. It is said to be absurd, to make what is incomprehensible an article of faith.

Ans. 1. Then it is absurd to make the infinity or spirituality of God articles of faith; for they are certainly incomprehensible.

2. If this objection be good, it is absurd to believe our own existence, or the existence of any thing else, as the *modus existendi* is in every case altogether incomprehensible.

3. The fact, and not the *quo modo*, is the thing to be believed. And this is no more incomprehensible than millions of facts which all receive.

Obj. IV. It is objected, that a Trinity in Unity is inconceivable.

Ans. It is not more so than the fact of our own existence, and the union of body and soul.

Obj. V. It is objected that this doctrine embarrasses and confounds the mind.

Ans. 1. It is not the fact, but the philosophy, or *quo modo*, that embarrasses the mind. You may as well confound yourself with the philosophy of your own existence, and maintain the materiality of mind to escape the union of two natures, as to confound yourself with the philosophy of this doctrine, and reject because you cannot comprehend it.

To avoid incomprehensibilities, some explain away the essential Unity, and others the Trinity of God; but no more relieve the difficulty, than materialists do, when they attempt to get rid of mystery by maintaining the intelligence of matter. The fact is, that we know nothing of infinity, only that it exists; and for ought we can know, an infinite mind may as well exist in ten thousand persons as one.

2. It is most remarkable, that many of those who have thought it highly unreasonable to affirm that God could exist in three persons, each possessing the powers of moral agency, are now adopting the Pantheistic philosophy, and maintaining that the Universe is God.

This is not only admitting but maintaining, that there are myriads of moral agents in one God. Not only so; but vegetables, trees, and animals, are so many parts of God. Marvelous consistency this!

To get rid of the doctrine of a Trinity, there must be a most manifest wresting of scripture, and a practical and total disregard of some of the most universally confessed rules of Biblical interpretation.

LECTURE XVIII.

DIVINITY OF CHRIST.

FIRST. Show what is intended by the Divinity of Christ.

SECOND. Show that Christ is truly Divine or that he is the true God.

THIRD. Answer objections.

FIRST. *What is intended by the Divinity of Christ.*

1. By the Divinity of Christ is not intended that he is a divine being in the sense in which angels are divine beings.
2. Nor in the sense in which super angelic creatures might be divine.
3. Nor that he is God in any subordinate sense of the term.
4. That he is properly and absolutely God.

SECOND. *Show that Christ is truly divine.*

The proof of the divinity of Christ is to be gathered of course from the Bible. In establishing it, I shall pursue very much the course that has been pursued by Pres. Dwight.

I. I adduce those texts in which the proper names of God are ascribed to Christ.

1. He is called God.

Gen. 32: 30: "And Jacob called the name of the place Peniel: for I have seen GOD face to face, and my life is preserved." Compared with—

Ex. 33: 20: "And he said thou canst not see my face; for there shall no man see me, and live." And—

John 1: 18: "No man hath seen God at any time; the only begotten Son, which is in the bosom of the Father, hath declared him." And—

John 6: 46: "Not that any man hath seen the Father, save he which is of God, he hath seen the Father."

Isa. 7: 14: "Therefore the Lord himself shall give you a sign; Behold, a virgin shall conceive, and bear a son, and shall call his name IMMANUEL." Compared with—

Mat. 1: 23: "Behold, a virgin shall be with child, and shall bring forth a son, and they shall call his name EMMANUEL, which, being interpreted, is, GOD with us." And—

John 1: 1: "In the beginning was the WORD, and the WORD was with God, and the WORD was GOD." And—

Rom. 9: 5: "Whose are the fathers, and of whom, as concerning the flesh, Christ came who is over all, GOD blessed for ever. Amen." And—

1 Tim. 3: 16: "And without controversy great is the mystery of godliness: GOD was manifest in the flesh, justified in the Spirit, seen of angels, preached unto the Gentiles, believed on in the world, and received up into glory."

Titus 1: 3: "But hath in due times manifested his word through preaching, which is committed unto me, according to the commandment of GOD our Savior."

Heb. 1: 8: "But unto the Son, he saith, Thy throne, O GOD, is for ever and ever; a sceptre of righteousness is the sceptre of thy kingdom."

Heb. 3: 4: "For every house is builded by some man; but he that built all things is God." Compared with—

John 1: 3, 10: "All things were made by HIM; and without HIM was not any thing made that was not made."

2. He is called the *true* God.

1 John 5: 20: "And we know that the Son of God is come and hath given us an understanding, that we may know him that is TRUE; and we are in him that is TRUE, even in his Son Jesus Christ. This is the TRUE God, and eternal life."

3. He is called the *mighty God.*

Isa. 9: 6: "For unto us a child is born, unto a son is given, and the government shall be upon his shoulder; and his name shall be called Wonderful, Counsellor, The MIGHTY God, The everlasting Father, The Prince of Peace."

4. He is called the Lord God *Almighty.*

Rev. 15: 3: "And they sing the song of Moses the servant of God, and the song of the Lamb, saying, Great and marvellous are thy works, Lord God Almighty; just and true are thy ways, thou King of saints."

5. He is called the *Almighty.*

Rev. 1: 8: "I am Alpha and Omega, the beginning and the ending, saith the Lord, which is, and which was, and which is to come, the ALMIGHTY."

6. He is called the *only wise God.*

Jude 25: "To the ONLY WISE God our Savior, be glory and majesty, dominion and power, both now and ever. Amen."

7. He is called the *great God.*

Titus 2: 13: "Looking for that blessed hope, and the glorious appearing of the GREAT GOD and our Savior Jesus Christ."

8. He is called the *God of Israel.*

Ex. 24: 9, 10: "Then went up Moses and Aaron, Nadab and Abihu, and seventy of the elders of Israel; and they saw the God of Israel: and there was under his feet as it were a paved work of a sapphire-stone, and as it were the body of heaven in his clearness." Compared with—

Ex. 33: 20: "And he said, Thou canst not see my face: for there shall no man see me, and live." And—

John 1: 18: "No man hath seen God at any time; the only begotten Son, which is in the bosom of the Father, he hath decared him." And—

John 6: 46: "Not that any man hath seen the Father, save he which is of God, he hath seen the Father."

9. He is called *Jehovah* in several instances, in the 12th chapter of Zechariah.

Isa. 6: 1, 3, 5, 8, 11, 12: "In the year that king Uzziah died I saw also the Lord sitting upon a throne, high and lifted up, and his train filled the temple." "And one cried unto another, and said, Holy, holy, holy is the Lord of Hosts; the whole earth is full of his glory." "Then said I, Woe is me! for I am undone; because I am a man of unclean lips, and I dwell in the midst of a people of unclean lips; for mine eyes have seen the King, the Lord of Hosts." "Also I heard the voice of the Lord, saying, Whom shall I send, and who will go for us? Then said I, Here am I, send me." "Then said I, Lord, how long? And he answered, Until the cities be wasted without inhabitants, and the houses without man, and the land be utterly desolate, and the Lord have removed men far away, and there be a great forsaking in the midst of the land." Compared with—

John 12: 40, 41: "He hath blinded their eyes, and hardened their heart; that they should not see with their eyes, nor understand with their heart, and be converted, and I should heal them. These things said Esias, when he saw his glory, and spake of him."

10. He is called *Jehovah of Hosts.*

Isa. 6: 3, 5: "And one cried unto another, and said Holy, holy, holy is the Lord of Hosts; the whole earth is full of his glory." "Then said I, Woe is me! for I am undone; because I am a man of unclean lips, and I dwell in the midst of a people of unclean lips: for mine eyes have seen the King, the Lord of Hosts."

In the original this is Jehovah of Hosts.

II. The natural attributes of God are ascribed to Christ.

1. Eternity.

Rev. 1: 10: 11: "I was in the Spirit on the Lord's day, and heard behind me a great voice, as of a trnmpet, saying, I am Alpha and Omega, the first and the last; and what thou seest, write in a book, and send it unto the seven churches which are in Asia; unto

Ephesus, and unto Smyrna, and unto Pergamos, and unto Thyatira, and unto Sardis, and unto Philadelphia, and unto Laodicea."

Rev. 2 : 8 : "And unto the angel of the church of Smyrna write : These things saith the FIRST and the LAST, which was dead, and is alive."

Isa. 44 : 6 : "Thus saith, the Lord the King of Israel, and his Redeemer the Lord of Hosts ; I am the first, and I am the LAST ; and besides me there is no God."

2. Omniscience.

John 21 : 17 : "He said unto him the third time, Simon, son of Jonas, lovest thou me ? Peter was grieved because he said unto him the third time, Lovest thou me ? And he said unto him, Lord, thou KNOWEST ALL THINGS ; thou knowest that I love thee."

Mat. 11 : 27 : "ALL THINGS are delivered unto me of my Father ; and no man knoweth the Son, but the Father ; neither knoweth any man the Father, save the Son, and he to whomsoever the Son will reveal him."

Rev. 2 : 23 : "And I will kill her children with death ; and all the churches shall know that I am he which searcheth the reins and hearts ; and I will give unto every one of you according to your works."

That searching the heart implies omniscience is manifest.

1 Kings 8 : 39 : "Then hear thou in heaven thy dwelling place, and forgive, and do, and give unto every man according to his ways, whose heart thou knowest ; for thou, even thou only knowest the hearts of all the children of men."

John 2 : 23, 24 : "Now when he was in Jerusalem at the passover, in the feast-day, many believed in his name, when they saw the miracles which he did. But Jesus did not commit himself unto them, because he knew all men."

3. Omnipresence.

Mat. 18 : 20. 'For where two or three are gathered together in my name, there am I in the midst of them.'

Mat. 28 : 20. 'Teaching them to observe all things whatsoever I have commanded you ; and lo, I am with you alway, even unto the end of the world.'

4. Omnipotence.

Rev. 1 : 8. 'I am Alpha and Omega, the beginning and the ending, saith the Lord, which is, and which was, and which is to come, the Almighty.'

Heb. 1 : 2. 'Hath in these last days spoken unto us by his Son, whom he hath appointed heir of all things, by whom also he made the worlds.'

John 1: 3. 'All things were made by him; and without him was not any thing made that was made.'

5. Immutability.

Heb. 13: 8. 'Jesus Christ the same yesterday, and to-day, and for ever.'

Ps. 102: 27. 'But thou art the same, and thy years shall have no end." Compared with—

Heb. 1: 10. 'And, Thou, Lord, in the beginning hast laid the foundation of the earth; and the heavens are the works of thine hands.'

III. The works of God are ascribed to Christ.

1. Creation.

John 1: 3, 10. 'All things were made by him; and without him was not any thing made that was made.'

Ps. 33: 6. 'By the word of the Lord were the heavens made; and all the hosts of them by the breath of his mouth."

Col. 1: 16. 'For by him were all things created that are in heaven, and that are in earth, visible and invisible, whether they be thrones, or dominions, or principalities, or powers; all things were created by him, and for him.'

Eph. 3: 9. 'And to make all men see what is the fellowship of the mystery, which from the beginning of the world hath been hid in God, who created all things by Jesus Christ.'

Heb. 1: 2. 'Hath in these last days spoken unto us by his Son, whom he hath appointed heir of all things, by whom also he made the worlds.'

Heb. 4: 11. "Thou art worthy, O Lord, to receive glory, and honor, and power; for thou hast created all things, and for thy pleasure they are and were created."

2. He governs the universe.

Isa. 6: 5. 'Then said I, Woe is me! for I am undone; because I am a man of unclean lips, and I dwell in the midst of a people of unclean lips; for mine eyes have seen the KING, the Lord of Hosts.'

Here he is called the King of the universe.

Isa. 9: 6, 7. 'For unto us a child is born, unto us a son is given, and the government shall be upon his shoulder; and his name shall be called Wonderful, Counsellor, The mighty God, the everlasting Father, the Prince of Peace. Of the increase of his government and peace there shall be no end, upon the throne of David, and upon his kingdom, to order it, and to establish it with judgment and with justice, from henceforth even for ever. The zeal of the Lord of Hosts will perform this.'

Dan. 7: 13, 14. 'I saw in the night-visions, and, behold, one like the Son of man came with the clouds of heaven, and came to the Ancient of days, and they brought him near before him. And there was given him dominion, and glory, and a kingdom, that all people, nations and languages, should serve him; his dominion is an everlasting dominion, which shall not pass away, and his kingdom that which shall not be destroyed.'

Acts. 10: 36. "The word which God sent unto the children of Israel preaching peace by Jesus Christ; he is Lord of all.'

Ps. 45: 6. 'Thy throne, O God, is for ever and ever; the scepter of thy kingdom is a right sceptre.'

Rom. 9: 5. 'Whose are the fathers, and of whom, as concerning the flesh, Christ came, who is over all, God blessed forever. Amen.'

1 Cor. 15: 25. 'For he must reign, till he hath put all enemies under his feet.'

Eph. 1: 20. 'Which he wrought in Christ, when he raised him from the dead, and set him at his own right hand in the heavenly places.'

Phil. 2: 9—11. 'Wherefore God also hath highly exalted him, and given him a name which is above every name; that at the name of Jesus every knee should bow, of things in heaven, and things in earth, and things under the earth.'

The whole of the 2d and 72d Psalm represent Christ as the governor of the world.'

3. He raised the dead.

John 5: 28, 29. 'Marvel not at this; for the hour is coming, in the which all that are in their graves shall hear his voice. And shall come forth; they that have done good, unto the resurrection of life; and they that have done evil, unto the resurrection of damnation.

John 10: 17, 18. 'Therefore doth my Father love me, because I lay down my life, that I might take it again. No man taketh it from me, but I lay it down of myself; I have power to lay it down, and I have power to take it again. This commandment have I received of my Father.'

John 6: 39, 40, 44, 54, 'And this is the Father's will which hath sent me, that of all which he hath given me I should lose nothing, but should raise it up again at the last day.' 'No man can come to me, except the Father, which hath sent me draw, him; and I will raise him up at the last day.' 'And this is the will of him that hath sent me, that every one which seeth the Son, and believeth on him may have everlasting life; and I will raise him up at the last day.' 'Whoso eateth my flesh, and drinketh my blood, hath eternal life; and I will raise him up at the last day.'

4. He forgives sins.

Mat. 9: 2—7. 'And, behold they brought to him a man sick of the palsy, lying on a bed; and Jesus, seeing their faith, said unto the sick of the palsy, Son, be of good cheer, thy sins be FORGIVEN thee. And, behold, certain of the scribes said within themselves, This man blasphemeth. And Jesus knowing their thoughts, said, Wherefore think ye evil in your hearts? For whether is easier to say, Thy sins be forgiven thee; or to say, Arise and walk? But that ye may know that the Son of man hath power on earth to FORGIVE sins, (then saith he to the sick of the palsy,) Arise, take up thy bed, and go unto thine house. And he arose, and departed to his house.'

5. He gives eternal life to men.

John 10: 27, 28. 'My sheep hear my voice, and I know them, and they follow me; and I give unto them ETERNAL LIFE; and they shall never perish, neither shall any pluck them out of my hand.'

Rev. 21: 6. 'And he said unto me, It is done. I am Alpha and Omega, the beginning and the end; I will give unto him that is athirst of the fountain of the water of life freely.'

Rev. 2: 7, 17, 28. 'He that hath an ear, let him hear what the Spirit saith unto the churches; To him that overcometh will I give to eat of the tree of life, which is in the midst of the paradise of God.' 'He that hath an ear, let him hear what the Spirit saith unto the churches; To him that overcometh will I give to eat of the hidden manna, and will give him a white stone, and in the stone a new name written, which no man knoweth saving he that receiveth it.' 'And I will give him the morning-star.'

6. He shall judge the world.

Acts. 17: 31. 'Because he hath appointed a day, in the which he will JUDGE the world in righteousness by that man whom he hath ordained; whereof he hath given assurance unto all men, in that he hath raised him from the dead.'

John 5: 22. 'For the Father judgeth no man, but hath committed all JUDGMENT unto the Son.'

Also, Mat. 2: 5.

7 He upholds all things.

Heb. 1: 3. 'Who being the brightness of his glory, and the express image of his person, and UPHOLDING ALL THINGS by the word of his power, when he had by himself purged our sins, sat down on the right hand of the Majesty on high.'

8. He inspired the prophets.

1 Pet. 1: 11. 'Searching what, or what manner of time, the Spirit of Christ which was in them, did signify, when it testified beforehand the sufferings of Christ, and the glory that should follow.'

9. He commissions ambassadors.

2 Cor. 5: 20. 'Now then we are ambassadors for Christ, as though God did beseech you by us; we pray you in Christ's, stead be ye reconciled to God."

IV. He sustains the relations of God to his creatures.

1. He is King.

John 1: 49. 'Nathaniel answered and said unto him, Rabbi, thou art the Son of God; thou art the KING of Israel.'

Isa. 6: 5. 'Then said I, Woe is me! for I am undone; because I am a man of unclean lips, and I dwell in the midst of a people of unclean lips; for I have seen the KING, the Lord of Hosts.'

Ps. 2: 6. 'Yet have I set my KING upon my holy hill of Zion.'

Luke 23: 2. 'And they began to accuse him, saying, We found this fellow perverting the nation, and forbidding to give tribute to Cæsar, saying that he himself is Christ a KING.'

John 18: 37. 'Pilate therefore said unto him, Art thou a KING then? Jesus answered, Thou sayest that I am a KING. To this end was I born, and for this cause came I into the world, that I should bear witness unto the truth. Every one that is of the truth heareth my voice.'

1 Tim. 1: 17. 'Now unto the KING eternal, immortal, invisible, the only wise God, be honor and glory for ever and ever. Amen.'

1 Tim. 6: 15. 'Which in his times he shall shew, who is the blessed and only Potentate, the KING of kings, and Lord of lords.'

2. He is the Creator of mankind.

John 1: 2. 'All things were made by him; and without him was not any thing made that was made.'

3. He is the Redeemer.

1 Cor. 1: 30. 'But of him are ye in Christ Jesus, who of God is made unto us wisdom, and righteousness, and sanctification, and REDEMPTION.'

Eph. 1: 7. 'In whom we have REDEMPTION through his blood, the forgiveness of sins, according to the riches of his grace.'

Heb. 9: 12. 'Neither by the blood of goats and calves, but by his own blood, he entered in once into the holy place, having obtained eternal REDEMPTION for us.'

Rev. 5: 9. 'And they sang a new song, saying, Thou art worthy to take the book, and to open the seals thereof; for thou wast slain, and hast REDEEMED us to God by thy blood out of every kindred, and tongue, and nation.'

4. He is the Sanctifier of mankind.

1 Cor. 1: 30. (As quoted above.)

5. He is the Judge of mankind.

Acts 17: 31. 'Because he hath appointed a day, in the which he will JUDGE the world in righteousness by that man whom he hath ordained; whereof he hath given assurance unto all men, in that he hath raised him from the dead.'

Acts 10: 42. 'And he commanded us to preach unto the people, and to testify that it is he which was ordained of God, to be the JUDGE of quick and dead.'

Rom. 2: 16. 'In the day when God shall JUDGE the secrects of men by Jesus Christ, according to my gospel.'

Acts 14: 10. 'But why dost thou judge thy brother? or why dost thou set at nought thy brother? for we shall all stand before the JUDGMENT-SEAT of Christ.'

To the above I will add several other proofs.

1. The fulness of the God-head is ascribed to him.

Col. 2: 9. 'For in him dwelleth all the FULNESS of the Godhead bodily.'

All the divine perfections are in him.

2. He is the express image of God.

Heb. 1: 3. 'Who, being the brightness of his glory, and the EXPRESS IMAGE of his person, and upholding all things by the word of his power, when he had by himself purged our sins, sat down on the right hand of the Majesty on high.'

3. He thought it not it robbery to be equal with God.

Phil. 2: 6. 'Who being in the form of God, thought it not robbery to be equal with God.'

4. He is the image of the invisible God.

1 Cor. 11: 7. 'For a man indeed ought not to cover his head, forasmuch as he is the IMAGE and glory of God.'

2 Cor. 4: 4. 'In whom the god of this world hath blinded the minds of them which believe not, lest the light of the glorious gospel of Christ, who is the IMAGE of God, should shine unto them.'

Col. 1: 15. 'Who is the IMAGE of the invisible God, the first-born of every creature.'

5. He is the Jehovah which Moses saw in the burning bush.

Ex. 3: 2—6. 'And the Angel of the Lord appeared unto him in a flame of fire out of the midst of a bush; and he looked, and, behold, the bush burned with fire, and the bush was not consumed. And Moses said, I will now turn aside and see this great sight, why the bush is not burned. And when the Lord saw that he turned aside to see, God called unto him out of the midst of the bush, and said, Moses, Moses. And he said, Here am I. And he said, Draw not nigh hither; put off thy shoes from off thy feet; for the place whereon thou standest is holy ground. Moreover he said, I am the God of thy father, the God of Abraham, the God of Isaac, and the God of Jacob. And Moses hid his face; for he was afraid to look upon God.' Compared with—

Ex. 33: 20. 'And he said, Thou canst not see my face; for there shall no man see me, and live.' And—

John 1: 18. 'No man hath seen God at any time; the only begotten Son, which is in the bosom of the Father, he hath declared him.' And—

John 6: 46. 'Not that any man hath seen the Father, save he which is of God, he hath seen the Father.'

6. He claimed, and received divine honors.

John 5: 23. 'That all men should HONOR the Son, even as they honor the Father. He that honoreth not the Son, honoreth not the Father which hath sent him.'

Mat. 2: 11. 'And when they were come into the house, they saw the young child with Mary his mother, and fell down and WORSHIPPED him.

Mat. 8: 2. 'And, behold, there came a leper, and WORSHIPPED him, saying, Lord, if thou wilt, thou canst make me clean.'

Mat. 14: 13. 'When Jesus heard of it, he departed thence by ship into a desert place apart; and when the people had heard thereof, they followed on foot out of the cities.'

7. He is worshipped in heaven.

Rev. 5: 12, 14. 'Saying with a loud voice, Worthy is the Lamb that was slain to receive power, and riches, and wisdom, and strength, and honor, and glory, and blessing.' 'And the four beasts said, Amen. And the four and twenty elders fell down and WORSHIPPED him that liveth for ever and ever.'

Isa. 6: 1—5. 'In the year that king Uzziah died, I saw also the Lord sitting upon a throne, high, and lifted up, and his train filled the temple. Above it stood the seraphim; each one had six wings; with twain he did fly. And one cried unto another, and said, Holy, holy, holy, is the Lord of Hosts; the whole earth is full of his glory. And the posts of the door moved at the voice of him that cried, and the house was filled with smoke. Then said I, Woe is me! for I am undone; because I am a man of unclean lips, and I dwell in the midst of a people of unclean lips; for mine eyes have seen the King, the Lord of Hosts.'

8. The Father commanded angels to worship him.

Heb. 1: 6. 'And again, when he bringeth in the first-begotten into the world, he saith, And let all the angels of God WORSHIP him.'

9. He was understood by the Jews to assert his own absolute divinity.

10. He wrought miracles in his own name, and by his own power.

11. He claimed power to raise himself from the dead.

John 10: 18. 'No man taketh it from me, but I lay it down of myself; I have power to lay it down, and I have power to take it again. This commandment have I received of my Father.'

12. If not God, he was an impostor, and a blasphemer; and according to the Jewish law, was justly put to death.'

13. If not God, he has made no Atonement, but only suffered as a martyr.

14. Set aside the doctrine of Christ's divinity, and you destroy the moral power of the gospel.

15. If not God, the Christian Church are, and always have been idolaters.

16. It is incredible that the Church should have been so greatly blessed by the outpouring of the Holy Spirit in the very act of worshipping Christ as God, unless he is the true God.

17. Those Churches who deny the divinity of Christ are not blessed with the effusions of the Holy Spirit as are those Churches that maintain his divinity, and worship him as God.

18. If Christ is not God, God the Father has deceived us by giving Christ the power to work miracles in confirmation of his assertion that he is God.

19. If he is not God, the Prophets and Apostles have been deceived, and have led the Church into idolatry.

20. It is a fact which cannot be denied that the Churches planted by the Apostles held the proper divinity of Christ.

21. If he is not God, it does not appears that there is any God revealed in the Bible.

22. If he is not God, the Bible is the most blasphemous book in the world.

23. If Christ is not God, it is truly unaccountable that the Bible

should speak of him in a manner so entirely different from that in which it speaks of any created being.

24. Christians are led by the Holy Spirit to commune with Christ as God.

25. The saints naturally pray to him as God.

Acts 9 : 13, 14. 'Then Ananias answered, Lord, I have heard by many of this man, how much evil he hath done to thy saints at Jerusalem; and here he hath authority from the chief priests to bind all that call on thy name.'

26. If Christ is not God, we have no means of being undeceived. As the Bible stands, we are bound to receive the doctrine of his divinity.

27. If he is not God, the more diligent, honest, and studious we are in biblical research, the more certain are we to be deceived.

28. If not God, none have held the truth upon this subject, but the mutilators of the Bible, and those who have held very loose notions of its divine inspiration and authority.

39. Those who have rejected the divinity of Christ have exhibited the loosest morality that has been seen in the christian world.

30. If this doctrine is not true, then the preaching and belief of this heresy have occasioned a purer morality, and have exerted altogether a better influence than has ever resulted from preaching the truth, or from a denial of this doctrine.

31. But this is impossible. Falsehood cannot promote a pure morality. If a belief in the divinity of Christ naturally results in the purest and the most perfect virtue, it must be true.

THIRD. *Answer objections.*

Obj. I. To the proper divinity of the Lord Jesus Christ, it is objected that he often and in many ways acknowledged his inferiority to, and dependence upon God. He prayed to God, and affirmed that God was greater than he.

Ans. 1. It has been common for those who deny the divinity of the Lord Jesus Christ, to quote that class of passages that prove his humanity, dependence, and inferiority to the Father, and there stop, taking it for granted that they have proved that he is not God.

2. This is unfair and absurd, for it is admitted and maintained by by Trinitarians, as well as by themselves, that he was a man, and as such, dependent on and inferior to his Father. But it is also maintained that he is likewise God, independent, omnipotent, and eternal.

3. There is, to say the least, as large a class of scriptures to prove his divinity as his humanity. They seem as explicit, full, and unequivocal as could be expressed in words.

4. To get rid of the mystery of the union of two natures in one person, some explain away his humanity, and others his divinity. The same rule of criticism, resorted to in the one case, is equally

effectual and conclusive in the other. And were the application made, it would be equally efficient in destroying the testimony of both these classes of passages, and rendering it uncertain whether he was either God, or man, or any thing else.

5. As Mediator, Christ was both inferior to, and dependent upon the Father.

Obj. II. It is objected that the union of the divine and human natures is utterly inconceivable.

Ans. It is true that we can have no conception of the *quo modo* of this union. Nor can we have any conception of the manner in which our soul and body are united. In the one case we can believe the fact on the testimony of God, and in the other, on the testimony of our own consciousness.

Obj. III. It is objected that the union of the divine and human natures should not be made an article of faith, because it cannot possibly be believed, inasmuch as it cannot be understood.

Ans. The thing to be believed can be understood. We are not called upon to believe any thing about the mode or manner of the union. It is not a question of philosophy, but of fact, that we are called upon to believe. The fact we can understand and believe.

LECTURE XIX.

HUMANITY OF CHRIST.

First. Notice the various opinions that have prevailed upon this subject.

Second. Show what is intended by the Humanity of Christ.

Third. Prove the doctrine.

First. *Notice the various opinions that have prevailed upon this subject.*

1. The Docetæ and Gnostics admitted the proper divinity of Christ, but denied that he possessed a human body. They held that he had a body and suffered only in appearance. This opinion originated in the philosophy of physical depravity, or the philosophy which teaches that moral evil has its seat in matter. They of course felt it necessary to deny that Christ had a material body.

2. The Sabellians admitted the divinity of Christ, and that he possessed a real human body; also that he suffered for the sins of men. But they deny his having a human soul.

Second. *What is intended by the Humanity of Christ.*

The common doctrine of the Church upon this subject, is that Christ was in all respects a perfect human being, possessing both a human body and human soul, with all the attributes of a perfect man.

Third. *Prove the Humanity of Christ.*

That he had a real body is evident.

1. From the fact that he was conceived by, and born of a woman.

Isa. 7: 14: "Therefore the Lord himself shall give you a sign; Behold, a virgin shall conceive, and bear a son, and shall call his name Immanuel," Compared with—

Mat. 1: 23: "Behold, a virgin shall be with child, and shall bring forth a son, and they shall call his name Emanuel, which being interpreted, is, God with us." And—

Luke 1: 31: "And, behold, thou shalt conceive in thy womb, and bring forth a son, and shalt call his name Jesus."

Luke 2: 11, 12: "For unto you is born this day, in the city of David, a Savior, which is Christ the Lord. And this shall be a sign unto you; Ye shall find the babe wrapped in swaddling-clothes, lying in a manger."

2. He was circumcised according to the law of Moses.

Luke 2: 21: "And when eight days were accomplished for the circumcising of the child, his name was called Jesus, which was so named of the angel before he was conceived in the womb."

3. He grew.

Luke 2: 40: "And the child GREW, and waxed strong in spirit, filled with wisdom; and the grace of God was upon him."

4. He was hungry.

Mat. 4: 2: "And when he had fasted forty days and forty nights, he was afterwards an HUNGERED."

Luke 4: 2: "Being forty days tempted of the devil, and in those days he did eat nothing; and when they were ended, he afterward HUNGERED."

5. He was thirsty.

John 19: 28: "After this, Jesus knowing that all things were now accomplished, that the scripture might be fulfilled, saith, I THIRST."

6. He ate and drank.

Mark 2: 16: "And when the scribes and Pharisees saw him EAT with publicans and sinners, they said unto his disciples, How is it that he EATETH and DRINKETH with publicans and sinners?"

7. He walked, labored, rested, slept, was weary, lived, and died, like other men. He sweat, bled, was buried, like other men.

8. He declared himself to have a body of flesh and bones.

Luke 24: 39: "Behold my hands and my feet, that it is myself: handle me, and see; for a spirit hath not FLESH and BONES, as ye see ME HAVE."

John 20: 20, 27: "And when he had so said, he shewed unto them his HANDS and his SIDE. Then were the disciples glad when they saw the Lord." "Then said he to Thomas, Reach hither thy finger, and behold my HANDS; and reach hither thy hand, and thrust it into my SIDE: and be not faithless, but believing."

Heb. 10: 5: "Wherefore, when he cometh into the world, he saith, Sacrifice and offering thou wouldst not, but a BODY hast thou prepared me."

9. It is repeatedly asserted of him that he had a body.

John 2: 21: "But he spake of the temple of his BODY."

Luke 23: 55: "And the women also, which came with him from Galilee, followed after, and beheld the sepulchre, and how his BODY was laid."

Luke 24: 3, 23: "And they entered in, and found not the BODY of the Lord Jesus." "And when they found not his BODY, they came, saying, that they had also seen a vision of angels, which said that he was alive."

Heb. 10: 10: "By the which will we are sanctified, through the offering of the BODY of Jesus Christ once for all."

John 20: 12: "And seeth two angels in white sitting, the one at the head, and the other at the feet, where the BODY of Jesus had lain."

Mark 14: 8: "She hath done what she could; she is come aforehand to anoint my BODY to the burying."

Also, Mark 14: 45—47; Heb. 2: 14; John 1: 14; Acts 2: 3, 30, 31; Rom. 1: 3; 1 Pet. 2: 24; which need not be quoted.

10. Those that knew him had the testimony of their senses that he had a body.

11. There is the same evidence that he had a real body, as there is that the Apostles had bodies, or that any man has a body.

12. The denial of his having a human body is regarded by the Apostles as fatal heresy.

1 John 1: 1: "That which was from the beginning, which we have heard, which we have seen with our eyes, which we have looked upon, and our hands have handled, of the Word of life."

1 John 4: 3: "And every spirit that confesses not that Jesus Christ is come in the FLESH is not of God: and this is that spirit of

anti-christ, whereof ye have heard that it should come; and even now already is it in the world."

13. Any rule of biblical interpretation that would set aside the evidence of this truth, would, if carried out, blot out every fundamental doctrine of the Bible.

That he had a human soul, I remark:

1. It is the soul, and not the body that constitutes a man.

2. A human body without a soul, is not a human being.

3. If Christ had no human soul, but was merely God dwelling in a human body, he was infinitely far from being a man.

4. He is often called a man in the Bible.

John 1: 30: "This is he of whom I have said, After me cometh a MAN which is preferred before me; for he was before me."

John 8: 40: "But now ye seek to kill me, a MAN that hath told you the truth, which I have heard of God: this did not Abraham."

Acts 2: 22: "Ye men of Israel, hear these words; Jesus of Nazareth, a MAN approved of God among you by miracles, and wonders, and signs, which God did by him in the midst of you, as ye yourselves also know."

Acts 17: 31: "Because he hath appointed a day, in the which he will judge the world in righteousness by that MAN whom he hath ordained; whereof he hath given assurance unto all men, in that he hath raised him from the dead."

1 Tim. 2: 5: "For there is one God, and one mediator between God and men, the MAN Christ Jesus."

Isa. 53: 3: "He is despised and rejected of men; a MAN of sorrows, and acquainted with grief; and we hid as it were our faces from him; he was despised, and we esteemed him not."

5. He is called the Son of man seventy-one times in the Bible.

6. He is often spoken of in the Bible as having a soul,

Isa. 53: 10, 11, 12: "Yet it pleased the Lord to bruise him; he hath put him to grief: when thou shalt make his SOUL an offering for sin, he shall see his seed, he shall prolong his days, and the pleasure of the Lord shall prosper in his hand. He shall see the travail of his SOUL, and shall be satisfied: by his knowledge shall my righteous servant justify many; for he shall bear their iniquities. Therefore will I divide him a portion with the great, and he shall divide the spoil with the strong; because he hath poured out his SOUL unto death; and he was numbered with the transgressors; and he bare the sins of many, and made intercession for the transgressors."

Ps. 16: 10: "For thou wilt not leave my soul in hell; neither wilt thou suffer thine Holy One to see corruption."

Acts 2: 27: "Because thou wilt not leave my SOUL in hell, neither wilt thou suffer thine Holy One to see corruption."

Mat. 26: 38: "Then saith he unto them, My SOUL is exceeding sorrowful, even unto death: tarry ye here, and watch with me."

John 12: 27: "Now is my SOUL troubled; and what shall I say? Father, save me from this hour: but for this cause came I unto this hour."

7. The sympathies and feelings of a human being are ascribed to him."

Isa. 53: 3, 4, 7, 10, 11: "He is despised and rejected of men; a man of SORROWS, and acquainted with GRIEF; and we hid as it were our faces from him: he was despised and we esteemed him not; Surely he hath borne our GRIEFS, and carried our SORROWS; ye we did esteem him STRICKEN, SMITTEN of God, and AFFLICTED." "He was OPPRESSED, and he was AFFLICTED." "Yet it pleased the Lord to BRUISE him; he hath put him to GRIEF." "He shall see of the TRAVAIL of his soul, and shall be satisfied: by his knowledge shall my righteous servant justify many; for he shall BEAR their iniquities."

John 12: 27: "Now is my soul TROUBLED: and what shall I say? Father save me from this hour: but for this cause came I unto this hour."

John 13: 21: "When Jesus had thus said, he was TROUBLED in spirit, and testified, and said, Verily, verily, I say unto you, That one of you shall betray me."

Mat. 26: 38: "Then saith he unto them, My soul is exceeding SORROWFUL, even unto death."

Luke 22: 44: "And being in an AGONY, he prayed more earnestly: and his sweat was as it were great drops of blood falling down to the ground."

8. He was in all things made like unto his brethren.

Heb. 2: 17: "Wherefore in all things it behoved him to be made like unto his brethren, that he might be a merciful and faithful high priest in things pertaining to God, to make reconciliation for the sins of the people."

9. He was tempted in all respects as we are.

Heb. 4: 15: "For we have not a high priest which cannot be touched with the feeling of our infirmities; but was in all points TEMPTED liks as we are, yet without sin."

But if he had no human soul, he was infinitely unlike his brethren.

10. He suffered under temptation.

Heb. 2: 18: "For in that he himself hath SUFFERED, being tempted, he is able to succor them that are tempted."

11. He was at first an infant in knowledge.

12. He grew in wisdom.

Luke 2: 52: "And Jesus INCREASED in WISDOM and stature, and in favor with God and man."

13. He was until the day of his death ignorant of some, and probably of many things.

Mark 13: 32: "But of that day and that hour KNOWETH NO MAN, no, not the angels which are in heaven, NEITHER the SON, but the Father."

Mat. 26: 38—42: "Then saith he unto them, My soul is exceeding sorrowful, even unto death: tarry ye here, and watch with me. And he went a little farther, and fell on his face, and prayed, saying, O my Father, IF it is POSSIBLE, let this cup pass from me: nevertheless, not as I will, but as thou wilt. And he cometh unto his disciples, and findeth them asleep, and saith unto Peter, What! could ye not watch with me one hour? Watch and pray that ye enter not into temptation: the spirit indeed is willing, but the flesh is weak. He went away again the second time, and prayed, saying, O my Father, IF this cup MAY not pass away from me, except I drink it, thy will be done."

To all this proof it is objected, by those who deny that he had a human soul, that all that is said of his ignorance, suffering, being tempted, increasing in wisdom, &c., might result from the connection of the divine mind with the human body; that if the divine nature was dependent on a human body for its developments, it might be attended with all the circumstances ascribed to Christ.

To this I answer:

(1.) This objection seems to be a begging of the question, or taking for granted the thing that needs to be, but never can be proved.

(2.) The supposition is absurd, because it assumes that infinite knowledge, and the other infinite attributes of God can become finite, and even infantile.

13. There appears to be the same evidence that Christ had a human soul, as there is that any man has a soul.

14. Any rule of interpretation that would set aside this doctrine as not taught in the Bible, would, if carried out in its application, blot out every doctrine of the Bible.

REMARKS.

1. Christ unites the sympathies of a man with the attributes of God.

2. He still possesses human nature in union with the divine nature.

3. He will greatly exalt human beings as his brethren; as sustaining a nearer relation to him than any other order of creatures.

LECTURE XX.

PERSONALITY AND DIVINITY OF THE HOLY SPIRIT.

First. Show what is not intended by the Divinity of the Holy Spirit.

Second. That he is truly God.

Third. What is intended by the Personality of the Holy Spirit.

Fourth. Prove that he is a Divine Person.

First. *What is not intended by the Divinity of the Holy Spirit.*

1. By the Divinity of the Holy Spirit is not intended, that he is a mere attribute of God.

2. Nor by his Divinity is it intended that he is a mere Divine operation or influence.

Second. *By the Divinity of the Holy Spirit, is intended that he is truly and properly God.*

PROOF.

I. The *names* of God are ascribed to him:

2 Cor. 3: 17. "Now the Lord is that Spirit; and where the Spirit of the Lord is there is liberty."

1 Cor. 2: 16. "For who hath known the mind of the Lord, that he may instruct him? But we have the mind of Christ." Compared with—

Isa. 40: 13. "Who hath directed the Spirit of the Lord, or being his counsellor hath taught him?"

Acts 5: 3, 4. "But Peter said, Ananias, why hath Satan filled thy heart to lie to the Holy Ghost, and to keep back part of the price of the land? While it remained was it not thine own? and after it was sold, was it not in thine own power? why hast thou conceived this thing in thy heart? thou hast not lied unto men, but unto God."

Acts 4: 24–26. "They lifted up their voice to God, with one accord, and said Lord, thou art God, which hast made heaven and earth, and the sea, and all that in them is; who, by the mouth of thy servant David, hast said, Why did the heathen rage, and the people imagine vain things? The kings of the earth stood up, and the rulers were gathered together, against the Lord, and against his Christ." Compared with—

Acts 1: 16. "Men and brethren, this scripture must needs have been fulfilled, which the Holy Ghost by the mouth of David spake before concerning Judas, which was guide to them that took Jesus."

Acts 28: 25. 'And when they agreed not among themselves, they departed, after that Paul had spoken one word, 'Well spake the Holy Ghost by Esaias [Isaiah] the prophet unto our fathers,' &c. Compared with—

Isa. 6: 8. 'I heard the voice of the Lord saying, Whom shall I send, and who will go for us?'

Heb. 3: 7–9. 'Wherefore, as the Holy Ghost saith, To-day, if ye will hear his voice, harden not your hearts as in the provocation, in the day of temptation in the wilderness, when your fathers tempted me, proved me, and saw my works forty years.' Compared with—

Ps. 95: 7. 'For he is our God; and we are the people of his pasture, and the sheep of his hand. To-day, if ye will hear his voice,' &c.

Heb. 10: 15, 16. 'Whereof the Holy Ghost also is a witness to us; for after that he had said before, This is the covenant that I will make with them after those days, saith the Lord; I will put my laws into their hearts, and in their minds will I write them.' Compared with—

Jer. 31: 33, 34. 'But this shall be the covenant that I will make with the house of Israel; after those days, saith the Lord, I will put my law in their inward parts, and write it in their hearts; and will be their God, and they shall be my people. And they shall teach no more every man his neighbor, and every man his brother, saying, Know the Lord; for they shall all know me, from the least of them unto the greatest of them, saith the Lord; for I will forgive their iniquity, and I will remember their sin no more.'

II. The *attributes* of God are ascribed to him.

1. Eternity. Heb. 9: 14. 'How much more shall the blood of Christ, who through the Eternal Spirit offered himself without spot to God, purge your conscience from dead works to serve the living God!'

2. Omnipresence. Ps. 139: 7. 'Whither shall I go from thy Spirit? or whither shall I flee from thy presence?'

3. Omniscience. 1 Cor. 2: 10, 11. 'For the Spirit searcheth all things, yea the deep things of God. For what man knoweth the things of a man, save the spirit of a man which is in him? even so the things of God knoweth no man, but the Spirit of God.'

4. Power. Rom. 15: 13, 19. 'Now the God of hope fill you with all joy and peace in believing, that ye may abound in hope,

through the *power* of the Holy Ghost.' 'By the *power* of the Spirit of God.'

5. The possession of Divine Attributes is implied in the works ascribed to him, as we shall presently see.

III. To these passages I will add several other proofs of his Divinity.

1. He is joined with the Father and the Son in the ordinance of baptism.

2. Also in the Apostolic Benediction.

3. Blaspheming against him is represented as an unpardonable sin.

4. If the Holy Spirit is not God, the Church are deceived.

5. If not, the Bible is exactly calculated to deceive mankind.

6. If not, it is God's own fault that we are deceived, as the Bible is written in such a manner, that no rational rules of interpretation can bring us to any other conclusions than that the Holy Spirit is truly God. Therefore,

7. If the Holy Spirit is not truly God, we have no means of being undeceived.

8. Suppose you substitute *power*, for the Holy Ghost, in Baptism and in the Apostolic Benediction, and read—'I baptize you in the name of the Father, of the Son, and of the Holy Power;' and, 'May the grace of our Lord Jesus Christ, with the love of God, and the communion of the Holy Power, be with you.'

THIRD. *The Personality of the Holy Spirit.*

By the Personality of the Holy Spirit, it is intended:

1. That he is a moral agent.

2. That as an agent he is distinct from the Father and the Son, though not separate in the substratum of his existence.

3. That he is in such a sense a distinct person as to render the application of the personal pronouns I, thou, he, to him strictly proper.

FOURTH. *Prove that the Holy Ghost is a Divine Person.*

I. The attributes of a personal agent are ascribed to the Holy Spirit.

1. Knowledge. 1 Cor. 2 : 10, 11. 'God hath revealed them unto us by his Spirit; for the Spirit searcheth all things, yea the deep things of God. For what man knoweth the things of a man, save the spirit of man which is in him? even so the things of God knoweth no man, but the Spirit of God.' And—

Isa. 11 : 2. 'And the Spirit of the Lord shall rest upon him, the Spirit of wisdom and understanding, the Spirit of counsel and might, the Spirit of knowledge, and of the fear of the Lord.'

2. Wisdom. Isa. 11 : 2: (as quoted above.) Acts 6 : 3. 'Wherefore, brethren, look ye out seven men of honest report, full of the Holy Ghost and wisdom, whom we may appoint over this business.' And—

Eph. 1: 17. 'That the God of our Lord Jesus Christ, the Father of glory, may give unto you the Spirit of Wisdom and revelation in the knowledge of him.'

3. Power. Rom. 15: 13, 19. 'Now the God of hope fill you with all joy and peace in believing, that ye may abound in hope, through the power of the Holy Ghost.' 'Through mighty signs and wonders, by the power of the Spirit of God.'

4. Goodness. Ps. 143: 10. 'Teach me to do thy will; for thou art my God; thy Spirit is GOOD.' And—

Neh. 9: 20. 'Thou gavest also thy GOOD Spirit to instruct them.'

5. Holiness, often.

II. The works of a personal agent are ascribed to him.

1. Creation. Job 33: 4. 'The Spirit of God hath made me, and the breath of the Almighty hath given me life.' And—

Ps. 104: 30. 'Thou sendest forth thy Spirit, they are created.'

2. He is said to *search*. 1 Cor. 2: 10, 11: (as cited above.)

3. To *strive*. Gen. 6: 3. 'My Spirit shall not always strive with man.'

4. To be *sent forth*. Gal. 4: 6. 'And because ye are sons, God hath sent forth the Spirit of his Son into your hearts, crying Abba, Father.' And—

John 15: 26. 'But when the Comforter is come, whom I will send unto you from the Father, even the Spirit of truth, which proceedeth from the Father, he shall testify of me.'

5. To *move*. Gen. 1: 2. 'And the Spirit of God moved upon the face of the waters.'

6. To *know*. 1 Cor. 2: 10, 11: (as above cited.)

7. To *speak*. John 16: 13. 'Howbeit, when he, the Spirit of trutn is come, he will guide you into all truth; for he shall not speak of himself; but whatsoever he shall hear, that shall he speak; and he will show you things to come.' And—

Acts 10: 19. 'While Peter thought on the vision, the Spirit said unto him, Behold, three men seek thee.' And—

Acts 11: 12. 'And the Spirit bade me go with them, nothing doubting.' And—

1 Tim. 4: 1. 'Now the Spirit speaketh expressly, that in the latter times some shall depart from the faith, giving heed to seducing spirits, and doctrines of devils.' And—

Rev. 14: 13. 'And I heard a voice from heaven, saying unto me, 'Write, Blessed are the dead, which die in the Lord from henceforth, Yea,' saith the Spirit, 'that they rest from their labors, and their works do follow them.'

8. To *guide*. John 16: 13. (Quoted above.)

9. To *lead*. Rom. 8: 14. 'For as many as are led by the Spirit of God, they are the sons of God.' And—

Gal. 5: 18. 'But if ye be led by the Spirit, ye are not under the law.'

10. To *help.* Rom. 8 : 26. 'For we know not what we should pray for as we ought; but the Spirit itself maketh intercession for us with groanings which cannot be uttered.'

11. To *testify.* Rom. 8: 16. 'The Spirit itself beareth witness with our spirit, that we are the children of God.' And—

John 15: 26. 'The Spirit of truth, which proceedeth from the Father, he shall testify of me.'

12. To *reveal.* Eph. 3 : 5. 'Now revealed unto his holy Apostles and prophets by the Spirit.'

13. To *prophesy.* John 16: 13. 1 Tim. 4: 1. (Both quoted above.)

14. To *intercede.* Rom. 8 : 26. (Quoted above.)

15. To *give gifts.* 1 Cor. 12: 4, 8–11. 'Now there are diversities of gifts, but the same Spirit.' 'For to one is given by the Spirit the word of wisdom; to another, the word of knowledge by the same Spirit; to another, faith by the same Spirit; to another the gift of healing by the same Spirit; to another, the working of miracles; to another, prophecy; to another, discerning of spirits; to another, divers kinds of tongues; to another, the interpretation of tongues. But all these worketh that one and the self-same Spirit, dividing to every man severally as he will.'

16. To *work miracles.* Rom. 15 : 19. 'Through mighty signs and wonders, by the power of the Spirit of God; so that from Jerusalem and round about unto Illyricum, I have fully preached the gospel of Christ.'

17. To *sanctify.* 1 Cor. 6: 11. 'And such were some of you; but ye are washed, but ye are sanctified, but ye are justified in the name of the Lord Jesus, and by the Spirit of our God.' And—

2 Thess. 2: 13. 'But we are bound to give thanks always to God for you, brethren beloved of the Lord, because God hath from the beginning chosen you to salvation, through sanctification of the Spirit.' And—

1 Pet. 1 : 2. 'Elect according to the foreknowledge of God the Father, through sanctification of the Spirit unto obedience, and sprinkling of the blood of Jesus Christ.'

18. To *quicken or give life.* John 6 : 63. 'It is the Spirit that quickeneth; the flesh profiteth nothing; the words that I speak unto you, they are spirit, and they are life.' And—

1 Pet. 3: 18. 'For Christ also hath once suffered for sins, the just for the unjust, that he might bring us to God, being put to death in the flesh, but quickened by the Spirit.'

19. To *send teachers* to the Church. Acts 13 : 2, 4. 'As they ministered to the Lord, and fasted, the Holy Ghost said, Separate me Barnabas and Saul for the work whereunto I have called them.' 'So they being sent forth by the Holy Ghost, departed unto Seleucia.' And—

Acts 20: 28. 'Take heed therefore unto yourselves, and to all the flock over the which the Holy Ghost hath made you overseers, to feed the Church of God.'

20. Teachers are said to *receive their knowledge* from the Holy Spirit. Luke 2: 26. 'And it was revealed unto him by the Holy Ghost, that he should not see death, before he had seen the LORD'S CHRIST.' And—

John 16: 13. 'When he, the Spirit of truth is come, he will guide you into all truth.' 'He will show you things to come.' And—

John 14: 26. 'But the Comforter, which is the Holy Ghost, whom the Father will send in my name, he shall teach you all things, and bring all things to your remembrance, whatsoever I have said unto you.'

21. He is said to *speak by them.* Mark 13: 11. 'When they shall lead you, and deliver you up, take no thought beforehand what ye shall speak, neither do ye premeditate; but whatsoever shall be given you in that hour, that speak ye; for *it is not ye that speak, but the Holy Ghost.*' And—

2 Pet. 1: 21. 'The prophecy came not in old time by the will of man; but holy men of God spake *as they were moved by the Holy Ghost.*'

22. He is said to *dwell in his people.* John 14: 17. 'Even the Spirit of truth; whom the world cannot receive, because it seeth him not, neither knowith him; but ye know him; for he dwelleth with you, and shall be in you.' And—

Rom. 8: 11. 'If the Spirit of him that raised up Jesus from the dead dwell in you, he that raised up Christ from the dead shall also quicken your mortal bodies by his Spirit that dwelleth in you.' And—

1 Cor. 6: 19. 'What! know ye not that your body is the temple of the Holy Ghost which is in you, which ye have of God, and ye are not your own? And—

1 Cor. 3: 16. 'Know ye not that ye are the temple of God, and that the Spirit of God dwelleth in you?'

23. He *raises the dead.* 1 Pet. 3: 18. 'Being put to death in the flesh, but quickened by the Spirit.'

24. He *reproves or convinces of sin.* John 16: 7, 8. 'It is expedient for you that I go away; for if I go not away, the Comforter will not come unto you; but if I depart, I will send him unto you. And when he is come, he will reprove the world of sin, and of righteousness, and of judgment.'

25. He is represented as having *the will and feelings of a personal agent.* Rom. 8: 27. 'He that searcheth the hearts knoweth what is the mind of the Spirit, because he maketh intercession for the saints, according to the will of God.'

26. He is *pleased.* Acts 15: 28. 'For it seemed good to the Holy Ghost, and to us, to lay upon you no greater burden than these necessary things.'

27. To be *grieved*. Eph. 4 : 30. 'Grieve not the Holy Spirit of God, whereby ye are sealed unto the day of redemption.'

28. To be *vexed*. Isa. 63 : 10. 'They rebelled and vexed his Holy Spirit; therefore he was turned to be their enemy, and he fought against them.'

29. To be *resisted*. Acts 7 : 51. 'Ye stiff-necked! and uncircumcised in heart and ears! ye do always resist the Holy Ghost; as your fathers did, so do ye.'

30. To be *blasphemed*. Mat. 12 : 31. 'All manner of sin and blasphemy shall be forgiven unto men; but the blasphemy against the Holy Ghost shall not be forgiven unto men.''

To suppose the Holy Spirit to be the attribute of power would make nonsense of the Bible. Acts 10 : 38. 'God anointed Jesus of Nazareth with the Holy Ghost and with power.' If the Holy Ghost is the attribute of power, this passage means that God anointed Jesus of Nazareth with the holy power and with power.

Rom. 15 : 13. 'Now the God of hope fill you with all joy and peace in believing, that ye may abound in hope, through the power of the Holy Ghost!' That is—through the power of the holy power. And—Verse 19. 'By the power of the Spirit of God.' By the power of the power of God. And—

1 Cor. 2 : 4. 'My speech and my preaching was not with enticing words of man's wisdom, but in demonstration of the Spirit and of power.' That is—In demonstration of the power and of power. Who can believe that the Bible utters such nonsense as this would be, if the Holy Spirit is but the attribute of power.

Objection. To all the passages that establish the personality of the Holy Spirit, it is objected, that in the Book of Proverbs, Wisdom is personified and spoken of as a personal agent, and it may be, that all these passages are nothing more than a personification of the attribute of power.

Ans. Personification is admissible in poetic language; but not in prose, and the plain language of narrative. The book of Proverbs is written in poetic language; but these attributes, words, works, feelings, and ways, are ascribed to the Holy Spirit in plain prose and in the simple language of narrative, and in such connections as to forbid the idea of his being an attribute personified.

REMARKS.

1. It is unnecessary to attempt the proof of the Divinity of the Father, as this is not questioned.

2. The denial of the Divinity of the Son, and of the Divinity and personality of the Holy Spirit, is necessary, to get rid of the doctrine of the Trinity.

3. Although the doctrine of the Trinity is in different ways taught in the Bible; yet the most satisfactory method is by establishing the personality and Divinity of the three persons, especially of the Son and Holy Spirit; as neither the personality or Divinity of the Father is questioned.

4. The appeal of the Unitarians to the Bible is absurd, inasmuch as their business with the Bible upon this point, is to explain it away.

5. The same rules of interpretation, that would expunge the doctrine of the personality and Divinity of the Holy Spirit from the Bible, would do the same with the personality and Divinity of the Father and of the Son.

LECTURE XXI.

PROVIDENCE OF GOD.

FIRST. Show what is intended by the providence of God.

SECOND. Prove that God administers over the universe a providential government.

THIRD. Notice the different theories that have prevailed respecting the Providence of God, with the principal arguments by which they have been supported, and show what seems to be the truth upon the subject.

FIRST. *What is intended by the Providence of God.*

1. All believers in Revelation have maintained that God administers a providential government, but have differed widely in respect to the *manner* in which he administers it.

2. It has been common for the different schools, or those who maintain different views upon the subject, to give such a definition of the providence of God, as to take for granted the truth of their own theory.

3. As the *quo modo* of divine Providence, has always been a subject of debate, it seems important, if possible, to give such a definition of Providence as shall not take for granted the truth of any theory in respect to the *quo modo*.

4. So to define Providence as to take the truth of either theory for granted, is to maintain by implication at least, that those who reject this particular theory, are altogether infidels in respect to the Providence of God, which is far from being true.

5. The true idea of Providence is, PROVISION. The Providence of God is an adequate provision on his part for the fulfillment of

all his designs. In other words, it consists in a sufficient provision for securing the highest practicable well being of the universe. This definition is sufficiently general to cover the whole ground, and yet takes nothing for granted in respect to the *quo modo*.

SECOND. *Prove that God administers a Providential Government.*

Some of the principal arguments in support of the doctrine of divine providence are,

1. Creation could not have been an *end* but must have been a *means* to some end.

2. That end, whatever it was, could not be accomplished without a provision for it, either in creation itself, or by exercising a subsequent superintendence and control, or both of these together.

3. The structure of the universe clearly indicates that the end of its creation was to glorify God in the promotion and diffusion of happiness.

4. This is manifest from the every where abounding proofs of benevolent design, the manifold contrivances for the promotion of happiness.

5. The proof is conclusive that there is a provision in the structure and movements of the universe for the promotion of happiness.

6. As happiness is a good in itself, it is self-evident that the promotion of happiness must have been an end in the creation of the universe. In this remark I include of course the happiness and glory of God.

7. The doctrine of a divine Providence then is a just inference from the fact of creation.

8. The necessities of the universe demand that God should administer over it a providential government.

9. Since God has created the universe, he is under an obligation to administer over it a providential government.

10. All nations have believed that God exercises over the universe a providential control. This is abundantly manifest in their public religious rites.

11. The Bible fully declares that God administers over the universe a providential government, that " He worketh all things after the counsel of his own will."

Ps. 103 : 19. 'The Lord hath prepared his throne in the heavens : and his kingdom ruleth over all.'

Dan. 4 : 17, 25. 'This matter is by the decree of the watchers, and the demand by the word of the holy ones ; to the intent that the living may know that the most High ruleth in the kingdom of men, and giveth it to whomsoever he will, and setteth up over it the basest of men.' 'That they shall drive thee from men, and thy dwelling shall be with the beasts of the field, and they shall make thee to eat grass as oxen, and they shall wet thee with the dew of heaven, and seven times shall pass over thee, till thou know that the most High ruleth in the kingdom of men, and giveth it to whomsoever he will.' 'And all the inhabitants of the earth are reputed as nothing: and he doeth according to his will in the army of heaven, and among the inhabitants of the earth; and none can stay his hand, or say unto him, What doest thou?'

12. A great part of the Bible is little less than a history of the Providence of God.

THIRD. *Notice the different theories of divine Providence, with the principal arguments by which they have been supported, and show what seems to be the truth upon the subject.*

I. The first theory that prevailed was that of OCCASIONALISM. The occasionalists maintained that all motion or action whether of mind or matter, was the result of a direct, divine, irresistible efficiency. They denied that any creature could be a cause, but that all creatures and things were only occasions of the divine conduct, and that God was properly the only active agent in the universe. This was a philosophic theory, and inclined strongly to Pantheism. It denied the efficiency of the inherent properties and laws of both matter and mind. Some of its advocates went so far as to maintain that the moral character of every act was to be ascribed to God. They maintained that what are generally termed the laws of nature, are only the mode of divine operation.

The arguments in support of this theory are,

1. The Bible declares the universal agency of God.

Ans. The Bible does indeed teach that 'God worketh all things after the counsel of his own will;' but it teaches nothing in respect to the *modus operandi*, which is the very point in question. It is admitted on all hands, that God is in some way concerned in every event of the universe; that he is either actively or permissively in such a sense concerned as that, in an important sense, all events may be ascribed to him. But the question at issue is, in what manner and by what agency does God work every thing after the counsel of his own will? Of this the Bible teaches nothing, in respect at least to myriads of events.

2. They alledge that God cannot create a system, that shall have the powers of operation in itself.

Ans. It may be true that God cannot create a universe that shall act independently of his sustaining agency; but that he cannot create a universe, that can have the power of operation lodged in its own properties and laws, so that nothing but a sustaining agency is necessary to produce a given result, has not been, and it is presumed cannot be shown.

3. They affirm that the laws of nature can be nothing else than the *modus operandi Dei*.

Ans. This is a mere begging of the question.

4. They alledge that we can conceive of no other way in which God can fulfill his purposes and prophecies.

Ans. 1. If we could not, it would be no proof of this theory. Is it to be supposed, that God does not possess resources of which we have no conception?

2. But we can conceive how God can influence moral agents, so as to produce a certain result without subjecting them to the law of necessity.

5. They affirm that this theory exalts God as a sovereign.

Ans. Yes; as an arbitrary and unrighteous one.

6. It is said that this theory impresses the mind with awe, as it brings us to regard God as the efficient agent and actor in every event.

Ans. It does impress the mind with abhorrence, as it ascribes all the wickedness in earth and hell to God, as its efficient cause.

Some of the objections to this theory are the following:

1. It is manifestly inconsistent with any rational idea of moral agency and accountability.

2. It is manifestly inconsistent with our own consciousness. We are as conscious of the freedom of our own actions, and of being the efficient cause of our own volitions, as we are of our own existence.

3. It makes God the only agent in the universe. This I have said is admitted by some, though denied by most of the advocates of this system. But if the theory be true, it is a palpable matter of fact, that God is the only agent, and that all creatures are but instruments. This seems to be implied in the very name of the theory. Occasionalism, or that God is the cause, and creatures the occasion of all action of mind and matter, seems to put the question, that God is regarded as the only agent, beyond a doubt.

4. Another objection to this theory is, that it is wholly inconsistent with any rational idea of moral government, of moral character, and of moral influence.

5. It excludes the idea of infernal agency from the universe, or makes God an accomplice with Satan. According to this theory, Satan could not tempt, without being caused to do so by a direct Divine efficiency. Nor could any creature yield to temptation and sin in view of it, without a direct Divine efficiency, to produce his yielding and sinning.

6. It makes God the author of sin in the worst sense.

7. It impeaches his sincerity and blackens his whole character.

II. A second theory that prevailed, was the Mechanical Theory, or the theory that in creation itself, God had made provision for securing the occurrence of all events, physical and moral, as they actually take place, without any superintendence or control being exercised over the universe—that in creating both mind and matter, they were constituted with such inherent properties and placed in such circumstances, and impressed with such laws as to secure the final and desired result, without any subsequent interference or control on the part of God. Thus making the universe a vast machine; working out its results by the force of its own inherent properties and laws. This is the direct opposite of the first theory.

The principal arguments in support of this theory are the following:

1. God was able to create such a universe.

Ans. This is taking for granted what needs to be proved. It is by no means self-evident, that it was naturally possible to create a universe like this, containing myriads of free moral agents, whose moral agency implies the power of resisting every degree of moral influence, in such a manner as that a given result would inevitably be secured without superintendence and control.

2. Another argument in support of this theory is, that such a creation of the universe as would avoid the necessity of subsequent superintendence and control, is a higher manifestation of the wisdom of God, than could otherwise have been made.

Ans. This also is begging the question. It assumes that a universe so created as to leave God in idleness, without the necessity of superintending and controling it, would have been the perfection of wisdom. But this is by no means self-evident.

3. Another argument is, that unless this theory be true, the creation of the universe was imperfect.

Ans. This again is begging the question. Because it assumes that the most perfect universe, would be that which should leave God in idleness, without at all concerning himself about its government and control. But this is not self-evident, for it should be remembered that the happiness of God, was infinitely the most important item in the *end* of creation. If God found a happiness in creating the universe it is not unreasonable to suppose that he takes a great pleasure in superintending and controling its movements.

If to this it be objected, that God must have been infinitely happy, previously to the work of creation; I answer, that as all eternity is present to God, he always enjoyed the work of creation and providence, and his happiness eternally consisted in the excellence of his character. And the excellence of his character is made up of the aggregate influences which have been and ever will be exerted by him for the promotion of virtue and happiness.

When it has been objected to this theory, as it justly may be, that it excludes the influence of prayer, and sets aside the idea that God interferes with the movements of the universe, in granting answers to prayer, it has been stated, that prayer is a necessary link in the chain of events, as originally established in the constitution of the universe.

To this it may be replied, that the answer either admits what the theory denies, or it is nonsense. The theory denies that God ever interferes in any case whatever, with the movements of the universe. What then can be intended by prayer's being a necessary link in the great chain of events? Is it meant that prayer is necessary to induce God to interfere with the movements of the universe, and so control things as to bring about an answer? If it means this, it admits what the theory denies. Or does it mean that prayer is a necessary link in the great chain of events, sustaining the relation of cause to its effect? If this be its meaning it is utter nonsense; for how can prayer sustain the relation of a cause to a storm of rain, or the stilling of a tempest, or of a fruitful season, or of any physical event whatever?

4. Another argument is, that to say the least it is consistent with the representations of scripture upon the subject of divine providence.

Ans. No. The representations of the Bible manifestly are, that God exercises a superintendence and control of all things. And not merely that he has so constructed the universe as that it needs no superintendence and control.

5. Again, it is asserted in support of this theory, that the Bible virtually asserts it, in saying that "God rested from all his works that he had created and made."

Ans. The Bible only affirms that he rested from the work of creation, and in no case intimates that he sat down in a state of inaction, without exercising any superintending control of the universe which he had made.

To this *theory* it may be objected:

1. That the laws of matter are uniform, and so far as we can see or conceive, cannot be so accommodated to the government of mind as to produce certain results, without superintendence. Therefore, if this theory might be true, were the universe all matter, it cannot be admitted when we take into consideration the fact, that so great a part of the universe is made up of moral agents.

2. It may be farther objected, that it is the doctrine of fate.

3. It is inconsistent with the holiness and happiness of moral beings, as it excludes God from any agency in the government and control of the universe, it annihilates their sense of dependence, and has a manifestly injurious tendency.

4. It is inconsistent with the Bible, which as I have already said, every where inculcates the doctrine of a divine universal superintendence and control.

5. It contradicts the general belief of all nations. The expiatory sacrifices, prayers, and multitudes of other public manifestations of belief, demonstrate that all nations have had the conviction that God continually interferes in the affairs of men, and exercises a universally superintending agency in the universe.

6. Another objection to this theory is, that it manifestly sets aside the use and influence of prayer, as a means of procuring blessings from God.

7. This theory is contrary to the experience of all saints.

8. It is inconsistent with the doctrine of the Spirit's influence and agency, in the conversion and sanctification of sinners.

9. It is inconsistent with the Atonement and all divine interference, for the salvation of the world.

10. Its manifestly demoralizing tendency gave birth to the next theory, which seems to take a middle ground between the first two.

III. This theory regards Providence as general and particular.

General Providence is the general provision made in the properties and laws of both matter and mind, for the accomplishment of his designs. It regards both matter and mind, not only as real existences, but as possessing inherent properties and laws, which, however, are not self-existent, and self-efficient, but require the upholding or sustaining power of God.

Particular Providence is that divine interference and control which is required by the exigencies of moral government. This theory maintains that God is directly or indirectly, actively or permissively concerned in every event.

Before adducing the arguments in proof of this theory, I will notice the objections to it.

Obj. I. It is objected, that it is inconsistent with the wisdom of God, to suppose that he has so created the universe as that it will need superintendence and control.

This has been sufficiently answered, in the examination of the second theory.

Obj. II. Another objection is, that it lays God under the necessity of constant exertion.

Ans. 1. This is not a weariness but a pleasure.

2. It is just what the Bible teaches.

3. This objection also has been sufficiently answered, in the examination of the second theory.

Obj. III. Another objection to this theory is, that it represents God as violating his own laws, and by a divine interference, setting aside their regular action.

Ans. 1. He has an undoubted right to violate or suspend the operation of physical law, for wise and benevolent ends.

2. It is not necessary to suppose that he violates or at all sets aside the action of physical law, but simply so interferes as to modify the results of the action of those laws.

Some of the arguments in support of this theory are the following:

1. It better accords with the representations of the Bible.
2. It better accords with the common sense of mankind.

3. It better accords with the general experience of mankind, so far as experience can be brought to bear upon this point.

4. It is more in accordance with the general belief of mankind.

5. Its moral influence is decidedly better.

6. It accords with the facts in the kingdom of grace.

7. It encourages prayer.

8. It seems satisfactory to the human mind.

9. It keeps up an intercourse and sympathy between God and moral beings.

10. It begets faith and encourages dependence upon God.

11. It begets affection for God.

12. It makes us realize his presence and agency.

LECTURE XXII.

MORAL GOVERNMENT.—No. 1.

FIRST. Define Moral Government.
SECOND. Show what is implied in it.

FIRST. *Define Moral Government.*

1. *Moral* Government, when opposed to physical, is the government of mind in opposition to the government of matter.

2. It is a government of motive or moral suasion, in opposition to a government of force.

3. Moral Government is the influence of moral considerations over the minds of moral agents.

4. *Moral Government*, in its most extensive sense, includes the whole influence of God's character as revealed in his works, providence, and word, over the universe of moral beings. It includes whatever influence God exerts to control the minds of moral agents, in conformity with the eternal principles of righteousness.

SECOND. *Show what is implied in Moral Government.*

1. Moral Government cannot be an end, but a means; and therefore implies and end, to which it sustains the relation of a means.

2. All rightful Moral Government implies that the end to which it sustains the relation of a means is good.

3. Rightful Moral Government implies the mutual dependence of both the ruler and the subject upon this means for the promotion of the desired end.

4. Moral Government, therefore, implies a necessity for its existence.

5. It implies that both the ruler and the ruled are moral agents.

6. It implies the existence of moral law.

7. It implies that both the ruler and the ruled are under a moral obligation, to obey the law, so far as it is applicable to the circumstances of each.

8. It implies the existence of a ruler who has a right to enforce moral obligation.

9. It implies that the ruler is under moral obligation to do this.

LECTURE XXIII.

MORAL GOVERNMENT.—No. 2.

FOUNDATION OF MORAL OBLIGATION.

FIRST. Inquire what Moral Obligation is.
SECOND. State the conditions of Moral Obligation.
THIRD. What is the foundation of Moral Obligation.

Under this head I shall show:

I. The different answers that have been given to the inquiry, What is the foundation of Moral Obligation?

II. Show wherein they agree.

III. Wherein they differ.

IV. What the real question is not.

V. What it is.

VI. Answer the question, or show what the foundation of Moral Obligation is.

To avoid confusion in discussing this subject, I will premise the following things:

1. There is a difference between the *foundation or fundamental* reason of Moral Obligation, and other reasons that may exist.

2. The foundation of Moral Obligation must be the *ultimate* reason upon which the obligation rests.

3. An ultimate reason is a first truth, in support of which there can be no proof, and of which no more can be or need be said than that so it is.

4. There is a plain and important distinction between willing or prefering the *existence* of a thing, as that which is desirable in itself, and on its own account, and willing to *create*, *do*, or *give existence* to that thing. I may prefer or will the *existence* of what I cannot do; but I cannot will to do what I know I cannot do. For example, were a moral being so perfectly isolated that neither God nor any other being knew of his existence, and were he at the same time acquainted with the existence of God and the

universe, universal benevolence would be his duty, although his benevolence would remain forever unknown to every being but himself, and no one but himself could ever be effected by it. Nor could the fundamental reason of this obligation be, that benevolence would make *himself* happy, but that the good of God and the universe is infinitely valuable and desirable in itself, and for its own sake, and on this account he would be under obligation to will it. In this case it is plain that the obligation would be to will the good of the universe; but not to will *to do* them good, as this were impossible; that is, it would be impossible to do them good, or to will to do it.

5. It may be my duty to be benevolent toward, or to will the happiness of a being, as a good in itself, whose happiness I am not at *liberty to promote*. For example, God and all beings are under obligation to exercise benevolence towards Satan and yet *may not will to make him happy*. This shows,

6. That to will the good of others for its own sake is benevolence, but to will to *do them good*, may or may not be an expression of benevolence, according to the circumstances of the case.

7. Benevolence is always right, because benevolence is good willing, or willing the good of the universe; and the good of the universe is desirable on its own account, and for its own sake.

8. Good willing is right, not merely because it is right, but because good is good, and to be willed on its own account.

9. Benevolence is right, not merely because it is useful, but because the thing which benevolence wills or the object willed is a good in itself, and to be willed for its own sake.

10. There is a difference between a law's being a *rule* of duty and the reasons for conforming to that rule. The *rule* is one thing, and the *reasons* for that rule are an other thing.

First. *Inquire what moral obligation is.*

Obligation is that which binds. Moral Obligation is the binding force of moral law, upon moral agents.

Second. *Conditions of moral obligation.*

1. Moral agency. I have given in the first of this course of lectures an outline of what constitutes a moral agent, and need not repeat it here.

2. Moral law, or a rule of right, is another condition of Moral Obligation.

3. Some degree of knowledge of this law or rule of right, and of its application to the point in question.

Third. *What is the foundation of Moral Obligation?*

Under this head I am to show,

I. The different answers that are given to this question.

1. Some affirm that the will of God is the foundation of Moral Obligation; and that moral beings are under obligation to conform

themselves to the law of God, simply and only because such is his will.

2. Others affirm that *right* is the foundation of Moral Obligation; that moral agents are bound to do right, simply and only because it is right.

3. Others affirm that *utility* is the foundation of Moral Obligation; that the tendency of virtue to promote happiness is the fundamental reason why moral agents should be virtuous, and of course the foundation of moral obligation.

4. Others affirm that the nature and relations of moral agents is the foundation of Moral Obligation.

5. Others affirm that the foundation of Moral Obligation lies partly in the nature and relations of moral beings, partly in the nature or intrinsic value of virtue, and partly in the nature and intrinsic value of happiness.

6. Others affirm that the foundation of Moral Obligation lies in the nature or intrinsic value of virtue and happiness; that they are an ultimate good, and therefore to be chosen for their own sake.

7. Others still deny that right or virtue is an *ultimate* good; and affirm that the foundation of Moral Obligation is in the nature and intrinsic value of happiness alone. They affirm that that cannot be an *ultimate* good which naturally and necessarily results in some other good beyond itself, of which it is not only a condition, but a cause. They affirm that consciousness testifies that right or virtue naturally, and so far as we can perceive necessarily results in happiness; and that therefore it is not in itself an *ultimate* good, but only a condition or cause of happiness, which is the only ultimate good; and that for this reason, *right* or virtue cannot be the foundation of Moral Obligation. They maintain that right or virtue are only the condition or cause of happiness, and not happiness itself; and that abstracted from the happiness in which it results, it is of no more intrinsic value than the motion of the planets. To this it is replied that right, or virtue is the ultimate good, and that happiness is only its reward, or an added blessing. To this it is answered, that happiness is a natural and necessary consequence of virtue, and not merely something given as a compensation, or as the reward of virtue; and if this is not so, it is inquired, who bestows the rewards of virtue upon God?

II. I am to show wherein they who maintain these different theories agree.

1. They agree in respect to what constitutes moral agency.

2. They agree that moral agency is an indispensible condition of Moral Obligation.

3. They agree in respect to all the conditions of Moral Obligation, as above specified.

4. They agree that all moral agents are under Moral Obligation.

5. They agree that God is a moral agent, and the subject of Moral Obligation; and that he could not be virtuous if he were not.

6. They agree that God, and all moral agents are under a moral and immutable obligation to will and act in perfect conformity with their nature and relations.

7. They agree that universal benevolence, or good willing is in precise conformity with the nature and relations of moral beings; and that it is therefore the substance and the whole of virtue.

They agree that right consists in volition, or right willing, and always resolves itself into benevolence, and that *right*, and *benevolence*, and *willing*, and *acting in conformity with the nature and relation of moral beings are indentical.*

9. They agree that right, benevolence, or acting in conformity with their nature and relations is universally obligatory on moral beings.

10. They agree that God does invariably will and act in conformity with his nature and relations, and the relations of all beings.

11. That his will is therefore always right or benevolent, and is therefore the *rule* of duty to all moral agents.

12. They agree that virtue is an indispensible condition of the happiness of moral beings.

13. They agree that virtue or benevolence naturally and necessarily results in the happiness of him who exercises it.

14. They agree that happiness is *a good* in itself, that it is *an ultimate good*, and to be chosen for its own sake.

15. They agree that misery is an evil in itself, and to be dreaded and rejected for its own sake.

16. They agree that moral agents are under Moral Obligation to will the happiness of all beings in proportion to their capacity for happiness.

17. They agree that right and utility are always at one; that what is upon the whole useful, is right; and that what is right, is upon the whole useful.

18. They agree in their definition of moral agency, and in their definition of Moral Obligation. They agree as to who are subjects of Moral Obligation. They agree as to the conditions of Moral Obligation; that right, and benevolence, and acting in conformity with the nature and relations of moral beings *are identical;* and that this course of willing and acting is universally obligatory on moral agents. But,

III. They differ in respect to the *why*, or in the fundamental reason of this obligation.

IV. But this leads me to show what the real point of inquiry is not.

1. It is not whether the will of God is obligatory upon all created moral agents. For this is on all hands admitted.

2. The inquiry is not what constitutes moral agency.

3. Nor whether moral agency is a condition of Moral Obligation.

4. Nor whether moral agents are bound to do right.

5. Nor whether moral agents are under obligation to act in conformity with their nature and relations.

6. Nor whether the utility of an act may not be one reason why it is obligatory.

7. Nor is the inquiry why *moral agents* are under obligation to do right, or act in conformity with their nature and relations any more than a *beast* is under Moral Obligation to do so; for in this case the plain and only answer would be, that they are under Moral Obligation, because they are moral agents; and that beasts are not, because they are not moral agents. This conducts us to the real point of inquiry.

V. The true and only question is, why are moral agents under Moral Obligation to do *right* rather than *wrong;* to be benevolent, rather than malevolent; to act in conformity with their nature and relations, rather than to act contrary to them? As right, benevolence, and acting in conformity with the nature and relations of moral beings are the same thing, the question is *one*, and may be stated thus: What is the fundamental reason why moral agents should be benevolent, or will the good of being? Suppose we consider this inquiry as respecting God, and ask: Why is God under obligation to be benevolent, or to will good?

VI. Answer the question, or show what the foundation of Moral Obligation is.

1. It is not the will of God.

(1.) It is plain that his obligation could not arise from, or be founded in his own will.

(2.) The will of God cannot be the foundation of Moral Obligation in created moral agents. It is admitted that God is himself the subject of Moral Obligation. If so, there is some reason, independent of his own will, why he wills as he does, some reason that imposes obligation upon him to will as he does will. His will, then, respecting the conduct of moral agents, is not the foundation reason of their obligation; but the foundation of their obligation must be that reason which induces God, or makes it obligatory on him to will in respect to the conduct of moral agents, just what he does.

(3.) If the will of God were the foundation of Moral Obligation, he could, by willing it, change the nature of virtue and vice.

(4.) If the will of God were the foundation of Moral Obligation, he not only can change the nature of virtue and vice, but has a right to do so; for if there is nothing back of his will that is as binding upon him as upon his creatures, he could at any time, by willing it, make malevolence a virtue, and benevolence a vice.

(5.) If the will of God be the foundation of Moral Obligation, we have no standard by which to judge of the moral character of his actions, and cannot know whether he is worthy of praise or blame.

(6.) If the will of God is the foundation of Moral Obligation, he has no standard by which to judge of his own character, as he has no rule with which to compare his own actions.

(7.) If the will of God is the foundation of Moral Obligation, he is not himself a subject of Moral Obligation. But,

(8.) If God is not a subject of Moral Obligation, he has no moral character; for virtue and vice are nothing else but conformity or non-conformity to Moral Obligation. The will of God, as expressed in his law, is the rule of duty to moral agents. It defines and marks out the path of duty, but the fundamental reason why moral agents ought to act in conformity to the will of God, is plainly not the will of God itself.

2. Right is not the foundation of Moral Obligation.

Let it be remembered, that right, benevolence, and acting in conformity with the nature and relations of moral beings are the same thing.

If the fundamental reason for doing right, being benevolent, or acting in conformity with our nature and relations, is simply because, and only because it is right, it must be that right, benevolence, or acting in conformity with our nature and relations, is the ultimate good, or a good in itself, entirely independent of any good that results from it. But this contradicts consciousness, and cannot therefore be true. If right be valuable in itself, it may so far be chosen for its own sake, and be *a* reason of Moral Obligation. Yet as it naturally and certainly results in a good beyond itself, it certainly is not the *ultimate* good, and therefore is not the *foundation* or *fundamental* reason of Moral Obligation. But we are not inquiring for all the reasons that may render virtue obligatory, but we are inquiring after the fundamental or ultimate reason, that which is at the bottom or foundation of all other reasons. This cannot be *right;* for right certainly is not the ultimate reason, as it naturally results in a good beyond itself. For this we have the testimony of consciousness. To this it is objected, as has been already shown, that right is the ultimate good, and that happiness is a reward or added blessing.

To this it has already been answered, that happiness is a natural and necessary consequence or result of virtue; and that although it is a reward of virtue, it is that in which virtue necessarily results, and if this were not so, it is inquired, who would bestow on God the rewards of virtue?

But to this view of the subject it is again objected, that moral agents affirm the *rightness* of any course of conduct as the reason for that course of conduct; and this must be the true reason, or it would not be virtuous.

To this it may be replied, that they may, and often do assign *a true* reason and *a good* reason for their conduct, when they do not assign *the fundamental* reason. They often assign the will of God as a reason; they often assign utility as a reason; they often assign the dictates of conscience as a reason. Each and all of these may, in some cases, be reasons, and good reasons, while neither of them is the fundamental reason.

Again it is asserted, that no other reason can be assigned for acting right, than that it is right, and that this runs us up to our first principle, and is a first or ultimate truth. But from the testimony of our consciousness we know this to be false. For although its being right may be *a* reason of Moral Obligation, it certainly is not the *only* reason, nor is it the *fundamental* reason; for we certainly know from consciousness that right naturally and necessarily results in happiness, which is a good beyond itself, and consequently that happiness is the fundamental or foundation reason of the obligation. This brings me to say,

3. That UTILITY is not the foundation of Moral Obligation. That benevolence will produce happiness, is not the foundation upon which the obligation to benevolence rests. For as happiness is a good in itself, to will its existence would be obligatory, if the willing it did not and could not produce it. Were a moral being completely insulated in his existence, universal benevolence would be his duty, did he know that other beings existed, although his benevolence could make no being in the universe happy. But if the foundation of the obligation to benevolence lay in the tendency of benevolence to promote the happiness of its object, if it were certain that his benevolence could do no one any good, the obligation would cease.

If to this it be replied, that in such circumstances he would be under obligation to be benevolent, because of its tendency to promote his own happiness; to this it may be answered, that it is impossible to be benevolent for that reason. Benevolence is good willing. Benevolence to others is willing good to others. But to will good to others for the sake of my own happiness, is a contradiction; for it is willing good to myself as an end, and willing good to others only as a means. This is not benevolence, but selfishness. In this case the supposition is that I am to be benevolent or to will the happiness of others, not because it is a good in itself, and therefore to be desired for its own sake, not because it will promote the happiness of its object, but simply and only because it will promote my own happiness.

Now it is not only impossible for me to be benevolent for this reason, as it contradicts the very nature of benevolence, but such an exercise, could it be put forth, could not promote my own happiness. It could promote my own happiness only as it was in accordance with the laws of my being; but my consciousness testifies and my reason affirms that happiness is a good in itself, that it is an ultimate good, and ought to be chosen for its own sake. If, therefore, I could will the happiness of other beings mainly for the sake of making myself happy, or as the means of my own happiness, this would not be acting in accordance with the laws of my being, and consequently could not make me happy. Therefore it is impossible that utility should be the foundation of Moral Obligation.

We have already seen that there is a difference between willing the *existence* of the happiness of all beings, in itself considered, and as a good in itself, and willing *to make* all beings or a particular being happy. The former is benevolence, and always, and universally obligatory. The latter is an expression or carrying out of benevolence, but its obligation is not universal, because the universal good demands that some wicked beings should be miserable and not happy.

Again. It is impossible to will *to do* what we know to be impossible. We may will the *existence* of what we know we cannot effect, but we cannot will *to do* what we know we cannot do. Hence we may and ought to will the happiness of all beings, as a good in itself, but we cannot will to make all beings happy.

4. The foundation of Moral Obligation does not lie in the nature and relations of moral beings. The affirmation that it does is founded in a mistaken apprehension of the real question in debate. As has been already said, the true question is not, why are moral agents under obligation to do right, to be benevolent, to act in conformity with their nature and relations, any more than brutes are under such obligation? If this were the inquiry, the true answer would doubtless be, because they are moral agents, and not brutes; because their nature and relations are what they are.

It should be remembered that the true inquiry is, why are moral agents under obligation to do right rather than wrong; to be benevolent, rather than malevolent; to act in conformity with their nature and relations, rather than contrary to them? If, then, to the question, why are moral agents under Moral Obligation to act in conformity with their nature and relations, rather than contrary to them, it be replied, that their nature and relations are the foundation of this obligation, this is only saying they are under obligation to act in conformity with their nature and relations rather than contrary to them, because they are under such obligation. This is only to assert their obligation, but is not assigning the reason. If to this it be replied, that no other reason can be assigned, it may be answered, that another, and a good and sufficient reason can be assigned, and ought to be assigned. Benevolence is willing in exact conformity with the nature and relations of moral beings. But benevolence is willing the existence of universal happiness as a good in itself.

This is a good, and sufficient, and infinitely weighty reason why moral beings should be benevolent, or act in conformity with their nature and relations. Acting contrary to their nature and relations is malevolence, or willing something inconsistent with universal happiness. But misery is an evil in itself, and therefore to be rejected for its own sake. This, then, is a good and sufficient reason why moral beings ought not to act contrary to their natures and relations.

The foundation of Moral Obligation, then, does not lie in the nature and relations of moral beings.

5. The foundation does not lie partly in the nature and relations of moral beings, partly in the nature or intrinsic value of virtue, and partly in the nature or intrinsic value of happiness. The affirmation that these are altogether the foundation of Moral Obligation is founded partly in a misapprehension of the real question at issue, and partly in the assumption that virtue or right is an ultimate good in itself, and apart from that happiness in which it results.

We have just seen that the foundation of Moral Obligation cannot be in the nature and relations of moral beings, because the question is not why are moral beings, rather than other beings, under Moral Obligation, but why are moral beings under obligation to do right rather than wrong? To say that the intrinsic value of right or virtue is the fundamental, or even *one* of the *fundamental* reasons of Moral Obligation, is to assume that right or virtue has an intrinsic value in itself. That its value is not ultimate, but that it results in something beyond itself, has already been shown; and should it be admitted, as perhaps it ought to be, that right or virtue is a good in itself, still it is not an *ultimate* good; and although it may be a reason of Moral Obligation, it is not the *fundamental* reason or *foundation* of Moral Obligation, as our consciousness testifies that there is another reason still below it. But the *foundation* of Moral Obligation is that after which we are inquiring.

6. The foundation of Moral Obligation does not lie in the nature and intrinsic value of both virtue and happiness. This has just been sufficiently shown. But,

7. The foundation of Moral Obligation does lie in the intrinsic value of happiness as an ultimate good. It has been shown that right always has its foundation in volition, and that right willing is always good willing, or benevolence. The foundation reason, then, why God and all moral beings should be benevolent, or will good, is that good is a good in itself, and to be willed for its own sake. The reason why they are under obligation not to be malevolent, to will evil, or to act contrary to their nature in willing evil to any being is that evil is an evil in itself, to be universally dreaded and rejected for its own sake. In other words, all Moral Obligation resolves itself into an obligation to will the universal good of being. The question is, why are moral agents under obligation to will the good of being? The answer is, because *good is good*. Happiness is an ultimate good, to be chosen for its own sake, and therefore the fundamental reason of Moral Obligation is, that good is good, and to be willed or chosen by all moral beings as a good, and an ultimate good in itself.

This, then, is the sum of the whole matter. Moral *right* consists in willing and acting in precise conformity with the nature and relations of moral agents.

Moral *Obligation* is the binding force of right upon moral agents.

The *foundation* of Moral Obligation to do right and not wrong, is not,

1. In the *nature* and *relations* of moral agents.

2. Not in *right*. These are reasons, but not the foundation.

Right is *benevolence* or *right willing*. *Right willing* is *good willing*, or *willing good*.

Moral agents are bound to will good, plainly, not because good willing will produce good, but because GOOD is GOOD.

REMARK.

This shows why the gospel offers a reward to virtue, and yet insists that that is not virtue in which reward isthe motive to action.

LECTURE XXIV.

MORAL GOVERNMENT.—No. 3.

WHOSE RIGHT IT IS TO GOVERN.

1. Moral beings exist.

2. They must of necessity be happy or miserable.

3. Happiness is a good in itself, and therefore desirable for its own sake.

4. Misery is an evil in itself and therefore to be dreaded for its own sake.

5. Moral law is that mode of moral action that exactly accords with the nature and relations of moral beings.

6. Conformity to this law is virtue.

7. Virtue is the cause of happiness.

8. Happiness is an ultimate good.

9. Happiness is the ultimate end of government.

10. Upon moral government as a means of promoting this end, both ruler and ruled are dependent.

11. He has a right to govern, who possesses such attributes, such a character, is so circumstanced, and sustains such relations as to be both able and willing to secure the highest good of the whole.

12. Upon him all eyes are, or ought to be turned, to sustain this office. It is both his right and his duty to govern; for upon him all are naturally dependent, for securing the highest interests of the whole.

13. It is therefore the right and the duty of God to administer

the moral government of the universe. In showing which I observe:

I. *That God is a moral being.*

A moral being is one who possesses understanding, reason, conscience and free will. That God is such a being has been already shown, in discussing his moral attributes. But in addition to what was there said, I remark:

1. That many of our notions of God are derived from our knowledge of ourselves. We are conscious of possessing the powers of moral agency. And because the works and providence of God exhibit phenomena corresponding to those of which we are conscious, we naturally and necessarily infer that he is a moral being like ourselves.

2. The whole argument for the *existence* of God, as fully establishes the truth that he is a *moral being* as that he *exists*. That the Maker of the universe must possess understanding, reason, conscience, and will, there can be no doubt.

3. We are conscious that all power to produce any effect without ourselves, consists in the will or power of volition. Understanding, reason, and conscience, might exist without any power to produce any effect without ourselves.

4. We conceive of the physical power of God as consisting in his will or volitions.

5. We are moral beings, and God is our Creator. God, therefore, must have had the *idea* of a moral being. He must have possessed the knowledge of what constitutes a moral being, or he could not have created one. But if he possessed sufficient knowledge of what constitutes a moral being, to enable him to create moral beings, with all the circumstances that render them responsible, he must be himself a moral being, *if his will is free.*

6. That the will of God is free, must be—

(1.) Because volition is nothing else but the will acting in view of motive.

(2.) It cannot but be free, if it has the power and liberty of choice, in view of motives.

(3.) Choice and necessity are terms of opposition.

(4.) It is as absurd to say that volition can be produced by physical force or necessity, as to say that the planets can be influenced by motives.

(5.) If God is not free he has no moral character.

(6.) But from the laws of our being, we must and do conceive of God as possessing moral character.

(7.) All nations have ascribed moral character to God.

(8.) The Bible every where represents God as a moral being, and as possessing the perfection of moral character.

II. *God is a Moral Governor.*

A moral governor is one who does or *has a right* to exercise a supreme moral control over moral beings. Under this head I remark:

1. That it is impossible that government should not exist.

2. Every thing must be governed by laws suited to its nature.

3. Matter must be governed by physical laws.

4. Mind must be governed by motives. And moral agents must be governed by moral considerations.

5. We are conscious of moral agency, and can be governed only by a moral government.

6. Our nature and circumstances demand that we should be under a moral government; because—

(1.) Moral happiness depends upon moral order.

(2.) Moral order depends upon the harmonious action of all our powers, as individuals and as members of society.

(3.) No community can perfectly harmonize in all their views and feelings, without perfect knowledge, or, to say the least, the same degree of knowledge on all subjects on which they are called to act.

(4.) But no community ever existed or will exist, in which every individual possesses exactly the same amount of knowledge, and where they are, therefore, entirely agreed in all their thoughts, views and opinions.

(5.) But if they are not agreed in opinion, or have not exactly the same amount of knowledge, they will not in every thing harmonize, as it respects their courses of conduct.

(6.) There must therefore be in every community some standard or rule of duty, to which all the subjects of the community are to conform themselves.

(7.) There must be some head or controlling mind, whose will shall be law, and whose decisions shall be regarded as infallible by all the subjects of the government.

(8.) However diverse their intellectual attainments are, in this they must all agree, that the will of the lawgiver is right, and universally the rule of duty.

(9.) This will must be authorative and not merely advisory.

(10.) There must of necessity be a penalty attached to and incurred by every act of disobedience to this will.

(11.) If disobedience be persisted in, exclusion from the privileges of the government is the lowest penalty that can consistently be inflicted.

(12.) The good then of the universe imperiously requires, that there should be a moral government and a moral governor.

That God is a Moral Governor, we infer—

1. From our own consciousness. From the very laws of our being we naturally feel ourselves responsible to him for our conduct. In the last lecture it was shown, that God is himself the subject of moral obligation, or under a moral obligation, to be benevolent. As God is our Creator, we are naturally responsible to him

for the right exercise of our moral powers. And as our good and his glory depend upon our conformity to the same rule, to which he conforms his whole being, he is under a moral obligation to require us to be holy as he is holy.

2. His natural attributes qualify him to sustain the relation of a moral governor to the universe.

3. His moral character, also, qualifies him to sustain this relation.

4. His relation to the universe as Creator and Preserver, when considered in connection with his nature and attributes, confers on him the right of universal government.

5. His relation to the universe, and our relations to him and to each other, render it obligatory upon him to establish and administer a moral government over the universe.

6. The honor of God demands that he should administer such a government.

7. His conscience must demand it. He must know that it would be wrong for him to create a universe of moral beings, and then refuse or neglect to administer over them a moral government.

8. His happiness must demand it, as he could not be happy unless he acted in accordance with his conscience.

9. If God is not a moral governor, he is not wise. Wisdom consists in the choice of the best ends, and in the use of the most appropriate means to accomplish those ends. If God is not a moral governor, it is inconceivable that he should have had any important end in view in the creation of moral beings, or that he should have chosen the best or any suitable means for the accomplishment of the most desirable ends.

10. The conduct or providence of God plainly indicates a design to exert a moral influence over moral agents.

11. His providence plainly indicates that the universe of mind is governed by moral laws, or by laws suited to the nature of moral agents.

12. Consciousness proves the existence of an inward law, or knowledge of the moral quality of actions.

13. This inward moral consciousness or conscience implies the existence of a rule of duty which is obligatory upon us. This rule implies a ruler, and this ruler must be God.

14. If God is not a moral governor, our very nature deceives us.

15. If God is not a moral governor, the whole universe, so far as we have the means of knowing it, is calculated to mislead mankind in respect to this fundamental truth.

16. If there is no such thing as moral government, there is, in reality, no such thing as moral character.

17. All nations have believed that God is a moral governor.

18. Our nature is such, that we must believe it. The conviction of our moral accountability to God, is in such a sense the dictate of our moral nature, that we cannot escape from it.

19. We must abhor God, if we ever come to a knowledge of

the fact that he created moral agents and then exercised over them no moral government.

20. The connection between moral delinquency and suffering is such as to render it certain that moral government does, as a matter of fact, exist.

21. The Bible, which has been proved to be a revelation from God, contains a most simple and yet comprehensive system of moral government.

22. If we are deceived in respect to our being subjects of moral government, we are sure of nothing.

REMARKS.

1. If God's government is moral, it is easy to see how sin came to exist. That a want of experience in the universe, in regard to the nature and natural tendencies and results of sin, prevented the due influence of motive.

2. If God's government is moral, we see that all the developments of sin are enlarging the experience of the universe in regard to its nature and tendencies, and thus confirm the influence of moral government over virtuous minds.

3. If God's government is moral, we can understand the design and tendency of the Atonement.

4. If God's government is moral, we can understand the philosophy of the Spirit's influences in convicting and sanctifying the soul.

5. If the government of God is moral, we can understand the influence and necessity of faith.

6. If God's government is moral, faith will produce obedience, with the same certainty as if it acted by force.

7. If God's government is moral, we can see the necessity and power of Christian example.

8. If God's government is moral, his natural or physical omnipotence is no proof that all men will be saved.

9. If God's government is moral, we see the importance of watchfulness, and girding up the loins of our minds.

10. If God's government is moral, we see the necessity of a well instructed ministry, able to wield the motives necessary to sway mind.

11. If God's government is moral, we see the philosophical bearings, tendencies, and power of the providence, law, and gospel of God, in the great work of man's salvation.

LECTURE. XXV.

MORAL GOVERNMENT.—No. 4.

WHAT IS IMPLIED IN THE RIGHT TO GOVERN.

1. The right to govern does not imply, that the will of the ruler can make law.
2. Nor the right to pass or enforce any arbitrary law. But—
3. It implies the right to declare and define the law of nature.
4. It implies the right to enforce obedience, with sanctions equivalent to its importance.
5. The *right* to govern implies the *duty* to govern.
6. The right of government implies, the obligations of obedience on the part of the governed.
7. It implies, that it is both the right and the duty, to execute penal sanctions, when the interests of the government demand the execution of them.

RECIPROCAL DUTIES OF THE RULER AND RULED.

1. They are under mutual obligation to aim, with single eye, at promoting the great end of government.
2. The ruler is under obligation to keep in view the foundation of his right to govern, and never assume or exercise authority that is not essential to the promotion of the highest good.
3. He is under obligation to regard and treat every interest according to its relative value.
4. He is never, in any case, to depart from the true spirit and principles of government.
5. He is invariably to reward virtue.
6. He is always to inflict penal evil upon transgressors, unless the highest good can as well, or better be secured in another way.
7. He is under obligation to pursue that course that will, upon the whole, result in the least evil, and promote the highest good.
8. The ruled are bound to co-operate with the ruler in this, with all their powers, with all they are and have.
9. They are under obligation to be obedient in all things, so far as, and no farther than the laws are in accordance with and promotive of the highest good of the whole.
10. They are bound to be disinterested; that is—to discard all selfishness, and to regard and treat every interest according to its relative value.
11. Both ruler and ruled are under obligation to exercise all that self-denial that is essential to the promotion of the highest good.

12. As it is the ruler's duty to inflict, so it is the subject's duty to submit to any penal inflictions that are deserved, and important to the highest interests of the government.

LECTURE XXVI.

MORAL GOVERNMENT.—No. 5.

MORAL LAW.

In discussing this part of the subject, I shall show:

FIRST. What law is.

SECOND. Define moral law.

THIRD. That all moral law is a unit.

FOURTH. That no being can make law.

FIFTH. That the will of the ruler can be obligatory only as it is declaratory of what the law is.

FIRST. *What law is.*

Law is a rule of action, and in its most extensive sense, it is applicable to all actions, whether of matter or mind.

SECOND. *Define Moral Law.*

1. Moral law is a rule of moral action.

2. It is the law of motive, and not of force.

3. Moral law is a rule, to which moral beings are under obligation to conform all their actions.

4. Moral law is the law of nature; that is—it is that rule of action that is founded in the nature and relations of moral beings.

5. It is that rule which, under the same circumstances, would be equally binding on all moral beings. Its essential elements are—

(1.) A declaratory, but authoritative precept, as distinguished from counsel or compact.

(2.) The precept should forbid all that is naturally wrong, or in any degree inconsistent with the nature, relations and highest happiness of moral beings.

(3.) It should define and require all that is according to the nature, and relations, and essential to the highest happiness of moral beings.

(4.) Another essential element of law is, requisite sanctions. Sanctions are the motives to obedience. They should be remuneratory and vindicatory.

(5.) Moral law naturally and necessarily connects happiness

with obedience, and misery with disobedience; and thus far the sanctions of moral law belong to its own nature. But—

(6.) In addition to this, there should be superadded, to obedience, the favor of the ruler, and to disobedience his displeasure.

(7.) The sanctions should be equivalent to the value of the precept.

(8.) Prescription, or publication, is essential to the binding obligation of law.

THIRD. *Law is a unit.*

1. The *nature* of moral agents is one.
2. The laws of their being are precisely similar.
3. That which will secure the highest good of one, will secure the highest good of all.
4. Perfect conformity of heart and life to the nature and relations of moral beings, will promote the highest good of all.
5. This course of conduct is universally obligatory.
6. It is, therefore, universal law.
7. It is and must be the only law.
8. It is the common law of the universe.
9. No enactment or statute of God or man, is morally obligatory, only as it is declaratory, and an application of this only law.

FOURTH. *No being can make law.*

1. God's existence and nature are necessary.
2. Moral law is that course of action which is in conformity with the laws of his being.
3. It is, therefore, obligatory upon him.
4. God could make moral *agents*, but not moral *law*; for when they exist, this rule is law to them, and would be, whether God willed it or not.
5. Law is that course of action demanded by the nature and relations of moral beings. Therefore—

FIFTH. *Neither the will of God, nor of any other being, can make law, or be obligatory any farther than it is declaratory of what the law of nature is.*

1. The true idea of government is that kind and degree of control, the object and tendency of which is, to promote the highest good.
2. The rule, conformity to which is essential to the promotion of the highest good, is founded in the nature, and relations, and circumstances of all the parties concerned, entirely independent of the will of any being.
3. The business of the ruler, is to declare and enforce this rule.
4. Thus far his will is obligatory, and no farther.
5. All legislation, human or divine, not declaratory of and in ac-

cordance with the law of nature, or with the nature and relations of moral beings, would be utterly null and void.

6. All positive legislation, except that which is declaratory of natural law is arbitrary and tyrannical, and therefore nugatory.

LECTURE XXVII.

MORAL GOVERNMENT.—No. 6.

LAW OF GOD.

FIRST. Show what is intended by the Law of God.

SECOND. That all the commandments, or specific requirements of God, are declaratory, and are but the spirit, meaning, and application of the one only law of love.

THIRD. That the ten commandments, or decalogue, are proofs and illustrations of this truth.

FOURTH. Consider the sanctions of the Law of God.

FIRST. *What is intended by the Law of God.*

1. We are not to understand that the arbitrary will of God is law.

2. Nor that any thing is law, merely because it is his will.

3. Nor that he in any case creates or makes moral law. But—

4. By the Law of God is intended that rule of universal benevolence, which is obligatory upon him as being in accordance with the laws of his own being.

5. The Law of God is that rule, to which he invariably conforms all his actions, or that law of his being which he himself obeys.

6. The Law of God is that rule of universal, perfect benevolence, which it is both his right and his duty to declare and enforce upon all moral agents for their good and his glory.

7. By the Law of God is intended that rule of universal benevolence to which himself and all moral beings are under immutable obligations, to conform their whole being.

8. The Law of God then is a unit. It is one, and only one principle. It is the one grand rule that every moral being shall regard and treat every being, interest, and thing, according to its relative value.

SECOND. *All the commandments are declaratory, &c.*

1. All God's moral attributes are modifications of one principle; that is—benevolence. This we have already seen in a former lecture.

2. Benevolence expresses his whole character, including his affections and acts.

3. All virtue in moral beings is only different modifications of benevolence.

4. Perfect, perpetual, and universal benevolence, modified by the relations and circumstances of moral beings, is their whole duty.

5. Complacency in right character, is only a modification of benevolence.

6. If benevolence, in its various modifications, is the whole of virtue, then all God's requirements must be in spirit one. Love expresses and comprehends the whole.

7. The command to love God with all the heart, and soul, and mind, and strength, is identical in spirit and meaning with the command, Thou shalt love thy neighbor as thyself.

8. These two commands might both be united in one precept: Thou shalt regard and treat all interests, beings and things according to their relative value.

9. Thus it appears, that what are called the two great principles of the law are really one in essence though two in form. They are identical in spirit, yet two in their letter.

THIRD. *The ten commandments are proofs and illustrations of this truth.*

FIRST COMMANDMENT.

Ex. 20: 3. 'Thou shalt have no other gods before me.'

I. Reasons for this commandment:

1. God's happiness is infinitely the greatest good in the universe, and therefore, thus to regard and treat it is right in itself.

2. God's virtue is infinitely greater than that of all other beings. Therefore, to love him with all possible complacency is right in itself.

3. We have infinitely greater cause of gratitude to God, than to any other and all other beings. Therefore, the highest degree of the love of gratitude is right in itself.

4. To render to God the highest degree of benevolence, gratitude, and complacent love, is demanded by the very laws of our being.

5. No moral being can be truly happy without it.

6. Nor can any moral being fail of being happy, if he exercise the perfection of these modifications of love to God.

7. The one universal law of benevolence requires it. It is, therefore, God's duty to require it.

8. He can neither abrogate nor relax the obligation.

II. The true meaning and spirit of this command:

1. Every law has its letter and its spirit. Its letter is its general statement in words. Its spirit is its real meaning as applied to specific cases and circumstances.

2. To the letter of the law there may be exceptions. To the spirit and meaning of the law never.

3. As no will can create law, so no will can make exceptions to the spirit of law.

4. This command prohibits the love of any being or thing more than God.

5. It prohibits the loving of any being or thing in comparison with God.

6. It requires the highest degree of benevolence or good will to God, of which we are capable.

7. It requires that this benevolence be real; that is—good will to God, or willing his good and happiness for its own sake, as infinitely valuable and desirable in itself, irrespective of its resulting in or being promotive of our own happiness.

8. It requires that this benevolence be uninterrupted.

9. That in all possible ways, the most perfect regard to the feelings, happiness, and glory of God be expressed.

10. It requires the highest degree of complacency in him of which we are capable.

11. That this complacency be expressed in all possible acts of obedience.

12. That this love of complacency be perpetual and perpetually expressed, in every appropriate way.

13. It requires the highest degree of the love of gratitude, of which we are capable.

14. That this love of gratitude be perpetual and perpetually expressed in every appropriate way.

15. This command requires the most perfect confidence.

16. That this confidence be perpetual and perpetually expressed, as above.

17. It requires the deepest repentance on the part of sinners, of which they are naturally capable, and that this repentance be as perpetual and as perpetually and fully expressed, in every appropriate way, as is consistent with their natural ability.

18. It requires the most perfect self-abhorrence and self-abasement, perpetual and perpetually expressed, of which the sinner is capable.

19. It requires the most perfect and perpetual subjection of our will to his, in all things.

20. It requires the most perfect and perpetual consecration of our whole being, time, talent, possessions, and all we have and are, to God.

21. All this must be implied in the command, 'Thou shalt have no other gods before me.'

22. It is plainly only a declaratory precept or a specific and authoritative application of the only law of love, universally obligatory on all moral agents, as will readily be seen, by comparing the expositions of it which have been given with the reasons for its enactment.

SECOND COMMANDMENT.

Ex. 20 : 4–6. 'Thou shalt not make unto thee any graven image, or any likeness of any thing that is in heaven above, or that is in the earth beneath, or that is in the water under the earth: thou shalt not bow down thyself to them, nor serve them: for I the Lord thy God am a jealous God, visiting the iniquity of the fathers upon the children to the third and fourth generation of them that hate me; and showing mercy unto thousands of them that love me, and keep my commandments.'

I. Reasons for this commandment:

1. God is a Spirit.

2. All sensible representations of God, by pictures, images, or other means, are utterly deceptive, and convey gross, false, abominable, and ruinous ideas of God.

3. Therefore, all such attempts to convey to our own minds, or the minds of others, any apprehensions of the true God, by any image, picture, resemblance, or sensible manifestations whatever, are inconsistent with the great and only law of benevolence, or good-willing.

II. This shows the true meaning and spirit of the law to prohibit any attempt to give human beings the knowledge of God, by pictures, images, visible or tangible representations of any kind whatever.

THIRD COMMANDMENT.

Ex. 20: 7. 'Thou shalt not take the name of the Lord thy God in vain; for the Lord will not hold him guiltless that taketh his name in vain.'

I. The true spirit of this requirement:

1. It does not imply that the word expressing the name of God, is more sacred than any other word.

2. It prohibits all unnecessary mention of the name of God.

3. It prohibits every light and irreverent use of it.

4. It prohibits every feeling that might lead to this.

5. It requires a feeling of the utmost holy awe, reverence, love, and respect for God.

6. It requires a constant and perfect recognition of what he is, of what we are, of his relations to us, and ours to him, so far as our circumstances and natural capabilities will allow.

7. It admits the use of the name of God, only when necessary, and then only in accordance with a perfect state of heart.

II. Reasons for this commandment:

1. God's infinite greatness and excellence.

2. His relation to the universe as Supreme Ruler.

3. The strength, stability, and influence of his government, depend upon the estimation in which he is held by his subjects.

4. Every light and irreverent mention of his name, tends to diminish awe, veneration, confidence, and respect, and of course to weaken his influence, and the power of his government.

5. The happiness of the universe depends on their virtue. Their virtue consists in obedience to God; and their obedience to God depends upon the light in which they regard him.

6. Therefore, the highest good of the universe demands that God should respect his own name, and never suffer it to be trifled with.

7. The highest good of the universe also demands that all moral beings should treat the name of God with the utmost awe, veneration, and respect.

8. Therefore, this command as above explained, is only a declaratory precept, and an application of the one great and only law of love, equally obligatory upon God, and upon all moral beings.

LECTURE XXVIII.

MORAL GOVERNMENT.—No. 7.

FOURTH COMMANDMENT.

Ex. 20: 9—11. 'Six days shalt thou labor, and do all thy work: but the seventh day is the Sabbath of the Lord thy God: in it thou shalt not do any work, thou, nor thy son, nor thy daughter, thy man-servant, nor thy maid-servant, nor thy cattle, nor thy stranger that is within thy gates: for in six days the Lord made heaven and earth, the sea, and all that in them is, and rested the seventh day: wherefore the Lord blessed the Sabbath-day and hallowed it.'

As several questions of importance upon which there has been much discussion, are connected with this commandment, I shall go a little more at length into its examination, embracing the question of its change from the seventh to the first day of the week.

FIRST. When the Sabbath was instituted.
SECOND. Its design.
THIRD. Its necessity.
FOURTH. Its perpetual and universal obligation.
FIFTH. The manner in which it should be observed.
SIXTH. Its change from the seventh to the first day of the week.

FIRST. *When the Sabbath was instituted.*

1. At the close of the six days' work of creation; or the first day after the work was done.

Gen. 2: 2, 3. 'And on the seventh day God ended his work which he had made; and he rested on the seventh day from all his work which he had made. And God blessed the seventh day, and sanctified it; because that in it he had rested from all his work which God had created and made.'

That the Sabbath here mentioned was observed by mankind, at least some of them, before the law was given at Mount Sinai, I argue,

1. From the fact that time was divided into weeks before the giving of the law at Sinai.

Gen. 8: 10—12. 'And he stayed yet other SEVEN DAYS, and again he sent forth the dove out of the ark: and the dove came in to him in the evening, and, lo, in her mouth was an olive leaf pluckt off. So Noah knew that the waters were abated from off the earth. And he stayed yet other SEVEN DAYS, and sent forth the dove, which returned not again unto him any more.'

2. The Sabbath was actually observed by the Israelites before the giving of the law at Sinai, and before we have any account of their having received any commandment concerning it.

Ex. 16: 22—26. 'And it came to pass, that on the sixth day they gathered twice as much bread, two omers for one man: and all the rulers of the congregation came and told Moses. And he said unto them, This is that which the Lord hath said, To-morrow is the rest of the holy Sabbath unto the Lord: bake that which ye will bake to-day, and seethe that ye will seethe; and that which remaineth over lay up for you, to be kept until the morning. And they laid it up till the morning, as Moses bade; and it did not stink, neither was there any worm therein. And Moses said, Eat that to-day; for to-day is a Sabbath unto the Lord: to-day ye shall not find it in the field. Six days shalt thou gather it; but on the seventh day, which is the Sabbath, in it there shall be none.'

Gen. 29: 27. 28. 'Fulfill her WEEK, and we will give thee this also.' 'And Jacob did so, and fulfilled her WEEK.'

All this took place before the law was given at Sinai.

3. The Sabbath is spoken of in the decalogue as an institution already existing. "*Remember* the Sabbath," &c.

Obj. If the Sabbath existed from the creation of the world, why is it not mentioned for so long a time after what is said of its first institution.

Ans. 1. Because the history of those times is so very brief.

2. It might as well be asked why the Sabbath is not mentioned from Joshua to the reign of David.

3. Or why is not circumcision mentioned from Joshua to Jeremiah? Can it be that the Prophets and pious Judges and Jews did

not observe the Sabbath or circumcision during those periods? and yet they are not once named.

4. Many ancient writers bear testimony to the existence and observance of the Sabbath in various nations. A few only are subjoined from Humphrey on the Sabbath.

a. Homer and Hesiod both speak of the seventh day as holy.

b. Porphyry says: "The Phœnicians consecrated one day in seven as holy."

c. Philo says: "The Sabbath is not a festival peculiar to any one people or country, but is common to all the world, and that it may be named the general and public feast, or the feast of the nativity of the world." That is, a celebration of the world's birthday.

d. Josephus affirms: "That there is no city either of Greeks or barbarians, or any other nation, where the religion of the Sabbath is not known."

e. Lampidius tells us that Alexander Severus, the Roman Emperor, usually went on the seventh day into the temple of the Gods, there to offer sacrifice to the Gods.

f. Grotius says: "That the memory of the creation being performed in seven days, was preserved not only among the Greeks and Italians, but among the Celts and Indians, all of whom divided their time into weeks."

Humphrey adds: "The same is affirmed of the Assyrians, Egyptians, Romans, Gauls, Britons, and Germans.

5. These facts show that the Sabbath was not a Jewish institution, but was known and acknowledged by various nations.

SECOND. *Its design.*

1. To commemorate the work of creation.

Gen. 2: 2, 3. 'And on the seventh day God ended his work which he had made; and he rested on the seventh day from all his work which he had made. And God blessed the seventh day, and sanctified it; because that in it he had rested from all his work which God created and made.'

Ex. 20: 11. 'For in six days the Lord made heaven and earth, the sea, and all that in them is, and rested the seventh day: wherefore the Lord blessed the Sabbath-day, and hallowed it.'

Ex. 31: 17. 'It is a sign between me and the children of Israel for ever: for in six days the Lord made heaven and earth, and on the seventh day he rested, and was refreshed.'

2. It was designed as a day of rest from ordinary employments or labors.

Gen. 2: 2, 3. (As above quoted.)

Ex. 20: 10, 11. 'But the seventh day is the Sabbath of the Lord thy God: in it thou shalt not do any work, thou, nor thy son, nor thy daughter, thy man-servant, nor thy maid-servant, nor thy cattle, nor thy stranger that is within thy gates. For in six days the Lord made heaven and earth, the sea, and all that in them is, and rested the seventh day: wherefore the Lord blessed the Sabbath-day, and hallowed it.'

Ex. 31: 13, 17. 'Speak thou also unto the children of Israel, saying, Verily my Sabbaths ye shall keep: for it is a sign between me and you throughout your generations; that ye may know that I am the Lord that doth sanctify you.' 'It is a sign between me and the children of Israel for ever: for in six days the Lord made heaven and earth, and on the seventh day he rested, and was refreshed.'

Deut. 5: 13, 14. 'Six days thou shalt labor, and do all thy work; but the seventh day is the Sabbath of the Lord thy God: in it thou shalt not do any work, thou, nor thy son, nor thy daughter, nor thy man-servant, nor thy maid-servant, nor thine ox, nor thine ass, nor any of thy cattle, nor thy stranger that is within thy gates; that thy man-servant and thy maid servant may rest as well as thou.'

3. It was designed as a means of spiritual knowledge. This is implied in its being both blessed and sanctified; that is, set apart to the service God.

Gen. 2: 3. (as quoted above.)

4. It was designed as a means of increasing holiness in holy beings. N. B. It was instituted before the fall.

5. It was designed to afford the means of grace for sinners. It must have had respect to the foreseen fall of man.

Third. *Its necessity.*

1. It is a well established fact that man and all laboring animals need to rest, at least one day in seven, from their ordinary employments.

2. That they will not only live longer, but actually perform more labor in a given time, by resting one day in seven.

3. That this is true, whether the labor be intellectual or corporeal.

4. Its necessity may be inferred from its existence.

5. Both the physical and moral wants of mankind demand it.

6. Mankind, as an ignorant fallen race, cannot possibly be sanctified and saved without it.

7. Men must have religious instruction.

8. This instruction must be public, as it cannot be given in private, inasmuch as it would require too great a number of religious teachers.

9. If the instruction be public, it must be upon a day when there is a general agreement among mankind to attend to it.

10. Upon such a day men would never agree among themselves, therefore it was necessary that God should authoritatively appoint such a day.

11. No government can be permanent without it.

FOURTH. *Its universal and perpetual obligation.*

I. It is universally obligatory.
1. It was made for *man as a race.*

Mark 2: 27. 'And he said unto them, The Sabbath was made for man, and not man for the Sabbath.'

2. If Adam needed it when holy, how much more do all men now need its moral influence.
3. All men need both its moral and physical influence.
4. It is like marriage founded in the moral and physical necessities of our race.
5. It is a command of the decalogue, and therefore a moral, and not a ceremonial or civil institution.

Obj. I. A moral precept is one of universal obligation wherever moral beings exist; but the law of the Sabbath will not be binding in heaven, therefore it is not a *moral* but a civil precept.

Ans. 1. The true idea of a *moral* precept, is that it is universally binding on moral beings whose circumstances are similar.

2. Men are universally in similar circumstances in this world, in respect to the design and necessity of the Sabbath. To them it is a moral precept and universally obligatory.

6. All the reasons for its *existence* hold equally in favor of its *universal* obligation.

II. It is perpetually obligatory.
1. All the reasons for its institution are reasons for its perpetual observance.
2. All the reasons for its *universal* obligation are equally good reasons for its *perpetual* obligation.
3. True religion would soon cease from the earth, but for the Sabbath.
4. Its perpetuity as a matter of fact is taught in the Bible.

Isa. 56: 6—8. 'Also the sons of the stranger, that join themselves to the Lord to serve him, and to love the name of the Lord, to be his servants, every one that keepeth the Sabbath from polluting it, and taketh hold of my covenant; even them will I bring to my holy mountain, and make them joyful in my house of prayer: their burnt-offerings and their sacrifices shall be accepted upon mine altar; for mine house shall be called an house of prayer for all people. The Lord God, which gathereth the outcasts of Israel, saith, Yet will I gather others to him, besides those that are gathered unto him.'

This passage refers to the gospel day, and to the time of Zion's great prosperity. Then there will be a Sabbath.

5. As the law of the Sabbath is founded in the nature and relations of moral beings, as they exist in this world, it is *common law*, and of course universally and perpetually obligatory.

FIFTH. *The manner in which it is to be observed.*

I. Every law has its letter and its spirit.

1. To the letter of a moral law there may be exceptions. To its *spirit never.*

2. The spirit of a law is its real meaning, or the real intention of the law-giver, as applicable to any and every set of circumstances.

For example; "The Priests," says Christ, "profane the Sabbath, and are blameless." That is, their labor in the Temple service, under the circumstances, is not a breach of the *spirit*, although it is of the letter of the law.

So David ate of the shew-bread, which was lawful only for the Priests, and was yet blameless, because under his circumstances of necessity his eating of that bread was not a violation of the *spirit*, although it was of the letter of the law.

The disciples rubbing the ears of corn, and Christ healing the sick are examples of the same kind.

II. The Sabbath is to be sanctified, or kept holy.

The inquiry is, what is implied in this?

1. It does not imply that works strictly of necessity and mercy are unlawful upon the Sabbath.

2. It does not imply the unlawfulness of sleep and any needed degree of physical and mental repose on the Sabbath.

3. It does not imply that the necessary labors of ministers or other religious teachers are unlawful upon the Sabbath.

4. It does not imply the necessity of very early rising, and of incessant and intense excitement, and running from one meeting to another all day on the Sabbath, regardless of health.

But it does imply:

1. Holiness of heart and right intentions in all we do on the Sabbath. That love and not legal considerations actuate us.

2. Complete rest from our ordinary labors, whether of body or mind, so far as is consistent with performing labors of strict necessity and mercy.

3. The abstraction of thought from those employments and labors.

4. The abstaining from conversation upon those subjects that constitute our secular employments.

Isa. 58: 13. 'If thou turn away thy foot from the Sabbath, from doing thy pleasure on my holy day; and call the Sabbath a delight, the holy of the Lord, honorable; and shalt honor him, not doing thine own ways, nor finding thine own pleasure, nor speaking thine own words,' &c.

5. That neither ourselves nor our beasts, nor any person under our control be either employed or allowed to engage in such labors.

Ex. 20: 10. 'But the seventh day is the Sabbath of the Lord thy God: in it thou shalt not do any work, thou, nor thy son, nor thy daughter, thy man-servant, nor thy maid-servant, nor thy cattle, nor thy stranger that is within thy gates.'

6. It implies the spending of that day in devotional exercises, public, private, and social, as opportunity affords, and health allows.

7. It implies the observance of twenty-four hours as a Sabbath, or a seventh part of time.

8. It implies the sacred application of our powers to the acquisition of holiness.

9. Those persons whose weekly labors are *bodily*, should let their bodies rest and employ their minds in devotional exercises, and in the acquisition of religious knowledge on the Sabbath.

10. Persons whose labors are of the *mind*, should rest from their mental application on that day.

11. The sanctification of the Sabbath implies that no unnecessary traveling, either by ministers going to preach, or by persons going to hear, shall be done upon that day.

12. It implies that all cooking, sweeping, cleansing dishes, and every kind of domestic labor shall be dispensed with, as far as is consistent with health and decency, upon that day.

13. It implies abstinence from all amusements.

14. It implies abstinence from walking or riding abroad for exercise.

15. It prohibits all unnecessary use of working animals.

16. That all this be done in the spirit of love to God, and not in a legal and self-righteous temper.

SIXTH. *Its change to the first day of the week.*

1. The change of the Sabbath from the seventh to the first day of the week, is a question entirely distinct from that of the perpetual obligation of the Sabbath.

2. If the evidence for a change in the day to be observed is found to be insufficient to warrant a belief in such a change, it follows that the seventh day is still the Sabbath, and to be universally observed.

3. Those who are opposed to the Sabbath gain nothing by contending against the change of the day; for if they neglect the first they are bound to keep the seventh.

4. The Sabbath was instituted on the seventh day after creation began, or on the *first* after the work of creation was finished, and was commemorative of that event.

5. There is a plain distinction between the *institution of the Sabbath* and the particular day on which it is to be celebrated.

This distinction is plainly recognized by the law, the phraseology of which distinguishes between the *Sabbath as an institution and a day of rest*, and the *seventh* day on which it was then celebrated. "*Remember the Sabbath day to keep it holy*." The *Sabbath* then is to be *remembered* as something already existing. The law then proceeds to say, "Six days shalt thou labor," &c., "but the seventh *is* the Sabbath." This phraseology plainly intimates that the spirit and meaning of the law was, that a seventh part of the time should be observed as a Sabbath, and that at that time the seventh was the Sabbath. The phrascology seems to lay no stress on the particular day as indispensable to the institution itself.

7. If the particular portion of the seven days was material to the institution, the law would no doubt have specified at what particular hour it should begin and end, whether at sunset, midnight, or sunrising. The custom of the Jews in this particular could be no law to other nations. Besides, it is naturally impossible that nations inhabiting different latitudes and longitudes should observe the same time as a Sabbath. They may observe the same number of hours but not the same hours. The spirit of the law *must* be, that after six days' labor, at whatever punctum of time the six days may commence in different latitudes, longitudes, climates, and nations, the Sabbath shall be celebrated. The fact that the law does not settle the hour at which the Sabbath is to commence, renders it certain that nothing more was intended than that a seventh part of time, or every seventh day, was to be observed as a Sabbath. If more than this was intended, it cannot be known whether any part of mankind observe, or ever have, observed the identical hours which really constitute the Sabbath.

8. If the seventh day were essential to the *institution*, the law would or should have said, Thou shalt remember the *seventh* day to keep it holy, beginning and ending at a certain hour, and no distinction would have been necessary or proper between the Sabbath and the seventh day.

9. Inasmuch as the necessity for a Sabbath lies in the nature and relations of moral beings as they exist in this world, God cannot *abrogate the Sabbath as an institution* any more than he can set aside the whole moral law.

10. But while he cannot abrogate the *institution as such*, he can and ought to regulate the observance of it as it respects the particular day and other circumstances, so as to retain the essence and spirit of the institution, and to secure to man, so far as may be, the ends of its institution.

11. Christ claimed to be Lord of the Sabbath, and the connection shows that he claimed the right to regulate its observance.

Mark 2: 28. 'Therefore the Son of man is Lord also of the Sabbath.'

12. It was Christ who performed the six days' labor of creation,

and of course it was he who rested on the seventh day, and blessed and sanctified it as a Sabbath.

13. Christ originally instituted the Sabbath, among other reasons, to commemorate his own work of creation.

14. If, when he had toiled, and labored, and bled, and died, and risen, and completed the infinitely greater work of man's redemption, he was disposed so to change the day as to commemorate the latter instead of the former event, as being more worthy of commemoration, he had a right to do so.

15. It was highly proper and important that he should do so.

16. In comparing the work of creation with that of redemption, prophecy points out a time when the former shall, as it were, be forgotten, and be no more remembered in comparison with the latter.

Isa. 65: 17, 18. 'For, behold, I create new heavens, and a new earth: and the former shall not be remembered, nor come into mind. But be ye glad and rejoice forever in that which I create: for, behold, I create Jerusalem a rejoicing, and her people a joy.'

17. If the former work is to be forgotten, and come no more into remembrance, in comparison with the latter, it is highly reasonable to suppose that the latter, and not the former, will be commemorated by a change in the day on which the Sabbath is to be observed.

18. The example of Christ, the Lord of the Sabbath, and of his inspired Apostles, whom he had solemnly promised to guide into all truth, and whom he commissioned to set all things in order, is as good authority for a change of the day as an express command.

19. The Sabbath was originally instituted on the *first* day after his labor of creation was done. So it is natural to look for the change of the day to the first after the greater work of redemption was finished.

20. It is of vastly more importance to mankind to celebrate the first day, as commemorative of the work of redemption, than the seventh, as commemorative of the work of creation.

11. It is also more glorious to God to celebrate the former than the latter.

22. After the resurrection, Christ met repeatedly with his disciples on the first day of the week, but not at all on the seventh.

John 20: 19. 'Then the same day at evening, being the first day of the week, when the doors were shut where the disciples were assembled for fear of the Jews, came Jesus and stood in the midst, and saith unto them, Peace be unto you.'

23. He honored and sanctified the first day of the week by anointing his Apostles for their work, by the Holy Ghost, at Pentecost.

24. The Apostles ever after observed the first day of the week as the Sabbath.

1 Cor. 16: 2. 'Upon the first day of the week let every one

of you lay by him in store, as God hath prospered him, that there be no gatherings when I come.'

25. The first day of the week was called the Lord's day.

Rev. 1: 10. 'I was in the Spirit on the LORD'S DAY, and heard behind me a great voice, as of a trumpet.'

26. There seems to be an intimation of this day in,

Ps. 118: 22—24. 'The stone which the builders refused is become the head stone of the corner. This is the Lord's doing; it is marvellous in our eyes. THIS IS THE DAY which the Lord hath made; we will rejoice and be glad in it.'

This passage is applied to Christ.

Mat. 21: 42. 'Jesus saith unto them, Did ye never read in the scriptures, The stone which the builders rejected, the same is become the head of the corner: this is the Lord's doing, and it is marvellous in our eyes?'

Mark 12: 10. 'And have ye not read this scripture, The stone which the builders rejected is become the head of the corner?'

Luke 20: 17. 'And he beheld them, and said, What is this then that is written, The stone which the builders rejected, the same is become the head of the corner?'

Acts 4: 11. 'This is the stone which was set at nought of you builders, which is become the head of the corner.'

Eph. 2: 20. 'And are built upon the foundation of the Apostles and Prophets, Jesus Christ himself being the chief corner-stone.'

1 Pet. 2: 4, 7. 'To whom coming, as unto a living stone, disallowed indeed of men, but chosen of God, and precious.' 'Unto you therefore which believe he is precious: but unto them which be disobedient, the stone which the builders disallowed, the same is made the head of the corner.'

27. The early Christian fathers bear testimony that the first day was regarded by the Church as the Lord's day, and as the Sabbath.

Ignatius, a cotemporary with the Apostle John, says: "Let every man that loves Christ keep holy the Lord's day; the queen of days; the resurrection day; the highest of all days."

Justin Martyr says: "On the day commonly called Sunday, (by the brethren,) all meet together in the city and country for divine worship."

"No sooner," says Dr. Carr, "was Constantine come over to the Church, but his principal care was about the Lord's day: he commanded it to be solemnly observed, and that by all persons whatsoever: he made it a day of rest, that men might have nothing to do but to worship God and be better instructed in the faith."

Theophilus, Bishop of Antioch: "Both custom and reason challenge from us that we should honor the Lord's day; seeing on that day it was that our Lord Jesus Christ completed his resurrection from the dead."

The Synod of Laodicea adopted this canon: "That Christians should not *Judaize* and rest from all labor on the Sabbath, (i. e., the seventh day,) but follow their ordinary work: and should not entertain such thoughts of it, but that they should prefer the Lord's day, and on that day rest as Christians." (See Humphrey on the Sabbath.)

28. Christ has greatly blessed the Church in the observance of the first instead of the seventh day.

29. This could not have been if they had, without authority, changed the day, and by so doing set aside what was essential to the institution.

30. It is incredible that Christ should have sanctified a day in commemoration of his work of creation, and neither have changed it nor set apart a new day in commemoration of the infinitely more arduous, painful, and important work of redemption.

31. Several of the most important reasons for its original institution demand a change in the day.

(1.) The work of redemption should be celebrated in preference to that of creation.

(2.) The moral influence of observing the first day as commemorative of the work of redemption, is far better and greater than would be the observance of the seventh day, as commemorative of the work of creation.

32. There can be no good reason for again observing the seventh instead of the first day of the week.

33. The Apostle cautions the Colossians against observing the Jewish Sabbath.

Col. 2: 16: 'Let no man therefore judge you in meat, or in drink, or in respect of a holyday, or of the new-moon, or of the Sabbath-days.'

34. The example of Christ after his resurrection; his promise to lead his disciples into all truth; their anointing to their work on the first day of the week; their actual inspiration; the fact that they observed the first day of the week as the Sabbath; that this custom was universal with the Churches planted by them; and that God has always owned and blessed the keeping of the first day of the week as his Sabbath; these facts, together with the facts and arguments above mentioned, and the Bible upon the subject, both the Old and New Testaments, make out as clear a case, and are as substantial proof that the change is in accordance with the mind and will of God, as can be reasonably expected or desired.

Obj. I. There is no express command requiring the change.

Ans. 1. No such command was needed, as in other ways God sufficiently indicated his will.

2. No such express command was to be expected.

(1.) Because the Gentile Christians would naturally regard the first, and not the seventh day, as the Sabbath.

(2.) Because the Jewish state and polity were soon to come to an end, and their prejudices were so inveterate as to render it inexpedient to introduce this change among them by authority, considering the short period which the Apostles had to labor for their conversion before their dispersion.

(3.) God had compassion on them, and as the particular day was not essential to the institution, he did not shock their prejudices any further than was necessary, but tried to save as many of them as he could, by suffering them to observe their Sabbath for the time being, while Christians observed the first day of the week.

(4.) In thus leaving this question out of dispute, he no doubt saved many that could not else have been saved.

(5.) He also had compassion on his Apostles, and did not insist upon their immediately and authoritatively abrogating the Jewish Sabbath, as this would have but increased the persecution that raged against them.

(6.) The Apostles could meet with and instruct the Jews on the seventh day, and meet with and instruct the Christians on the first day of the week. Thus having, for the time being, and at this critical and important period, the advantage, as it were, of two Sabbaths in a week for the preaching of the infant kingdom of Christ.

(7.) As God foresaw the immediate destruction of the Jewish Church and polity, he saw that the first day of the week would of course be soon universally observed by his Church without an express command; and as so much present evil might and would result from interposing express authority on the subject at this time, it was like God, and what might have been expected of him, to bring about the change as he did.

(8.) He took the same course, and for the same reasons, in respect to Baptism and Circumcision. The institution of the Sabbath remains in all its force, and is universally and perpetually obligatory; but the first day of the week is now the day on which it is to be celebrated.

Obj. II. The Sabbath was a type of the rest of faith, and not needed by, nor binding upon those who have entered into the rest of faith. Having received the anti-type, they no longer need the type.

Ans. 1. The Sabbath was typical of both gospel rest and heavenly rest; they who have entered into the former need it as a type of the latter.

2. There were other and important reasons for the Sabbath, all of which render it still obligatory on all men.

3. They who make this objection overlook every reason and design of the Sabbath but one, while the reasons are many.

4. Those who have entered into the rest of faith need the Sabbath as a means of preserving them in this rest. This they will surely learn sooner or later.

5. They who have entered the rest of faith are bound to preserve its blessings to those who have not, and for this reason, if there were no other, they ought to, and must observe it.

Obj. III. The observance of the Sabbath leads to formality and self-righteousness, and therefore had better be laid aside.

Ans. This is an abuse of a good thing, and not a necessary result. This same objection is urged against the ordinances, prayer, public and social worship, &c. I might as reasonably reject my daily food on account of the dietetic abuses of mankind, as to reject the Sabbath, or any of the means of communion with God because they are perverted by so many.

LECTURE XXIX.

MORAL GOVERNMENT.—No. 8.

FIFTH COMMANDMENT.

Ex. 20 : 12. 'Honor thy father and thy mother: that thy days may be long upon the land which the Lord thy God giveth thee.'

I. Reasons for this commandment.

1. The parents have been instrumental in giving their children existence.

2. Children are naturally dependent upon their parents.

3. Their parents love and protect them, and provide for them.

4. Their parents are their natural instructors and guides.

5. Their own well-being demands that they should honor their parents, because it is in accordance with the laws of their being, and with the great law of gratitude.

6. The virtue, and of course the happiness of society, requires that children honor their parents.

7. The good of the world demands that children honor their parents.

8. The parent is the natural protector, and of course governor of his children while in a state of dependence.

9. The parents cannot protect and govern their children, unless they are respected and honored by them.

II. What is implied in this requirement.

1. This requirement implies that the parent practically recognize his relations to the child; for if he cast the child out helpless in the street, and refuse or neglect to recognize his relation, the true spirit of this command cannot require the child to honor him as a parent, but simply to regard him as a fellow-being, and to treat him according to the universal law of benevolence.

2. It implies, then, that the parent be at least decent in a moral point of view.

3. That he require of the child that only which is consistent with the universal law of benevolence and right, that he do not deny the child liberty of conscience, that he do not attempt to prevent his doing his whole duty to God, himself, and his neighbor.

4. It implies that the parent protect, provide for, and govern the child, upon the principles of right reason, so far as his circumstances and ability will allow. These things being implied and taken for granted, it follows—

III. That the true spirit and meaning of this requirement—

1. Prohibits the least feeling of disrespect.

2. Every kind and degree of ill-manners.

3. All trifling with the feelings of parents.

4. Every species of murmuring, self-will, and disobedience.

5. All inattention to their wants and necessities, when they are old or infirm.

6. It requires the most perfect benevolence towards them.

7. Complacency, so far as their characters are right.

8. The love of gratitude, so far as they have been obliged and benefitted by their parents.

9. All that obedience of heart and life which is consistent with the highest perfection of family order, love, and happiness.

10. A cheerful and prompt obedience in all things not inconsistent with the will of God.

11. It requires all reasonable efforts to promote the highest temporal and spiritual interests of their parents.

12. It requires reverence and respect for parents.

13. It requires that both parents and children should fulfill to each other all those duties that will, in the highest degree, promote their individual and domestic happiness, holiness, and peace.

14. It requires both parents and children to conduct towards each other in all things, in such a way as to promote the highest well-being of the universe, and the glory of God.

SIXTH COMMANDMENT.

Ex. 20: 13. 'Thou shalt not kill.'

I. What is prohibited by the letter of this precept.

The *letter* of this precept prohibits the unnecessary destruction of life, whether of men or animals.

II. What is the true spirit of this requirement.

1. This must be inferred from the express or implied exceptions to the letter. There can be no exceptions to the spirit of a commandment, but to the letter there may be many.

2. Exceptions with respect to taking the life of animals:

Gen. 9: 3. 'Every moving thing that liveth shall be meat for you; even as the green herb have I given you all things.'

Here is a general permission to kill animals for the food of man. Afterward exceptions are made, in regard to the use of certain animals as food.

Gen. 9: 5. 'And surely your blood of your lives will I require; at the hand of every beast will I require it, and at the hand of man; at the hand of every man's brother will I require the life of man.'

Here general authority is given for the destruction of those beasts that are injurious to men. This must be the spirit of this exception, for if a beast may be slain who has killed a man, certainly it must be lawful to anticipate the ravages of those animals who are known to be destructive to human life, and to slay them before they have committed their depredations. These are the only two exceptions in respect to taking the lives of animals. The true spirit of these exceptions is in precise accordance with the declaration of God to Adam:

Gen. 1: 28. 'God blessed them, and God said unto them, Be fruitful, and multiply, and replenish the earth, and subdue it: and have dominion over the fish of the sea, and over the fowl of the air, and over every living thing that moveth upon the earth.'

Here upon the first creation of the world, God gave mankind dominion over all animals. This law prohibits taking their lives, except for food, and in cases where they are injurious, and their death is demanded by the interests of human beings. In all other cases, to take the lives of animals is a violation of this commandment.

3. Exceptions in respect to the life of man:

(1.) Ex. 22: 2. 'If a thief be found breaking up, and be smitten that he die, there shall no blood be shed for him.'

The spirit of this exception plainly justifies taking life, strictly in self-defence. It also plainly justifies strictly defensive war. If a thief might be killed for breaking into our houses at night, or in attempting to rob, or murder, certainly the spirit of this exception justifies the repelling of foreign invasions, and the defence of our families, certainly against the ravages of thieves, pirates, marauders, banditti, and mobs.

(2.) Gen. 9: 6. 'Whoso sheddeth man's blood, by man shall his blood be shed.'

This allows and demands taking the life of man, for the crime of murder.

(3.) Ex. 21 : 12, 14. 'He that smiteth a man so that he die, shall be surely put to death.' 'But if a man come presumptuously upon his neighbor, to slay him with guile; thou shalt take him from mine altar, that he may die.' And—

Lev. 24: 17. 'He that killeth any man shall surely be put to death.'

(4.) There are several species of crime, for which the Law of God not only allows the punishment of death, but absolutely makes or did make such punishment obligatory.

(5.) Human life may be taken in offensive wars, when such wars are required by God. Taking human life cannot be wrong in itself, under all circumstances; for if it were, God could not authorize it. But he does authorize and command it. Cases in which it may be taken, are expressly or impliedly specified in various parts of the Bible. With these exceptions, and only with these, human life can in no instance be lawfully destroyed.

II. What is and what is not prohibited by the spirit of this requirement.

1. It does not prohibit the sacrifice of our own health and life, for the promotion of a greater good. If it did, Christ had no right to sacrifice his life for the salvation of men.

2. Nor is the spirit of this law different under the gospel, from what it was at first.

3. Nor can any command of the New Testament be at all inconsistent with the spirit of this law. The real spirit and meaning of law, is dependent on the will of no being. It has its foundation in the nature and relations of moral beings.

4. Hence God can never give two commandments, which shall be inconsistent with each other in spirit.

5. It prohibits all unnecessary taking the life of any thing that has life.

6. Especially, it prohibits taking human life, without the express or implied authority of God.

7. It prohibits taking human life, for any selfish reason whatever.

8. It prohibits taking human life, without a strict conformity to the spirit of a just and righteous government.

9. It prohibits all taking the life of any thing that has life, but for benevolent ends.

10. It prohibits all unnecessary violations of the laws of life and health.

11. It prohibits all unnecessary exposure of life and health in any way.

12. It prohibits every kind and degree of intemperance, and all unnecessary expenditure of health and life.

13. It prohibits the use of means to destroy the existence of human beings in embryo.

14. It prohibits all ill-will, and all selfish anger.

15. It prohibits every kind and degree of injurious treatment, that might effect the health and life.

III. What the true spirit and meaning of this command requires.

1. It requires human beings, under suitable circumstances, and at suitable age, to marry.

2. It requires them, within the bonds of lawful marriage, to propagate their species.

3. To encourage and promote the existence and life of sentient beings, so far as is good for the universe.

4. It enjoins entire benevolence to all beings that have life.

5. It enjoins obedience to all the laws of life and health, so far as consists with the general good.

6. It requires us to do what we can, to promote the life, and health, and well-being of others.

7. It requires us to treat our own health and life, and the health and life of all men and animals, according to their relative value in the scale of being.

IV. Reasons on which this command is founded.

1. Happiness is a good in itself.

2. Life is an indispensable condition of happiness.

3. The destruction and waste of life is a destruction and waste of the means of happiness.

4. The greater the amount of life, the greater the means of happiness.

5. The good of the universe demands, that life should be considered and treated as of great value.

6. As perfect and universal benevolence or good-willing, is the duty of all moral beings, so it is their duty to regard and treat life, as an indispensable means of promoting individual and universal happiness.

7. This precept is plainly only· declaratory of the one great universal law of love.

V. Some cases to be regarded as violations of this command.

1. All abuse, neglect, or treatment of animals, whereby their life is shortened.

2. All sporting with the life of animals.

3. All such treatment of human beings, as tends to injure their health and destroy their lives.

4. All duelling.

5. Every unnecessary violation of the laws of life and health, either in men or animals.

6. Every unnecessary disregard of the command to multiply the number of human beings.

7. Every selfish disposition to lessen the amount of animal life.

8. Every degree of ill-will or malevolent feeling toward any being.

9. All selfish anger. 'He that hateth his brother is a murderer.'

LECTURE XXX.

MORAL GOVERNMENT.—No. 9.

SEVENTH COMMANDMENT.

Ex. 20: 14. "Thou shalt not commit adultery.

I. Show what is implied in this command.

1. It implies the pre-existence of the institution of marriage.

2. It implies that marriage is recognized as not only already existing but as a divine institution.

II. Show what its true spirit prohibits.

1. All carnal commerce of married persons, with others than their lawful husband or wife.

2. All carnal commerce between unmarried persons.

3. All lewd and unchaste desires, thoughts, and affections:

Mat. 5: 28. 'I say unto you, That whosoever looketh on a woman to lust after her hath committed adultery with her already in his heart.'

4. All marriages and consequent carnal commerce between persons within those degrees of consanguinity, whose marriage is prohibited by the law of God. This is not only adultery but incest.

5. All marriages, and consequent carnal commerce, between unmarriageable persons, such as persons already having a husband or wife living, from whom they have not been properly divorced. Such as have been put away, or divorced, are considered by the law of God as unmarriageable persons:

Mat. 5: 32. 'Whosoever shall marry her that is divorced committeth adultery.'

6. It prohibits sodomy, or the crime against nature:

Lev. 20: 13. 'If a man lie with mankind, as he lieth with a woman, both of them have committed an abomination: they shall surely be put to death; their blood shall be upon them.'

7. It prohibits buggery, or carnal commerce between men and beasts:

Lev. 18 : 23. 'Neither shalt thou lie with any beast to defile thyself therewith : neither shall any woman stand before a beast to lie down thereto : it is confusion.' And—

Lev. 20 : 15. 'If a man lie with a beast he shall surely be put to death ; and ye shall slay the beast.' And—

Deut. 27 : 21. 'Cursed be he that lieth with any manner of beast.'

8. It prohibits Onanism, or self-pollution.

9. It prohibits every kind and degree of licentiousness, in word, thought, desire, and action.

10. It prohibits all writing, conversation, pictures, modes of dress, and whatever has a natural tendency to beget in any degree a licentious state of mind ; for he who provokes to lust is guilty of the crime of which he is the guilty cause.

III. Reasons of this command.

1. Marriage is a necessity of our nature, both moral and physical.

2. The species must be propagated.

3. So propagated as to secure the highest physical and moral perfection of the race.

4. Children must be born within the lawful bonds of marriage, to secure to them parental affection, with that nurture, training, and maintenance that is essential to their highest well-being.

5. Marriage is, therefore, wholly indispensable to the highest well-being of the race.

6. But the benefits of marriage will be entirely excluded, unless licentiousness be prevented. Every kind and degree of licentiousness is inconsistent with the highest well-being of man.

7. This command, therefore, is only declaratory, and an application of the principle of benevolence, to this particular relation.

8. It is therefore universally binding upon all men in all nations and ages.

9. While human beings exist in this world, the law of marriage cannot possibly be abrogated or altered in its spirit by the will of any being.

EIGHTH COMMANDMENT.

Ex. 20 : 15. 'Thou shalt not steal.'

I. What is implied in this command.

1. That the persons of human beings are their own, or that every human being has a property in himself, and that he is, so far as his fellow-men are concerned, his own proprietor. This law plainly implies this ; for if men do not own themselves, they certainly own nothing else, and of course nothing could be stolen from them.

2. It implies the right of property—that human beings can, with respect to their fellow-men, have a lawful right to their possessions.

3. It implies that self-ownership, and the right of property, are agreeable to the law of nature and of God.

4. It implies that these rights are based in the very nature and relations of human beings, and that while this nature and these relations exist, these rights can never be cancelled, or set aside, except by such infamous crimes as forfeit life and liberty.

II. What the true spirit of this command prohibits.

1. All appropriations of the property of another to ourselves, without his knowledge and consent.

2. It prohibits every kind and degree of fraud.

3. It prohibits taking any advantage in business, that is inconsistent with the rule, 'Thou shalt love thy neighbor as thyself.'

4. It prohibits the infliction of any injury upon the person, morals, education, reputation, family, or property of a human being, whereby he has less of good than he would have possessed but for your interference.

5. It prohibits every sinful omission, that naturally tends to the same result.

6. It prohibits every disposition to defraud, overreach, circumvent, or in any way inflict an injury on a human being.

III. Reasons for this commandment.

1. Self-ownership is implied in moral agency.

2. It is indispensable to accountability.

3. Hence self-ownership is indispensable to virtue.

4. It is also indispensable to that happiness which is the result of virtue.

5. The right of property is founded upon, and is necessarily connected with self-ownership.

6. Both these are indispensable to the highest well-being of individuals, and of the race.

7. Hence, the command 'Thou shalt not steal,' is only declaratory of the one great, universal law of benevolence.

IV. When the spirit of this law is violated.

1. Slavery is a flagrant and infamous violation of it.

2. Taking whatever belongs to another, for temporary use only, but without leave. Many think that nothing is stealing but the taking of property without leave, without any design of returning it; but taking the temporary use of a thing, without leave, is as absolute stealing, as to take the thing without the design of returning it. In the one case the thing itself is stolen, and in the other the use of it is stolen.

3. Every selfish use of your neighbor's property, although with his permission, such as living by borrowing and using your neighbor's things, when you are as able to provide them for yourself as he is to provide them for himself and for you too.

4. Using a borrowed article for a different purpose than that for which the consent was given.

5. Lending that which is not your own, and which you have no right to lend, is also a violation of the spirit of this commandment.

6. All careless, injurious, or improper use of a borrowed article.

7. All neglect to return a borrowed article in due time, whereby the owner's interest is made to suffer.

8. All keeping back the wages due to laborers.

9. All refusal or neglect to pay honest debts.

10. All refusal to bear your full proportion in building churches, supporting ministers, and sustaining all the institutions of religion. To receive these things gratuitously, is to make slaves of your neighbors, to receive their services for nought, and involves the very principle of theft.

11. Every wrong done or intended to a neighbor, is a violation of his rights, and a violation of the spirit of this commandment.

12. Every thing that is properly a speculation in business transactions; that is—where full equivalents are not given and received.

LECTURE. XXXI.

MORAL GOVERNMENT.—No. 10.

NINTH COMMANDMENT.

Ex. 20: 16. 'Thou shalt not bear false witness against thy neighbor.'

I. What this commandment implies.

1. It implies the duty, under certain circumstances, of being true witnesses for or against our neighbor.

2. It implies that all men are to be regarded as our neighbors.

II. What is not properly a violation of this commandment.

1. Testifying to the truth with benevolent intentions, in a court of justice, whether for or against a neighbor, is not a violation of this commandment.

2. Telling the truth under any circumstances, when the great law of benevolence requires it, does not violate it, whatever the bearing may be upon any particular individual.

3. Stating a falsehood through unavoidable mistake, or misunderstanding, or through failure of memory, is not a violation of this commandment.

4. Withholding truth upon any subject, from one who has no right to know it, is not a violation of this commandment.

III. What its true spirit prohibits.

1. It prohibits all designed, or careless, or malicious misrepresentation of the character, conduct, or views of another, in any way whatever.

2. It prohibits every disposition that naturally tends to slander and misrepresentation.

3. It prohibits taking up, or in any way giving the least countenance to an ill or slanderous report of our neighbor.

4. It prohibits all bearing testimony to the truth of such report, from motives of ill-will.

5. Or, giving unnecessary publicity to the faults of any one.

6. It prohibits every kind and degree of false coloring, in our representations of the character, motives, or conduct of our neighbor, or of whatever concerns him.

7. It prohibits every kind or degree of concealment that tends to the injury of any one.

8. It prohibits all withholding the truth upon any subject, from him who has a right to know it.

9. It prohibits every species of artifice, or designed deception, intended to make any impression contrary to truth, on any subject, upon one who has a right to know the truth upon that subject.

IV. Reasons for this commandment.

1. Individual and universal good.

2. This commandment is plainly declaratory of the law of universal benevolence.

TENTH COMMANDMENT.

Ex. 20: 17. 'Thou shalt not covet thy neighbor's house, thou shalt not covet thy neighbor's wife, nor his man-servant, nor his maid-servant, nor his ox, nor his ass, nor any thing that is thy neighbor's.'

I. What this commandment implies.

1. The right of property—that a thing may lawfully belong to a neighbor.

2. It implies a right to the exclusive possession and enjoyment of our wives and husbands as such.

3. It implies that the exclusive enjoyment and possession of our wives and husbands as such is not selfishness.

4. It implies that every desire to interfere with the exclusive enjoyment of wives by their husbands, or husbands by their wives, as such, is selfishness.

5. It implies that we have a lawful interest in, and a right to the enjoyment of our friends.

II. What is not a breach of this commandment.

1. The desire to possess what belongs to another, by rendering the possessor a full equivalent, is not a breach of this commandment.

2. Neither is it a breach of this commandment to purchase, with a full equivalent, and take possession in a lawful way, of that which did belong to a neighbor.

3. The desire to possess whatever in our just estimation would contribute to our highest well-being, is not a violation of the spirit of this commandment.

III. What the true spirit of this commandment prohibits and enjoins.

1. It prohibits every selfish disposition to possess what is our neighbor's.

2. It prohibits every selfish disposition to possess any thing which belongs to God.

3. It prohibits every selfish disposition to possess what is our neighbor's, without a disposition on our part to render a full equivalent.

4. It prohibits any disposition to possess whatever of our neighbor's we may not lawfully possess; for example, his wife.

5. It prohibits any disposition to possess that which our neighbor has, and needs as truly and as much as ourselves.

6. It prohibits every degree of selfishness.

7. It prohibits a disposition to possess any thing that is inconsistent with the will of God, and the highest good of the universe.

8. The spirit of this commandment enjoins perfect and universal benevolence.

9. It is plainly a declaratory summing up of the spirit of the law of universal benevolence.

IV. Reasons for this commandment.

1. This commandment is designed to regulate all the moral affections and emotions of the soul.

2. It is designed to show the spirituality of all the other commandments, and that they relate purely to the state of the mind.

3. It is designed to enjoin perfect and universal holiness of heart.

REMARKS.

1. The above commandments are to be regarded only as specimens of the manner of declaring and applying by express statute, the common law of the universe, or the one great, universal and only law of love.

2. Every precept of the Bible is a moral precept, and the usual division of the precepts of the Bible into moral, civil, ceremonial, and positive, is arbitrary, and in many respects incorrect.

3. Neither God nor any being can make that obligatory as law, which enjoins the observance of that which is indifferent in its own nature, and obligatory for no other reason, than that such is the will of the law-giver.

4. Neither God nor any other being has a right to require any course of conduct, without some good reason; and therefore, that can never be law, which is wholly indifferent in itself, and for the requiring of which the law-giver has no good reason.

5. That may be law, the reasons of which we are unacquainted with; but it is law only because there are good reasons, either known or unknown to us, for the requirement.

6. The common definition of moral law has been defective. It has been defined to be that which is universally binding on all moral agents, in all circumstances, and in all worlds. Hence what is called the civil, positive, and commercial institutions or laws of the Jews, have been distinguished from moral laws.

7. This distinction is not only inconvenient, but creates a false impression. If these laws were not moral, the violation of them would have no moral character; that is—it would not be the violation of moral principle.

8. The true definition of moral law, and that which I have given elsewhere, is, a rule of action, that is and would be universally binding upon all moral agents in similar circumstances. Hence—

9. The ceremonial code of the Jews were moral laws, in the sense, that under the circumstances, and for the same reasons, they would be, or would have been universally binding on all moral agents.

10. Any precept of the Bible, or any precept whatever, that is not founded in moral principle, or required by the circumstances of moral beings, is utterly null and void, and can never in any case be law.

11. All the prohibitions in regard to agriculture, and diet, and every other regulation and precept under the Old Testament dispensation is binding on all mankind, just as far as their circumstances are similar.

12. The idea, that the positive, civil, and ceremonial laws of the Jews were not moral laws, has done and is doing much to undermine the morality of the Church and the world.

13, All the commandments of God were properly summed up by our Savior, and condensed into the two great precepts, "Thou shalt love the Lord thy God with all thy heart, and soul, and mind, and strength; and thy neighbor as thyself." These two precepts are at once a condensation and a declaration of the whole duty of man to God and to his neighbor.

14. The spirit of moral law is one, and unalterable; dependent on the will of no being. And the duty of God is to declare and enforce it, with such sanctions as the importance of the law demands; but it can never be altered or repealed.

15. Antinomianism, under any form, is an utter abomination, both unreasonable, and impossible for God to sanction.

LECTURE XXXII.

MORAL GOVERNMENT.—No. 11.

SANCTIONS OF LAW.

FIRST. What constitutes the Sanctions of Law.
SECOND. There can be no law without Sanctions.
THIRD. In what light the Sanctions of Law are to be regarded.
FOURTH. The end to be secured by law and the execution of *penal* Sanctions.
FIFTH. The rule for graduating the Sanctions of Law.

FIRST. *What constitutes the Sanctions of Law.*

1. The Sanctions of Law are the motives to obedience, that which is to be the natural and the governmental consequence, or result of obedience.

2. They are *remuneratory*, i. e. they reward obedience.

3. They are *vindicatory*, i. e. they inflict punishment upon the disobedient.

4. They are natural, i. e.

(1.) All moral law is that rule of action which is in exact accordance with the nature and relations of moral beings.

(2.) Happiness is naturally connected with, and the necessary consequence of obedience to moral law.

(3.) Misery is naturally and necessarily connected with and results from disobedience to moral law, or from acting contrary to the nature and relations of moral beings.

5. Sanctions are governmental. By governmental sanctions are intended,

(1.) The favor of the government as due to obedience.

(2.) A positive reward bestowed upon the obedient by government.

(3.) The displeasure of government towards the disobedient.

(4.) Direct punishment inflicted by the government as due to disobedience.

6. All the happiness and misery resulting from obedience or disobedience, either natural or from the favor or frown of government, are to be regarded as constituting the sanctions of law.

SECOND. *There can be no Law without Sanctions.*

1. It has been said in a former lecture that precept without Sanction is only counsel or advice, and no law.

2. Nothing is law, but that rule of action which is founded in the nature and relations of moral beings. It is therefore absurd to say, that there should be no natural sanctions to this rule of action. It is the same absurdity as to say, that conformity with the laws of our being would not produce happiness, and that non-conformity to the laws of our being would not produce misery which is a contradiction, for what do we mean by acting in conformity to the laws of our being, but that course of conduct in which all the powers of our being will sweetly harmonize, and produce happiness. And what do we mean by non-conformity to the laws of our being, but that course of action that creates mutiny among our powers themselves, that produces discord instead of harmony, misery instead of happiness.

3. A precept, to have the nature and the force of law, must be founded in reason, i. e., it must have some reason for its existence. And it were unjust to hold out no motives to obedience where a law is founded in a necessity of our nature.

4. But whatever is unjust is no law. Therefore a precept without a sanction is not law.

5. Necessity is the foundation of all government. There would be and could be no just government, but for the necessities of the universe. But these necessities cannot be met, the great end of government cannot be secured without motives or sanctions. Therefore that is no government, no law, that has no sanctions.

THIRD. *In what light Sanctions are to be regarded.*

1. Sanctions are to be regarded as an expression of the benevolent regard of the law-giver to his subjects: the motives which he exhibits to induce in the subjects the course of conduct that will secure their highest well-being.

2. They are to be regarded as an expression of his estimation of the justice, necessity, and value of the precept.

3. They are to be regarded as an expression of the amount or strength of his desire to secure the happiness of his subjects.

4. They are to be regarded as an expression of his opinion in respect to the desert of disobedience.

5. The natural sanctions are to be regarded as a demonstration of the justice, necessity, and perfection of the precept.

FOURTH. *The end to be secured by Law, and the execution of penal Sanctions.*

1. The ultimate end of all government is happiness.

2. This is the ultimate end of the precept and Sanction of Law.

3. Happiness can be secured only by the prevention of sin and the promotion of holiness.

4. Confidence in the government is the *sine qua non* of all virtue.

5. Confidence results from a revelation of the lawgiver to his

subjects. Confidence in God results from a revelation of himself to his creatures.

6. The moral law, in its precepts and sanctions, is a revelation of God.

7. The execution of penal sanctions, is also a revelation of the mind, will, and character of the lawgiver.

8. The highest and most influential sanctions of government are those measures that most fully reveal the true character of God.

FIFTH. *The rule for graduating the Sanctions of Law.*

1. God has laid the foundations of the natural sanctions of Law, deep in the constitution of moral beings.

2. Therefore the natural Sanctions of law will always and necessarily be proportioned to the perfection of obedience and disobedience.

3. *Governmental* sanctions should always be graduated by the importance of the precept.

4. Moral law is a unit. Every sin is a violation of the eternal law of love, and its reward should be equal to the value of the precept.

5. Under moral government there can be no small sin, as evey sin is a breach of the whole and only law of benevolence, i. e. it is a violation of the principle which constitutes the law of God.

6. The Sanction of moral law should therefore in every case, be equal to the value of the eternal and unalterable law of benevolence, or as near its value as the nature of the case will admit.

LECTURE XXXIII.

MORAL GOVERNMENT.—No. 12.

SANCTIONS OF GOD'S LAW.

FIRST. God's law has Sanctions.

SECOND. What constitutes the remuneratory Sanctions of the law of God.

THIRD. The perfection and duration of the remuneratory Sanctions of the law of God.

FOURTH. What constitutes the vindicatory Sanctions of the law of God.

FIFTH. Their duration.

FIRST. *God's law has Sanctions.*

1. That sin or disobedience to the moral law, is attended with and results in misery, is a matter of consciousness.

2. That virtue or holiness is attended with and results in happiness, is also attested by consciousness.

3. Therefore that God's law has natural sanctions, both remuneratory and vindicatory, is a matter of fact.

4. That there are governmental sanctions added to the natural, must be true, or God in fact has no Government.

5. The Bible expressly and in every variety of form teaches that God will reward the righteous and punish the wicked.

SECOND. *The remuneratory sanctions of the law of God.*

1. The happiness that is naturally and necessarily connected with and results from holiness or obedience.

2. The merited favor, protection, and blessing of God.

3. All the natural and governmental rewards of virtue.

THIRD. *The perfection and duration of the remuneratory Sanctions of the Law of God.*

1. The perfection of the natural reward is and must be proportioned to the perfection of virtue.

2. The duration of the remuneratory sanction must be equal to the duration of obedience. This cannot possibly be otherwise.

3. If the existence and virtue of man are immortal his happiness must be endless.

4. The Bible most unequivocally asserts the immortality both of the existence and virtue of the righteous, and also that their happiness shall be endless.

5. The very design and end of government make it necessary that governmental rewards should be as perfect and unending as virtue.

FOURTH. *The vindicatory sanctions of the law of God.*

1. The misery naturally and necessarily connected with, and the result of disobedience to moral law. Here again let it be understood that moral law is nothing else than that rule of action which accords with the nature and relations of moral beings. Therefore the natural vindicatory sanction of the law of God is misery resulting from the violation of man's own moral nature.

2. The displeasure of God, the loss of his protection and governmental favor, together with that punishment which it is his duty to inflict upon the disobedient.

3. The rewards of holiness and the punishment of sin, are described in the Bible in figurative language. The rewards of virtue are called eternal life. The punishment of vice is called death. By life is intended, not only existence, but that happiness which makes life desirable. By death is intended, not annihilation, but that misery which renders existence an evil.

FIFTH. *The duration of the penal Sanctions of the Law of God.*

Here the inquiry is, what kind of death is intended where death is denounced against the transgressor as the penalty of the law of God?

I. It is not merely natural death, for

1. This would in reality be no penalty at all. But it would be offering a reward to sin. If natural death is all that is intended, and if persons, as soon as they are naturally dead have suffered the penalty of the law, and their souls go immediately to heaven, the case stands thus: If your obedience is perfect and perpetual, you shall live in this world forever: but if you sin you shall die and go right to heaven. This would be hire, and salary, and not punishment.

2. If natural death be the penalty of God's law, the righteous who are forgiven, should not die a natural death.

3. If natural death be the penalty of God's law there is no such thing as forgiveness, but all must actually endure the penalty.

4. If natural death be the penalty, then infants and animals suffer this penalty as well as the most abandoned transgressors.

5. If natural death be the penalty it sustains no proportion whatever to the guilt of sin.

6. Natural death would be no adequate expression of the importance of the precept.

II. The penalty of God's law is not spiritual death.

1. Because spiritual death is a state of entire sinfulness.

2. To make a state of entire sinfulness the penalty of the law of God, would be to make the penalty and the breach of the precept identical.

3. It would be making God the author of sin, and would represent him as compelling the sinner to commit one sin as the punishment for another, as forcing him into a state of total depravity as the reward of his first transgression.

III. But the penal sanction of the law of God is *eternal death* or that state of suffering which is the natural and governmental result of sin or spiritual death.

Before I proceed to the proof of this, I will notice an objection which is often urged against the doctrine of eternal punishments. The objection is *one*, but it is stated in three different forms. This, and every other objection to the doctrine of endless punishment, with which I am acquainted, is leveled against the justice of such a governmental infliction.

1. It is said that endless punishment is unjust because life is so short that men do not live long enough in this world to commit so great a number of sins as to deserve endless punishment. To this I answer,

(1.) That it is founded in a ridiculous ignorance or disregard of a universal principle of government, viz: that one breach of the precept always incurs the penalty of the law, whatever that penalty is.

(2.) The length of time employed in committing a sin, has nothing to do with its blameworthiness or guilt. It is the *design* which constitutes the moral character of the action, and not the length of time required for its accomplishment.

(3.) This objection takes for granted that it is the number of sins and not the intrinsic guilt of sin that constitutes its blameworthiness, whereas it is the intrinsic desert or guilt of sin, as we shall soon see, that renders it deserving of endless punishment.

2. Another form of the objection is, that a finite creature cannot commit an infinite sin. But none but an infinite sin can deserve endless punishment: therefore endless punishments are unjust.

(1.) This objection takes for granted that man is so diminutive a creature, so much less than the Creator, that he cannot deserve his endless frown.

(2.) The fact is, the greater the distance between the creature and the creator, the more aggravated is the guilt of insult or rebellion in the creature. Which is the greatest crime, for a child to insult his playfellow or his parent? Which would involve the most guilt, for a man to smite his neighbor and his equal, or his lawful sovereign?

(3.) The higher the ruler is exalted above the subject in his nature, character, and rightful authority, the greater is the guilt of transgression in the subject. Therefore the fact that man is so infinitely below his maker but enhances the guilt of his rebellion and renders him worthy of his endless frown.

3. A third form of the objection is, that sin is not an infinite evil, and therefore does not deserve endless punishment.

(1.) This objection may mean either that sin would not produce infinite mischief if unrestrained, or that it does not involve infinite guilt. It cannot mean the first, for it is agreed on all hands that misery must continue as long as sin does, and therefore that sin unrestrained would produce endless evil. The objection therefore must mean that sin does not involve infinite guilt. Observe then, the point at issue is, what is the intrinsic demerit or guilt of sin? What does all sin in its own nature deserve? They who deny the justice of endless punishment, manifestly consider the guilt of sin as a mere trifle. They who maintain the justice of endless punishment, consider sin as an evil of immeasurable magnitude, and as in its own nature deserving of endless punishment. Proof.

(1.) The guilt or blameworthiness of an action consists in its being the violation of an obligation. E. g.: Should a child refuse obedience to his father who has no natural or acquired claims upon his obedience, he would not be blameworthy. But should he refuse obedience to his parent who has both a natural and acquired claim to his obedience, this conduct would be blameworthy. This shows in what blameworthiness consists.

2. The guilt or blameworthiness of an action is equal to the amount of obligation, to do or omit that thing. We have just seen that the blameworthiness lies in its being the violation of an obligation. Hence the amount of blameworthiness must be equal

to the amount of obligation. If a child refuse to obey his fellow, he contracts no guilt. If he refuse to obey his parent, he contracts a degree of guilt equal to the amount of his obligation to obey. Suppose that some one upon whom he is a thousand times as dependent as upon his parent, and who therefore has a thousand times higher claim upon his obedience than his parent has, should command him to do or omit a certain thing. Should he in this case disobey, his guilt would be a thousand times as great as when he disobeyed his parents. Now suppose that God, upon whom every moral being is not only perfectly but endlessly dependent, requires the creature to love him with all his heart; who does not see that his guilt in refusing obedience must be as great as his obligation to obey.

3. The amount of obligation may be estimated in three ways.

(1.) By the claims of the law-giver. God's claims upon the obedience of man are equal.

a. To their dependence upon him.

b. Their obligation to exercise benevolence towards him, is equal to the value of his happiness, which is infinite.

c. Their obligation to exercise complacency in him, is equal to the amount of his virtue. When we say that God is lovely, we mean that he deserves to be loved. When we say that he deserves to be loved, we mean that moral beings are under an obligation to love him. If they are under an obligation to love him for his loveliness, their obligation to love him is equal to his loveliness. By this it is not intended that they are under an obligation to love him with affections infinitely strong; but they are under infinite obligation to love him with all their powers, whatever they are. When the amount, then, of an obligation to love God is thus estimated, it is seen to be infinite. The guilt of disobedience must therefore be infinite, and punishment, to be equal to our demerit, or as nearly so as the nature of the case admits, must be endless.

(2.) A second method of estimating the amount of obligation to obey a law, is by ascertaining the value of the law, or the amount of interest secured by it. It has been more than once said, that happiness certainly and necessarily results from obedience to moral law. It should here be said that the happiness of God and of all moral beings results from, and is dependent upon their obedience to moral law. Moral law, then, is as valuable as the infinite and eternal happiness of God, and the endless welfare of all moral beings. Who will deny, then, that the importance of the law is infinite? But the amount of guilt involved in a breach of the precept is as great as the value of the precept. Therefore viewed in this light, the guilt of sin is infinite.

(3.) A third method of ascertaining the amount of obligation to obey a law is by ascertaining the natural tendency of disobedience to defeat those interests which the law is intended to protect and secure. Among the tendencies of sin, the following are most manifest:

a. To destroy the present happiness of the sinner.

b. To make him perpetually miserable.

c. Another tendency of sin is to perpetuate and aggravate itself

d. Sin is contagious. Example is the highest moral influence that can be exerted. Consequently the disobedience of one tends to beget disobedience in others. And sin, if not counteracted, tends as naturally to spread and become universal, as a contagious disease does.

(*e.*) Sin tends to total and universal selfishness.

(*f.*) It tends to universal damnation.

(*g.*) It tends to bring the authority of God into universal contempt.

(*h.*) It tends to overthrow all government, all happiness. And as all rebellion is aimed at the throne and the life of the sovereign, the natural tendency of sin is not only to annihilate the authority, but the very being of God. Thus, in this respect also, sin involves infinite guilt.

Having disposed of these objections leveled at the justice of eternal punishments, and having also established the fact that sin in its very nature, involves infinite blame-worthiness or guilt, when viewed in any just point of light, I proceed to say:

4. That the law is infinitely unjust, if its penal sections are not endless. Law must be just in two respects.

(1.) The precept must be in accordance with the law of nature.

(2.) The penalty must be equal to the importance of the precept. That which has not these two peculiarities is not just, and therefore is not and cannot be law. Either, then, God has no law, or its penal sanctions are endless.

5. That the penal sanctions of the law of God are endless, is evident from the fact that a less penalty would not exhibit as high motives as the nature of the case admits, to restrain sin and promote virtue.

6. Natural justice demands that God should exhibit as high motives to secure obedience as the value of the law demands, and the nature of the case admits.

7. The justice, holiness, and benevolence of God demand that the penal sections of his law should be endless; and if they are not, God cannot be just, holy, or benevolent.

8. Unless the penal sanctions of the law of God are endless, they are virtually and really no penalty at all. If a man be threatened with punishment for one thousand, or ten thousand, or ten millions, or ten hundred millions of years, after which he is to come out, as a matter of justice, and go to heaven, there is beyond an absolute eternity of happiness. Now there is no sort of proportion between the longest finite period that can be named, or even conceived, and endless duration. If, therefore, limited punishment, ending in an eternity of heaven, be the penalty of God's law, the case stands thus: Be perfect, and you live here forever. Sin, and receive finite

suffering, with an eternity of heaven. This would be, after all, offering reward to sin.

9. Death is eternal in its nature. The fact, therefore, that this figure is used to express the future punishment of the wicked affords a plain inference that it is endless.

10. The tendency of sin to perpetuate and aggravate itself, affords another strong inference that the sinfulness and misery of the wicked will be eternal.

11. The fact that punishment has no tendency to beget disinterested love in a selfish mind towards him who inflicts the punishment, also affords a strong presumption that future punishment will be eternal.

12. The law makes no provision for terminating future punishment.

13. Sin deserves endless punishment just as fully as it deserves any punishment at all. If, therefore, it is not forgiven, if it be punished at all with penal suffering, the punishment must be endless.

14. To deny the justice of eternal punishments, involves the same principle as a denial of the justice of any degree of punishment.

15 To deny the justice of endless punishment, is virtually to deny the fact of moral evil. But to deny this is to deny moral obligation. To deny moral obligation we must deny moral agency. But of both moral obligation and moral agency, we are absolutely conscious. Therefore it follows to a demonstration, not only that moral evil does exist, but that it deserves endless punisment.

16. The Bible in a great many ways represents the future punishment of the wicked as eternal. It expresses the duration of the future punishment of the wicked by the same terms, and in every way as forcibly as it expresses the duration of the future happiness of the righteous.

Obj. Will all sinners be punished alike in a future world?
Ans. Not in degree, but only in duration.

LECTURE XXXIV.

MORAL GOVERNMENT.—No. 13.

GOVERNMENTAL PRINCIPLES.

1. The precept of the law must be intelligible.

2. That obedience shall be practicable.

3. That it shall be for the highest good of the subjects.

4. That it shall be impartial, and not contrary to the law of nature.

5. That the law-giver shall express in the sanctions the amount of his regard to the precept.

6. That perfect obedience shall be rewarded with the perpetual favor and protection of the law-giver.

7. That one breach of the precept shall incur the penalty of law.

8. That law makes no provision for repentance or forgiveness.

9. That a leading design of penal sanctions is prevention.

10. That disobedience cannot be pardoned unless some equally efficient preventive be substituted for the execution of law.

11. That where this can be done, pardon is in strict accordance with the perfection of government.

12. That in all cases of disobedience the executive is bound to inflict the penalty of the law, or see that some equivalent is rendered to public justice.

13. The only equivalent that can be rendered to public justice is some governmental measure that will as fully illustrate and manifest the righteousness of the government, as the execution of law would do.

14. The execution of law acts as a preventive, by demonstrating the righteousness of the law-giver, and thus begetting confidence and heart obedience.

15. That any act on the part of the government that will upon the whole set the character of the governor in as impressive and influential a light as the execution of the law would do, is a full satisfaction to public justice, and renders pardon not only proper but highly beneficial.

LECTURE. XXXV.

ATONEMENT.—No. 1.

In this lecture I shall show:
FIRST. What is intended by the Atonement.
SECOND. That an Atonement was necessary.

FIRST. *What is intended by the Atonement.*

The English word Atonement is synonymous with the Hebrew word *Cofer*. This is a noun from the verb *caufar*, to cover. The *cofer* or cover, was the name of the lid or cover of the ark of the covenant, and constituted what was called the mercy seat. The Greek word rendered Atonement is *katallage*. This means reconciliation, to favor; from *kallasso*, to change, or exchange. The term properly means substitution. An examination of these original words, in the connection in which they stand, will show that the Atonement is the substitution of the sufferings of Christ in the place of the sufferings of sinners. It is a covering of their sins, by his sufferings.

SECOND. *Its necessity.*

1. All nations have felt the necessity of expiatory sacrifices. This is evident from the fact that all nations have offered them. Hence *antipsucha*, or ransom for their souls, have been offered by nearly every nation under heaven. (See Buck's Theo. Dic. p. 539.)

2. The wisest heathen philosophers, who saw the intrinsic inefficacy of animal sacrifices, held that God could not forgive sin. This proves to a demonstration, that they felt the necessity of an atonement or expiatory sacrifice. And having too just views of God and his government, to suppose that either animal, or merely human sacrifices, could be efficacious under the government of God, they were unable to understand upon what principles sin could be forgiven.

3. The whole Jewish scriptures, especially the whole ceremonial dispensation of the Jews attest, most unequivocally, the necessity of an Atonement.

4. The New Testament is just as unequivocal in its testimony to the same point. The Apostle expressly asserts, that "without the shedding of blood, there is no remission of sin."

5. The necessity of an Atonement is fully implied in the fact, that an Atonement has been made.

6. The fact that the execution of the law of God on rebel angels had not and could not arrest the progress of rebellion in the universe, proves that something more needed to be done, in sup-

port of the authority of law, than the execution of its penalty upon rebels could do. While the execution of law may have a strong tendency to prevent the beginning of rebellion, and to awe and restrain rebellion, among the rebels themselves; yet penal inflictions, do not as a matter of fact, subdue the heart, under any government, whether human or divine.

7. As a matter of fact, the law, without Atonement, was only exasperating rebels, without confirming holy beings. Paul affirmed that the action of the law upon his own mind, while in impenitence, was, to beget in him all manner of concupisence. One grand reason for giving the law was, to develop the nature of sin, and to show that the carnal mind is not subject to the law of God, neither indeed can be. The law was, therefore, given that the offence might abound, that thereby it might be demonstrated, that without an Atonement there could be no salvation for rebels under the government of God.

8. The nature, degree, and execution of the penalty of the law, made the holiness and justice of God so prominent, as to absorb too much of public attention to be safe. Those features of his character were so fully revealed, by the execution of his law upon the rebel angels, that to have pursued the same course with the inhabitants of this world, without the offer of mercy, might have had, and doubtless would have had an injurious influence upon the universe, by creating more of fear than of love to God and his government.

9. Hence, a fuller revelation of the love and compassion of God was necessary, to guard against the influence of slavish fear.

10. Public justice required either that an Atonement should be made, or that the law should be executed upon every offender. By public justice is intended, that due administration of law, that shall secure in the highest manner the nature of the case admits, private and public interests, and establish the order and well-being of the universe. In establishing the government of the universe, God had given the pledge, both impliedly and expressly, that he would regard the public interests and by a due administration of the law, secure and promote, as far as possible, public and individual happiness.

11. Public justice could strictly require only the execution of law; for God had neither expressly or impliedly given a pledge to do any thing more for the promotion of virtue and happiness, than to administer due rewards to both the righteous and the wicked. Yet an Atonement, as we shall see, would more fully meet the necessities of the government, and act as a more efficient preventive of sin, and a more powerful persuasive to holiness, than the infliction of the penalty of his law would do.

12. An Atonement was needed, to contradict the slander of Satan. He had seduced our first parents, by the insinuation that God was selfish, in prohibiting their eating the fruit of a certain tree. Now the execution of the penalty of his law would not so tho-

roughly refute this abominable slander as would the great self-denial of God exhibited in the Atonement.

13. An Atonement was needed, for the removal of obstacles to the free exercise of benevolence towards our race. Without an Atonement, the race of man after the fall, sustained to the government of God the relation of rebels and outlaws. And before God, as the great executive magistrate of the universe, could suffer his benevolence to flow toward them, an Atonement must be decided upon and made known, as the reason upon which his favorable treatment of them was founded.

14. An Atonement was needed, to promote the glory and influence of God in the universe. But more of this hereafter.

15. An Atonement was needed, to present overpowering motives to repentance.

16. An Atonement was needed, that the offer of pardon might not seem like connivance at sin.

17. An Atonement was needed, to manifest the sincerity of God, in his legal enactments.

18. An Atonement was needed, to make it safe, to present the offer and promise of pardon.

19. An Atonement was needed, to inspire confidence in the offers and promises of pardon, and in all the promises of God to man.

20. An Atonement was needed, as the only means of reclaiming rebels.

21. An Atonement was needed, as the great and only means of sanctifying sinners:

Rom. 8: 3, 4. 'For what the law could not do, in that it was weak through the flesh, God, sending his own Son in the likeness of sinful flesh, and for sin, condemned sin in the flesh: that the righteousness of the law might be fulfilled in us, who walk not after the flesh, but after the Spirit.'

22. An Atonement was needed, not to render God merciful, but to reconcile pardon with a due administration of justice:

Rom. 3: 23–26. 'For all have sinned, and come short of the glory of God; being justified freely by his grace, through the redemption that is in Christ Jesus: whom God has set forth to be a propitiation through faith in his blood, to declare his righteousness for the remission of sins that are past, through the forbearance of God; to declare, I say, at this time, his righteousness: that he might be just, and the justifier of him which believeth in Jesus.'

LECTURE XXXVI.

ATONEMENT.—No. 2.

In this lecture I shall present several farther reasons why an Atonement under the government of God was preferable in the case of the inhabitants of this world, to punishment, or to the execution of the divine law. Several reasons have already been assigned in the last lecture, to which I will add the following, some of which are plainly revealed in the Bible; others are plainly inferred from what the Bible does reveal; and others still are plainly inferable from the very nature of the case:

1. God's great and disinterested love to sinners themselves was a prime reason for the Atonement.

John 3: 16. 'For God so loved the world, that he gave his only begotten Son, that whosoever believeth in him should not perish, but have everlasting life.'

2. His great love to the universe at large must have been another reason, inasmuch as it was impossible that the Atonement should not exert an amazing influence over moral beings, in whatever world they might exist.

3. Another reason for substituting the sufferings of Christ in the place of the eternal damnation of sinners, is that an infinite amount of suffering might be prevented. The relation of Christ to the universe rendered his sufferings so infinitely valuable and influential as an expression of God's abhorrence of sin on the one hand, and great love to his subjects on the other, that an infinitely less amount of suffering in him than must have been inflicted upon sinners, would be equally, and no doubt vastly more influential in supporting the government of God, than the execution of the law upon them would have been.

4. By this substitution an immense good might be gained. The eternal happiness of all that can be reclaimed from sin, together with all the augmented happiness of those who have never sinned that must result from this glorious revelation of God.

5. Another reason for preferring the Atonement to the punishment of sinners, must have been, that sin had afforded an opportunity for the highest exercise of virtue in God: the exercise of forbearance, mercy, self-denial, for enemies, and suffering for enemies that were within his own power, and for those from whom he could expect no equivalent in return.

6. It is impossible to conceive of a higher order of virtues than are exhibited in the Atonement of Christ.

7. It was vastly desirable that God should take advantage of such an opportunity to exhibit his true character, and shew to the universe what was in his heart.

8. Another reason for preferring Atonement was God's desire to lay open his heart to the inspection and imitation of moral beings.

9. Another reason is, because God is love, and prefers mercy when it can be safely exercised. The Bible represents him as delighting in mercy, and affirms that "judgment is his strange work."

10. Because he so much prefers mercy to judgment as to be willing to suffer as their substitute, to afford himself the opportunity to exercise pardon on principles that are consistent with a due administration of justice.

11. In the Atonement God consulted his own happiness and his own glory. To deny himself for the salvation of sinners was a part of his own infinite happiness, always intended by him, and therefore always enjoined.

12. In making the Atonement, God complied with the laws of his own mind, and did just that, all things considered, in the highest degree promotive of the universal good.

13. The self-denial exercised in the Atonement would secure to him the highest kind and degree of happiness.

14. The Atonement would present to creatures the highest possible motives to virtue.

15. It would beget among creatures the highest kind and degree of happiness, by leading them to contemplate and imitate his love.

16. The circumstances of his government rendered an Atonement necessary; as the execution of law was not, as a matter of fact, a sufficient preventive of sin. The annihilation of the wicked would not answer the purposes of government. A full revelation of mercy, blended with such an exhibition of justice, was called for by the circumstances of the universe.

17. To confirm holy beings.

18. To confound his enemies.

19. A just and necessary regard to his own reputation made him prefer Atonement to the punishment of sinners.

20. A desire to sustain his own reputation, as the only moral power that could support his own moral government, must have been a leading reason for the Atonement.

21. The Atonement was preferred as the best and perhaps only way to inspire an affectionate confidence in him.

22. Atonement must have been the most agreeable to God, and the most beneficial to the universe.

23. Atonement would afford him an oppportunity to always gratify his love in his kindness to sinners in using means for their salvation, in forgiving and saving them when they repent, without the danger of its being inferred in the universe that he had not a sufficient abhorrence of their sins.

24. The Atonement demonstrates the superior efficacy of love, as a moral influence, over penal inflictions.

25. Another reason for the Atonement was to counteract the influence of the Devil, whose whole influence is exerted in this world for the promotion of selfishness.

26. The Atonement would enable God to make the best use of the Devil which the nature of the case admitted.

27. To make the final punishment of the wicked more impressive in the light of the infinite love manifest in the Atonement.

28. The Atonement is the highest testimony that God can bear against selfishness. It is the testimony of his own example.

29. The Atonement is a higher expression of his regard for the public interests than the execution of law. It is therefore a fuller satisfaction to public justice.

30. The Atonement so reveals all the attributes of God as to complete the whole circle of motives needed to influence the minds of moral beings.

31. By dying in human nature, Christ exhibited his heart to both worlds.

LECTURE XXXVII.

ATONEMENT.—No. 3.

WHAT CONSTITUTES THE ATONEMENT.

In this lecture I will show:

FIRST. Not Christ's obedience to law as a covenant of works.

SECOND. That his sufferings, and especially his death, constitutes the Atonement.

THIRD. That his taking human nature and obeying unto death, under such circumstances, constituted a good reason for our being treated as righteous.

FOURTH The nature and kind of his sufferings.

FIFTH. The amount of his sufferings.

SIXTH. That the Atonement is not a commercial transaction.

SEVENTH. That the Atonement is to be regarded as a satisfaction of public justice.

FIRST. *Christ's obedience to the moral law, as a covenant of works, did not constitute the Atonement.*

1. Christ owed obedience to the moral law both as God and man. He was under as much obligation to be perfectly benevolent as any moral creature is. It was therefore impossible for him to to perform any works of supererogation; that is, so far as obedi-

ence to law was concerned, he could, neither as God, nor as man, do any thing more than his duty.

2. Had he *obeyed* for us, he would not have suffered for us. If his obedience was to be substituted for our obedience, he need not certainly have both fulfilled the law for us, as our substitute under a covenant of works, and at the same time have suffered, a substitute for the penalty of the law.

3. If he obeyed the law as our substitute, then why should our own personal obedience be insisted upon as a *sine qua non* of our salvation.

4. The idea that any part of the Atonement consisted in Christ's obeying the law for us, and in our stead and behalf, represents God as requiring:

(1.) The *obedience* of our substitute.

(2.) The same *suffering* as if no obedience had been rendered.

(3.) Our *repentance.*

(4.) Our *personal obedience.*

(5.) And then represents him as, after all, ascribing our salvation to grace. Strange grace this, that requires a debt to be paid sevral times over before the obligation is discharged!

SECOND. *The sufferings of Christ, and especially his death, constituted the Atonement.*

1. His sufferings were no part of them deserved by him. They must, therefore, have been vicarious or unjust. If they were vicarious, that is, voluntarily suffered by him as our substitute, no injustice was done. But if they were not vicarious, he could not have suffered at all under the government of God, without injustice having been done him.

2. That his sufferings were vicarious, is manifest from the fact that they were *all* occasioned by the sins of men.

3. The Bible represents *all* his sufferings as for us.

Isa. 53: 'Who hath believed our report? and to whom is the arm of the Lord revealed? For he shall grow up before him as a tender plant, and as a root out of a dry ground: he hath no form nor comeliness; and when we shall see him, there is no beauty that we should desire him. He is despised and rejected of men; a man of sorrows and acquainted with grief; and we hid as it were our faces from him; he was despised, and we esteemed him not. Surely he hath borne our griefs, and carried our sorrows; yet we did esteem him stricken, smitten of God, and afflicted. But he was wounded for our transgressions, he was bruised for our iniquities: the chastisement of our peace was upon him; and with his stripes we are healed. All we, like sheep, have gone astray; we have turned every one to his own way; and the Lord hath laid on him the iniquity of us all. He was oppressed, and he was afflicted; yet he opened not his mouth: he is brought as a lamb to the slaughter, and as a sheep before his shearers is dumb, so he opened not his mouth. He was taken from prison and from judgment: and who shall declare his generation? for he was cut off out of the land of the living: for the transgression of my people was he stricken. And he made his grave with the wicked, and with the rich in his death; because he had done no violence, neither was any deceit in his mouth. Yet it pleased the Lord to bruise him; he hath put him to grief: when thou shalt make his soul an offering for sin, he shall see his seed, he shall prolong his days, and the pleasure of the Lord shall prosper in his hand. He shall see of the travail of his soul, and shall be satisfied: by his knowledge shall my righteous servant justify many; for he shall bear their iniquities. Therefore will I divide him a portion with the great, and he shall divide the spoil with the strong; because he hath poured out his soul unto death: and he was numbered with the transgressors; and he bare the sins of many, and made intercession for the transgressors.'

Heb. 2: 10. 'For it became him, for whom are all things, and by whom are all things, in bringing many sons unto glory, to make the Captain of their salvation perfect through sufferings.'

4. The Bible especially, and almost every where represents his death, or the shedding of his blood, as a vicarious offering for our sins. The texts which prove this are too numerous to be quoted in a skeleton.

5. Perhaps his other sufferings are to be regarded as incidental to the work he had undertaken, and fitted to prepare him to sympathize with us, rather than as strictly vicarious.

Heb. 2: 17, 18. 'Wherefore in all things it behoved him to be made like unto his brethren, that he might be a merciful and faithful high priest in things pertaining to God, to make reconciliation for the sins of the people: For in that he himself hath suffered, being tempted, he is able to succor them that are tempted.'

Heb. 4: 15. 'For we have not a high priest which cannot be touched with the feeling of our infirmities; but was in all points tempted like as we are, yet without sin.'

THIRD. *His taking human nature, and obeying unto death, under such circumstances, constituted a good reason for our being treated as righteous.*

1. It is a common practice in human governments, and one that is founded in the nature and laws of mind, to reward distinguished public service by conferring favors on the children of those who had rendered this service, and treating them as if they had rendered it themselves. This is both benevolent and wise. Its governmental importance, its wisdom and excellent influence have been most abundantly attested in the experience of nations.

2. As a governmental transaction, this same principle prevails, and for the same reason, under the government of God. All that

are Christ's children and belong to him, are received for his sake, treated with favor, and the rewards of the righteous are bestowed upon them for his sake. And the public service which he has rendered the universe by laying down his life for the support of the divine government, has rendered it eminently wise that all who are united to him by faith should be treated as righteous for his sake.

Fourth. *The nature or kind of his sufferings.*

1. His sufferings were not those of a sinner, neither in kind nor degree. The sufferings of a sinner must consist, in a great measure, in remorse. But Christ could not feel remorse, having never sinned.

2. He could not have endured the literal penalty of the law of God, for this we have seen in a former skeleton was eternal death.

3. He did not endure the displeasure of God. On the contrary, God expressly affirmed that he was his "beloved Son in whom he was well pleased."

4. But a substitute for the curse due to sinners fell on him. In other words, he endured such sufferings, as our substitute, both in kind and degree, as fully to meet the demand of public justice.

Isa. 53: 4—12. 'Surely he hath borne our griefs, and carried our sorrows; yet we did esteem him stricken, smitten of God, and afflicted. But he was wounded for our transgressions, he was bruised for our iniquities: the chastisement of our peace was upon him; and with his stripes we are healed. All we, like sheep, have gone astray; we have turned every one his own way; and the Lord hath laid on him the iniquity of us all. He was oppressed, and he was afflicted; yet he opened not his mouth: he is brought as a lamb to the slaughter, and as a sheep before his shearers is dumb, so he opened not his mouth. He was taken from prison and from judgment: and who shall declare his generation? for he was cut off out of the land of the living: for the transgression of my people was he stricken. And he made his grave with the wicked, and with the rich in his death: because he had done no violence, neither was any deceit in his mouth. Yet it pleased the Lord to bruise him; he hath put him to grief: when thou shalt make his soul and offering for sin, he shall see his seed, he shall prolong his days, and the pleasure of the Lord shall prosper in his hand. He shall see the travail of his soul, and shall be satisfied: by his knowledge shall my righteous servant justify many; for he shall bear their iniquities. Therefore will I divide him a portion with the great, and he shall divide the spoil with the strong; because he hath poured out his soul unto death; and he was numbered with the transgressors; and he bare the sin of many, and made intercession for the transgressors.'

Rom. 4: 25. 'Who was delivered for our offences, and was raised again for our justification.'

2 Cor. 5: 21. 'For he hath made him to be sin for us, who knew no sin; that we might be made the righteousness of God in him.'

Heb. 9: 28. 'So Christ was once offered to bear the sins of many: and unto them that look for him shall he appear the second time, without sin, unto salvation.'

1 Pet. 2: 24. 'Who his own self bare our sins in his own body on the tree, that we, being dead to sins, should live unto righteousness: by whose stripes ye were healed.'

5. His sufferings were those of a holy mind voluntarily submited to, in support of law, under a dispensation of mercy.

FIFTH. *The amount of his sufferings.*

1. He did not suffer all that was due to sinners on the ground of retributive justice. This was naturally impossible, as each sinner deserved eternal death.
2. Inflicting upon him this amount of suffering would have been unjust, as his sufferings were infinitely more valuable than the sufferings of sinners.
3. Therefore such an amount of suffering was wholly unnecessary in him.
4. Had he suffered the same amount that was due to sinners, nothing would have been gained to the universe by this substitution, and therefore the Atonement would have been unwise.
5. Neither wisdom nor enlightened benevolence could consent that an innocent being should suffer, as a substitute for a guilty one, the same amount that was justly due to the guilty.
6. We are no where informed, nor is it possible for us to know, or perhaps to conceive, the exact amount of Christ's sufferings as a substitute for sinners. It is enough for us to know that his sufferings, both in kind and degree, were so ample a satisfaction to public justice as to render the universal offer of forgiveness to all the penitent consistent with the due administration of justice.

SIXTH: *The Atonement was not a commercial tranasaction.*

Some have regarded the Atonement simply in the light of the payment of a debt; and have represented Christ as purchasing the elect of the Father and paying down the same amouut of suffering in his own person that justice would have exacted of them. To this I answer:

1. It is naturally impossible, as it would require that satisfaction should be made to retributive justice.
2. But as we have seen in a former lecture, retributive justice must have inflicted on them eternal death. To suppose, therefore, that Christ suffered in amount all that was due to the elect, is to suppose that he suffered an eternal punishment multipled by the whole number of the elect.

SEVENTH. *The Atonement of Christ was intended as a satisfaction of public justice.*

1. Isa. 53: 10—12. 'Yet it pleased the Lord to bruise him; he hath put him to grief: when thou shalt make his soul an offering for sin, he shall see his seed, he shall prolong his days, and the pleasure of the Lord shall prosper in his hand. He shall see of the travail of his soul, and shall be satisfied: by his knowledge shall my righteous servant justify many; for he shall bear their iniquities. Therefore will I divide him a portion with the great, and he shall divide the spoil with the strong; because he hath poured out his soul unto death: and he was numbered with the transgressors; and he bare the sin of many, and made intercession for the transgressors.

Rom. 24—26. 'Being justified freely by his grace, through the redemption that is in Christ Jesus: whom God hath set forth to be a propitiation through faith in his blood, to declare his righteousness for the remission of sins that are past, through the forbearance of God; to declare, I say, at this time his righteousness; that he might be just, and the justifier of him which believeth in Jesus.'

2. Public justice requires:

(1.) That penalties shall be annexed to laws that are equal to the importance of the precept.

(2.) That when these penalties are incurred they shall be inflicted for the public good, as an expression of the law-giver's regard to the law, of his determination to support public order, and by a due administration of justice to secure the highest well being of the public. As has been seen in a former lecture, a leading design of the sanctions of law is prevention; and the execution of penal sanctions is demanded by public justice. The great design of sanctions, both remuneratory and vindicatory, is to prevent disobedience and secure obedience or universal happiness. This is done by such a revelation of the heart of the law-giver, through the precept, sanctions, and execution of his law, as to beget awe on the one hand, and the most entire confidence and love on the other.

3. Whatever can as effectually reveal God, make known his hatred to sin, his love of order, his determination to support government, and to promote the holiness and happpiness of his creatures, as the execution of his law would do, is a full satisfaction of public justice.

4. Atonement is, therefore, a part, and a most influential part of moral government. It is an auxiliary to a strictly legal government. It does not take the place of the execution of law in such a sense as to exclude penal inflictions from the universe. The execution of law still holds a place and makes up an indispensable part of the great circle of motives essential to the perfection of moral government. Fallen angels and the finally impenitent of this world will

receive the full execution of the penalty of the divine law. But Atonement is an expedient above law, not contrary to it, which adds new and vastly influential motives to induce obedience. I have said it is an auxiliary to law, adding to the precept and sanction of law an overpowering exhibition of love and compassion.

5. The Atonement is an illustrious exhibition of commutative justice, in which the government of God, by an act of infinite grace, commutes or substitutes the sufferings of Christ for the eternal damnation of sinners.

These various positions might be sustained by numerous quotations from scripture, but in this skeleton form they cannot conveniently be given; and besides, it is no part of my design to dispense with the necessity of your searching the Bible for the proof of these positions yourselves.

LECTURE XXXVIII.

ATONEMENT.—No. 4.

ITS VALUE.

In discussing the value of the Atonement, I shall—

FIRST. Show in what its value consists.

SECOND. How great its value is.

THIRD. For whose benefit it was intended.

FIRST. *Show in what its value consists.*

1. It is valuable only as it tends to promote the glory of God, and the virtue and happiness of the universe.

2. In order to understand, in what the value of the Atonement consists, we must understand:

(1.) That happiness is an ultimate good.

(2.) That virtue is indispensable to happiness.

(3.) That the knowledge of God is indispensable to virtue.

(4.) That Christ, who made the Atonement, is God.

(5.) That the work of Atonement was the most interesting and impressive exhibition of God that ever was made in this world and probably in the universe.

(6.) That, therefore, the Atonement is the highest means of promoting virtue that exists in this world, and perhaps in the universe. And that it is valuable only, and just so far as it reveals God, and tends to promote virtue and happiness.

(7.) That the work of Atonement was a gratification of the infinite benevolence of God.

(8.) It was a work eternally designed by him, and therefore eternally enjoyed.

(9.) It has eternally made no small part of the happiness of God.

(10.) The development or carrying out of this design, in the work of Atonement, highly promotes and will for ever promote his glory in the universe.

(11.) Its value consists in its adaptedness to promote the virtue and happiness of holy angels, and all moral agents who have never sinned. As it is a new and most stupendous revelation of God, it must of course greatly increase their knowledge of God, and be greatly promotive of their virtue and happiness.

(12.) Its value consists in its adaptedness to prevent farther rebellion against God in every part of the universe. The Atonement exhibits God in such a light, as must greatly strengthen the confidence of holy beings in his character and government. It is therefore calculated in the highest degree, to confirm holy beings in their allegiance to God, and thus prevent the further progress of rebellion.

Second. *Show how great its value is.*

1. Let it be remembered, the value of the Atonement consists in its moral power or tendency to promote virtue and happiness.

2. Moral power is the power of motive.

3. The highest moral power is the influence of example. Advice has moral power. Precept has moral power. Sanction has moral power. But example is the highest moral influence that can be exerted by any being.

4. Moral beings are so created as to be naturally influenced by the example of each other. The example of a child, as a moral influence, has power upon other children. The example of an adult, as a moral influence, has power. The example of great men and of angels has great moral power. But the example of God is the highest moral influence in the universe.

5. The word of God has power. His commands, threatenings, promises; but his example is a higher moral influence than his precepts or his threatenings.

6. Virtue consists in benevolence. God requires benevolence, threatens all his subjects with punishment, if they are not benevolent, and promises them eternal life if they are. All this has power. But his example, his own benevolence, his own disinterested love, as expressed in the Atonement, is a vastly higher moral influence than his word, or any other of his ways.

7. Christ is God. In the Atonement God has given us the influence of his own example, has exhibited his own love, his own compassion, his own self-denial, his own patience, his own long-suffering, under abuse from enemies. In the Atonement he has exhibited all the highest and most perfect virtues, has united himself with human nature, has exhibited these virtues to the inspection of

our senses, and labored, wept, suffered, bled, and died for man. This is not only the highest revelation of God, that could be given to man ; but is giving the whole weight of his own example in favor of all the virtues which he requires of man.

8. This is the highest possible moral influence. It is properly moral omnipotence ; that is—the influence of the Atonement, when apprehended by the mind, will accomplish whatever is an object of moral power. It cannot compel a moral agent, and set aside his freedom, for this is not an object of moral power ; but it will do all that motive can, in the nature of the case accomplish. It is the highest and most weighty motive that the mind of a moral being can conceive. It is the most moving, impressive, and influential consideration in the universe.

9. The value of the Atonement may be estimated then :

(1.) By the consideration, that it has from eternity made up no inconsiderable part of the happiness of God. We are not aware, and cannot know, that God has ever exercised a higher class of virtues, than were exercised and exhibited in the Atonement. His happiness arises out of, and is founded in, his virtue.

(2.) God has always been in that state of mind, so far as his will and design were concerned, in which he made the Atonement.

(3.) He has, therefore, always exercised those virtues, and always enjoyed the happiness resulting from them. And those virtues are certainly among the highest kind that can possibly be exercised by God, and as his happiness is in proportion to the perfection and strength of his virtue, we have good reason for believing, that the work of Atonement, or the virtues exercised or exhibited in it, have ever constituted a great share of the happiness of God.

(4.) Its value may be estimated, by its moral influence in the promotion of holiness among all holy beings :

a. Their love to God must depend upon their knowledge of him.

b. As he is infinite, and all creatures are finite, finite beings know him only as he is pleased to reveal himself.

c. The Atonement has disclosed or revealed to the universe of holy beings, a class and an order of virtues, as resident in the divine mind, which, but for the Atonement, would probably have for ever remained unknown.

d. As the Atonement is the most impressive revelation of God, of which we have any knowledge, or can form any conception, we have reason to believe that it has greatly increased the holiness and happiness of all holy creatures, that it has done more than any other and perhaps every other revelation of God, to exalt his character, strengthen his government, enlighten the universe, and increase its happiness.

e. The value of the Atonement may be estimated by the amount of good it has done and will do in this world. The Atonement is an exhibition of God suffering as a substitute for his rebellious subjects. His relation to the law and to the universe, is that which gives his sufferings such infinite value. I have said, in a former lecture, that the utility of executing penal sanctions consists in the exhibition it makes of the true character and designs of the law-giver. It creates public confidence, makes a public impression, and thus strengthens the influence of government, and is in this way promotive of order and happiness. The Atonement is the highest testimony that God could give of his holy abhorrence of sin; of his regard to his law; of his determination to support it; and, also, of his great love for his subjects; his great compassion for sinners; and his willingness to suffer himself in their stead; rather, on the one hand, than to punish them, and on the other, than to set aside the penalty without satisfaction being made to public justice.

f. The Atonement may be viewed in either of two points of light.

(a.) Christ may be considered as the law-giver, and attesting his sincerity, love of holiness, approbation of the law, and compassion for his subjects, by laying down his life as their substitute.

(b.) Or, Christ may be considered as the Son of the Supreme Ruler; and then we have the spectacle of a sovereign, giving his only begotten and well beloved Son, his greatest treasure, to die a shameful and agonizing death, in testimony of his great compassion for his rebellious subjects, and of his high regard for public justice.

g. The value of the Atonement may be estimated, by considering the fact that it provides for the pardon of sin, in a way that forbids the hope of impunity in any other case. This, the good of the universe imperiously demanded. If sin is to be forgiven at all, under the government of God, it should be known to be forgiven upon principles that will by no means encourage rebellion, or hold out the least hope of impunity, should rebellion break out in any other part of the universe.

h. The Atonement has settled the question, that sin can never be forgiven, under the government of God, simply on account of the repentance of any being. It has demonstrated, that sin can never be forgiven without full satisfaction being made to public justice, and that public justice can never be satisfied with any thing less than an Atonement made by God himself. Now, as it can never be expected, that the Atonement will be repeated, it is for ever settled, that rebellion in any other world than this, can have no hope of impunity. This answers the question so often asked by infidels, "If God was disposed to be merciful, why could he not forgive without an Atonement?" The answer is plain; he could not forgive sin, but upon such principles as would for ever preclude the hope of impunity, should rebellion ever break out in any other part of the universe.

i. From these considerations, it is manifest that the value of the Atonement is infinite. We have reason to believe, that Christ, by his Atonement, is not only the Savior of this world, but the Savior of the universe in an important sense. Rebellion once broke out in Heaven, and upon the rebel angels God executed his law, and sent them down to hell. It next broke out in this world; and as the execution of law was found by experience not to be a sufficient preventive against rebellion, there was no certainty that rebellion would not have spread until it had ruined the universe, but for that revelation of God which Christ has made in the Atonement. This exhibition of God has proved itself, not merely able to prevent rebellion among holy beings, but to reclaim and reform rebels. Millions of rebels have been reclaimed and reformed. This world is to be turned back to its allegiance to God, and the blessed Atonement of Christ has so unbosomed God before the universe, as, no doubt, not only to save other worlds from going into rebellion, but to save myriads of our already rebellious race from the depths of an eternal hell.

THIRD. *For whose benefit the Atonement was intended.*

1. God does all things for himself; that is—he consults his own glory and happiness, as the supreme and most influential reason for all his conduct. This is wise and right in him, because his own glory and happiness are infinitely the greatest good in the universe. He does what he does, because he loves to do it. He made the Atonement to gratify himself; that is—because he loved to do it. "God so loved the world, that he gave his only begotten Son, that whosoever believeth in him should not perish, but have everlasting life." God himself, then, was greatly benefitted by the Atonement. In other words, his happiness, in a great measure, consisted in it.

2. He made the Atonement for the benefit of the universe. All holy beings are and must be benefitted by it, from its very nature. As it gives them a higher knowledge of God, than they ever had before, or ever could have gained in any other way. The Atonement is the greatest work that he could have wrought for them, the most blessed, and excellent, and benevolent thing he could have done for them. For this reason, angels are described as desiring to look into the Atonement. The inhabitants of Heaven are represented as being deeply interested in the work of Atonement, and those displays of the character of God that are made in it. The Atonement is then, no doubt, one of the greatest blessings that ever God conferred upon the universe of holy beings.

3. The Atonement was made for the benefit particularly of the inhabitants of this world. From its very nature, it is calculated to benefit all the inhabitants of this world; as it is a most stupendous revelation of God to man. Its nature is adapted to benefit all mankind. All mankind can be pardoned, if they will be rightly affected and brought to repentance by it, as well as any part of mankind can.

4. The Bible delares that Christ tasted death for every man.

5. All do certainly receive many blessings on account of it. There is reason to believe, that but for the Atonement, none of our race, except the first human pair, would ever have had an existence.

6. But for the Atonement, no man could have been treated with any more lenity and forbearance than Satan can.

7. The lives, and all the blessings which all mankind enjoy, are conferred on them on account of the Atonement of Christ; that is—God could not consistently confer these blessings, were it not that Christ has made such a satisfaction to public justice, that God can consistently wait on sinners, and bless, and do all that the nature of the case admits to save them.

8. That it was made for all mankind, is evident, from the fact that it is offered to all, indiscriminately.

9. Sinners are universally condemned, for not receiving it.

10. If the Atonement is not intended for all mankind, God is insincere in making them the offer of salvation through the Atonement.

11. If the Atonement is not for all mankind, then God is partial.

12. If not, sinners in hell will see and know, that their salvation was never possible; that no Atonement was made for them; and that God was insincere, in offering them salvation.

13. If the Atonement is not for all men, no one can know for whom, in particular, it was intended, without direct revelation.

14. If the Atonement is for none but the elect, no man can know whether he has a right to embrace it, until by a direct revelation, God has made known to him that he is one of the elect.

15. If the Atonement was made but for the elect, no man can by any possibility embrace it without such a revelation. Why cannot Satan believe in, embrace, and be saved, by the Atonement? Simply because it was not made for him. If it was not made for the non-elect, they can no more embrace and be saved by it, than Satan can. If, therefore, the Atonement was made but for a part of mankind, it is entirely nugatory, unless a further revelation make known for whom in particular it was made.

16. If it was not made for all men, ministers do not know to whom they should offer it.

17. If ministers do not believe that it was made for all men, they cannot heartily and honestly press its acceptance upon any individual, or congregation in the world; for they cannot assure any individual, or congregation, that there is any Atonement for him or them, any more than there is for Satan.

LECTURE XXXIX.

MORAL GOVERNMENT.—No. 18.

ATONEMENT.—No. 5.

ITS INFLUENCE.

I have already anticipated many things that might be said under this head, some of which I shall glance at again, and to which several other considerations may be added.

1. The Atonement renders pardon consistent with the perfect administration of justice.

2. The Atonement, as it was made by the lawgiver, magnifies the law, and renders it infinitely more honorable and influential than the execution of the penalty upon sinners would have done.

3. It is the highest and most glorious expedient of moral government. It is adding to the influence of law the whole weight of the most moving manifestation of God, that men or angels ever saw or will see.

4. It completes the circle of governmental motives. It is a filling up of the revelation of God. It is a revealing of a department of his character, with which it would seem that nothing else could have made his creatures acquainted. It is, therefore, the highest possible support of moral government.

5. It greatly glorifies God, far above all his other works and ways.

6. It must be to him a source of the purest, most exalted, and eternal happiness.

7. It opens the channels of divine benevolence to state criminals.

8. It has united God with human nature.

9. It has opened a way of access to God, never opened to any creatures before.

10. It has abolished natural death, by procuring universal resurrection:

1 Cor. 15: 22. 'For as in Adam all die, even so in Christ shall all be made alive.'

11. It restores the life of God to the soul, by restoring to man the influence of the Holy Spirit.

12. It has introduced a new method of salvation, and made Christ the head of the New Covenant.

13. It has made Christ our surety:

Heb. 7: 22. 'By so much was Jesus made a surety of a better testament.'

14. It has arrayed such a public sentiment against rebellion, as to crush it whenever the Atonement is fairly understood and applied by the Holy Spirit.

15. It has procured the offer of pardon to all sinners of our race.

16. It has been the occasion of a new and most aggravated kind of sin.

17. It has, no doubt, added to the happiness of heaven.

18. It has more fully developed the nature and importance of the government of God.

19. It has more fully developed the nature of sin.

20. It has more fully developed the strength of sin.

21. It has more fully developed the total depravity and utter madness of sinners.

22. It has given scope to the long-suffering and forbearance of God.

23. It has formed a more intimate union between God and man, than between him and any other order of creatures.

24. It has elevated human nature, and the saints of God, into the stations of kings and priests to God.

25. It has opened new fields of usefulness, in which the benevolence of God, angels, and men may luxuriate in doing good.

26. It has developed and fully revealed the doctrine of the Trinity.

27. It has revealed the most influential and only efficacious method of government.

28. It has more fully developed those laws of our being upon which the strength of moral government depends.

29. It has given a standing illustration of the true interest, meaning, and excellency of the law of God. In the Atonement God has illustrated the meaning of his law by his own example.

30. The Atonement has fully illustrated the nature of virtue, and demonstrated that it consists in disinterested benevolence.

31. It has for ever condemned all selfishness, as entirely inconsistent with virtue.

32. It has established all the great principles and completed the power of moral government.

LECTURE XL.

MORAL GOVERNMENT.—No. 19.

ATONEMENT.—No. 6.

OBJECTIONS.

I. To the *fact* of Atonement. It is said that the doctrine of Atonement represents God as unmerciful.

Ans. 1. This objection supposes that the Atonement was demanded to satisfy retributive instead of public justice.

2. The Atonement was the exhibition of a merciful disposition. It was because God desired to pardon that he consented to give his own Son to die as the substitute of sinners.

3. The Atonement is infinitely the most illustrious exhibition of mercy ever made in the universe. The mere pardon of sin, as an act of mercy, cannot compare with the mercy displayed in the Atonement itself.

II. It is objected that the Atonement is unnecessary.

Ans. 1. The testimony of the world and of the consciences of all men is against this objection. This is universally attested by their expiatory sacrifices.

2. The Bible is against it.

3. A heathen philosopher can answer this.

III. It is objected that the doctrine of Atonement is inconsitent with the idea of mercy and forgiveness.

Ans. 1. This takes for granted that the Atonement was the literal payment of a debt, and that Christ suffered all that was due to all the sinners for whom he died. So that their discharge or pardon is an act of justice and not of mercy. But this was by no means the nature of the Atonement. The Atonement, as we have seen, had respect simply to *public*, and not at all to *retributive* justice. Christ suffered what was necessary to illustrate the feelings of God towards sin and towards his law. But the amount of his sufferings had no respect to the amount of punishment that might have justly been inflicted on the wicked.

2. The punishment of sinners is just as much deserved by them as if Christ had not suffered at all.

3. Their forgiveness, therefore, is just as much an act of mercy as if there had been no Atonement.

IV. It is objected that it is unjust to punish an innocent being instead of the guilty.

Ans. 1. Yes, it would not only be unjust, but it is impossible to *punish* an innocent individual at all. Punishment implies guilt. An innocent being may suffer, but he cannot be punished. Christ voluntarily "suffered, the just for the unjust." He had a right to exercise this self-denial; and as it was by his own voluntary consent, no injustice was done to any one.

2. If he had no right to make an Atonement, he had no right to consult and promote his own happiness; for it is said that "for the joy that was set before him he endured the cross, despising the shame."

V. It is objected that the doctrine of Atonement is utterly incredible.

To this I have replied in a former lecture; but will here again state, that it is utterly incredible upon any other supposition than that God is love. But if God is love, as the Bible expressly affirms that he is, the work of Atonement is just what might be expected of him under the circumstances; and the doctrine of Atonement is the most reasonable doctrine in the universe.

VI. It is objected to the doctrine of Atonement, that it is of a demoralizing tendency.

Ans. 1. There is a broad distinction between the natural tendency of a thing and such an abuse of a good thing as to make it the instrument of evil. The best things and doctrines may be, and often are, abused, and their natural tendency perverted.

2. The natural tendency of the Atonement is the direct opposite of demoralizing. Is the manifestation of deep disinterested love naturally calculated to beget enmity? Who does not know that the natural tendency of manifested love is to beget love in return?

3. Those who have the most fully believed in the Atonement, have exhibited the purest morality that has ever been exhibited in this world; while the rejecters of the Atonement, almost without exception, exhibit a loose morality. This is as might be expected from the very nature of Atonement.

VII. To a *general* Atonement it is objected, that the Bible represents Christ as laying down his life for his sheep, or for the elect only, and not for all mankind.

Ans. 1. It does indeed represent Christ as laying down his life for his sheep, and also for all mankind.

1 John 2: 2. 'And he is the propitiation for our sins; and not for ours only, but also for the sins of the WHOLE WORLD.

John 3: 17. 'For God sent not his Son into the WORLD to condemn the world; but that the WORLD through him might be saved.

Heb. 2: 9. 'But we see Jesus, who was made a little lower than the angels for the suffering of death, crowned with glory and honor; that he by the grace of God should taste death for EVERY MAN.'

2. Those who object to the general Atonement take substantially the same course to evade this doctrine that Unitarians do to set aside the doctrine of the trinity, and divinity of Christ. They quote those passages that prove the unity of God and the humanity of Christ, and then take it for granted that they have disproved the doctrine of the trinity and Christ's divinity. The asserters of limited Atonement in like manner quote those passages that prove that Christ died for the elect and for his saints, and then take it for granted that he died for none else. To the Unitarian we reply, we admit the unity of God, and the humanity of Christ, and the full meaning of those passages of scripture which you quote in proof of these doctrines; but we insist that this is not the whole truth, but there are still other classes of passages which prove the doctrine of the trinity and of the divinity of Christ. Just so to the asserters of limited Atonement we reply, we believe that Christ laid down his life for his sheep, as well as you; but we also believe that he tasted death for every man.

John 3: 16. 'For God so loved the world that he gave his only begotten Son, that whosoever believeth in him, should not perish, but have everlasting life.'

VIII. To the doctrine of general Atonement it is objected, that it would be folly in God to provide what he knew would be rejected; and that to suffer Christ to die for those whom he foresaw would not repent, would be a useless expenditure of blood and suffering.

Ans. 1. This objection assumes that the Atonement was a literal payment of a debt, which we have seen is not the nature of the Atonement.

2. If sinners do not accept it, no particle of the Atonement can be useless, as the great compassion of God in providing and offering them mercy will forever exalt his character in the estimation of holy beings, greatly strengthen his government, and therefore benefit the whole universe.

3. If all men rejected the Atonement it would nevertheless be of infinite value to the universe, as it is the most glorious revelation of God that was ever made.

IX. To the general Atonement it is objected, that it implies universal salvation.

Ans. 1. It does indeed imply this, upon the supposition that the Atonement is the literal payment of a debt. It was upon this view of the Atonement that Universalism first took its stand. Universalists taking it for granted that Christ had payed the debt of those for whom he died, and finding it fully revealed in the Bible that he died for all mankind, naturally, and if this were correct, properly inferred the doctrine of universal salvation. But we have seen that this is not the nature of the Atonement. Therefore this inference falls to the ground.

X. It is objected that if the Atonement was not a payment of the debt of sinners, but general in its nature, as we have mentioned, it secures the salvation of no one.

Ans. It is true that the Atonement itself does not secure the salvation of any one; but the promise and oath of God that Christ shall have a seed to serve him does.

REMARKS ON THE ATONEMENT.

1. The execution of the law of God on rebel angels must have created great awe in heaven.

2. Its action may have tended too much to fear.

3. The forbearance of God toward men previously to the Atonement of Christ may have been designed to counteract the superabundant tendency to fear, as it was the beginning of a revelation of compassion.

4. Sinners will not give up their enmity against God, nor believe that his is disinterested love, until they realize that he actually died as their substitute.

5. In this can be seen the exceeding strength of unbelief and prejudice against God.

6. But faith in the Atonement of Christ rolls a mountain weight of crushing considerations upon the heart of the sinner.

7. Thus the blood of Christ when apprehended and believed in, cleanses from all sin.

8. God's forbearance toward sinners must increase the wonder, admiration, love, and happiness of the universe.

9. The means which he uses to save mankind must produce the same effect.

10. Beyond certain limits, forbearance is no virtue, but would be manifestly injurious, and therefore wrong. A degree of forbearance that might justly create the impression that God was not infinitely holy and opposed to sin, would work infinite mischief in the universe.

11. When the forbearance of God has fully demonstrated his great love, and done all it can to sustain the moral government of God, without a fresh display of holiness and justice, God will no doubt come forth to execution, and make parallel displays of justice and mercy forever, by setting heaven and hell in eternal contrast.

12. Then the law and gospel will be seen to be one harmonious system of moral government, developing in the fullest manner the glorious character of God.

13. From this you can see the indispensable necessity of faith in the Atonement of Christ, and why it is that the gospel is the power of God unto salvation only to every one that believeth. If the Atonement is not believed, it is to that mind no revelation of God at all, and with such a mind the gospel has no moral power.

14. But the Atonement tends in the highest manner to beget in the believer the spirit of entire and universal consecration to God.

15. The Atonement shows how solid a foundation the saints have for unbroken and eternal repose and confidence in God. If God could make an Atonement for men, surely it is infinitely unreasonable to suppose that he will withhold from those that believe any thing which could be to them a real good.

16. We see that selfishness is the great hindrance to the exercise of faith. A selfish mind finds it exceedingly difficult to understand the Atonement, inasmuch as it is an exhibition of a state of mind which is the direct opposite of all that the sinner has ever experienced. His experience being wholly selfish renders it difficult for him to conceive aright what true religion is, and heartily to believe in the infinitely great and disinterested love of God.

LECTURE XLI.

MORAL GOVERNMENT.—No. 20.

HUMAN GOVERNMENTS ARE A PART OF THE MORAL GOVERNMENT OF GOD.

In this lecture I shall show:

First. That Human Governments are a necessity of human nature.

Second. That this necessity will continue as long as men exist in the present world.

Third. That Human Governments are plainly recognized in the Bible as a part of the government of God.

Fourth. Whose right and duty it is to govern.

Fifth. In what cases human legislation imposes moral obligation.

Sixth. That it is the duty of all men to aid in the establishment and support of Human Government.

Seventh. It is a ridiculous and absurd dream, to suppose that Human Government can ever be dispensed with in this world.

First. *Human Governments are a necessity of human nature.*

1. There is a material universe.

2. The bodies of men are material.

3. All action wastes these material bodies, and consequently they need continual sustenance.

4. Hence, we have many bodily wants.

5. Hence, the necessity of worldly goods and possessions.

6. There must be real estate.

7. It must belong to somebody.

8. There must, therefore, be all the forms of conveyancing, registry, and in short, all the forms of legal government, to settle and manage the real estate affairs of men.

9. Men have minds residing in a material body, and depending upon the organization and perfection of this body for mental development.

10. The mind receives its ideas of external objects, and the elements of all its knowledge through the bodily senses. It therefore needs books and other means of knowledge.

11. Hence, for this reason also men need property.

12. Moral beings will not agree in opinions on any subject without similar degrees of knowledge.

13. Hence, no human community exists or ever will exist, who on all subjects will agree in opinion.

14. This creates a necessity for human legislation and adjudication, to apply the great principle of moral law to all human affairs.

15. There are multitudes of human wants and necessities that cannot properly be met, except through the instrumentality of human governments.

Second. *This necessity will continue as long as human beings exist in this world.*

1. This is as certain as that the human body will always need sustenance, clothing, &c.

2. It is as certain as that the human soul will always need instruction, and that the means of instruction will not grow spontaneously, without expense or labor.

3. It is as certain as that men of all ages and circumstances will never possess equal degrees of information on all subjects.

4. If all men were perfectly holy and disposed to do right, the necessity of human governments would not be set aside, because this necessity is founded in the ignorance of mankind.

5. The decisions of legislators and judges must be authoritative, so as to settle questions of disagreement in opinion, bind and protect all parties.

6. The Bible represents human governments not only as existing, but as giving their authority and power to the support of the Church in its most prosperous state, or in the Millenium. It proves that human government will not be dispensed with when the world is holy:

Isa. 49: 22, 23. 'Thus saith the Lord God, Behold, I will lift up my hand to the Gentiles, and set up my standard to the people: and they shall bring thy sons in their arms, and thy daughters shall be carried upon their shoulders. And kings shall be thy nursing fathers, and their queens thy nursing mothers: they shall bow down to thee with their faces toward the earth, and lick up the dust of thy feet; and thou shalt know that I am the Lord: for they shall not be ashamed that wait for me.'

THIRD. *Human Governments are plainly recognized in the Bible as a part of the moral government of God.*

1. Dan. 2 : 21. 'He changeth the times and the seasons: he removeth kings, and setteth up kings: he giveth wisdom unto the wise, and knowledge to them that know understanding.'

Dan. 4 : 17, 25, 32. 'This matter is by the decree of the watchers, and the demand by the word of the holy ones; to the intent that the living may know that the Most High ruleth in the kingdom of men, and giveth it to whomsoever he will, and setteth up over it the basest of men.' 'They shall drive thee from men, and thy dwelling shall be with the beasts of the field, and they shall make thee to eat grass as oxen, and they shall wet thee with the dew of heaven, and seven times shall pass over thee, till thou know that the Most High ruleth in the kingdom of men, and giveth it to whomsoever he will.' 'And they shall drive thee from men, and thy dwelling shall be with the beasts of the field: they shall make thee to eat grass as oxen, and seven times shall pass over thee, until thou know that the Most High ruleth in the kingdom of men, and giveth it to whomsoever he will.'

Dan. 5: 21. 'He was driven from the sons of men; and his heart was made like the beasts, and his dwelling was with the wild asses: they fed him with grass like oxen, and his body was wet with the dew of heaven; till he knew that the Most High God ruleth in the kingdom of men, and that he appointeth over it whomsoever he will.'

Rom. 13: 1—7. 'Let every soul be subject unto the higher powers. For there is no power but of God: the powers that be are ordained of God. Whosoever therefore resisteth the power, resisteth the ordinance of God: and they that resist shall receive to themselves damnation. For rulers are not a terror to good works but to the evil. Wilt thou then not be afraid of the power? Do that which is good, and thou shalt have praise of the same: for he is the minister of God to thee for good. But if thou do that which is evil, be afraid; for he beareth not the sword in vain: for he is the minister of God, a revenger to execute wrath upon him that doeth evil. Wherefore ye must needs be subject, not only for wrath but also for conscience sake. For, for this cause pay ye tribute also: for they are God's ministers, attending continually upon this very thing. Render therefore to all their dues; tribute to whom tribute is due; custom to whom custom; fear to whom fear; honor to whom honor.'

Titus 3 : 1. 'Put them in mind to be subject to principalities and powers, to obey magistrates, to be ready to every good work.'

1 Peter 2: 13, 14. 'Submit yourselves to every ordinance of man for the Lord's sake: whether it be to the king, as supreme, or unto governors, as unto them that are sent by him for the punishment of evil doers, and for the praise of them that do well.'

These passages prove conclusively, that God establishes human governments, as parts of moral government.

2. It is a matter of fact, that God does exert moral influences through the instrumentality of human governments.

3. It is a matter of fact, that he often executes his law, punishes vice, and rewards virtue, through the instrumentality of human governments.

4. Under the Jewish Theocracy, where God was King, it was found indispensable to have the forms of the executive department of government.

FOURTH. *Whose right and duty it is to govern.*

1. I have said that government is a necessity. Human beings are, under God, dependent on human government to promote their highest well-being.

2. It is his right and duty to govern, who is both able and willing, in the highest and most effectual manner, to secure and promote individual and public virtue and happiness.

3. Upon him all eyes are or ought to be turned, as one whose right and whose duty it is, to sustain to them the relation of ruler.

FIFTH. *In what cases human legislation imposes moral obligation.*

1. Not when it requires what is inconsistent with moral law.

2. Not when it is arbitrary, or not founded in right reason.

3. But it always imposes moral obligation when it is in accordance with moral law, or the law of nature.

SIXTH. *It is the duty of all men to aid in the establishment and support of Human Governments.*

1. Because human governments are founded in the necessities of human beings.

2. As all men are in some way dependent upon them, it is the duty of every man to aid in their establishment and support.

3. As the great law of benevolence, or universal good-willing, demands the existence of human governments, all men are under a perpetual and unalterable moral obligation to aid in their establishment and support.

4. In popular or elective governments, every man having a right to vote, and every human being who has moral influence, is bound to exert that influence, in the promotion of virtue and happiness. And as human governments are plainly indispensable to the highest good of man, they are bound to exert their influence to secure a legislation that is in accordance with the law of God.

5. The obligation of human beings to support and obey human governments, while they legislate upon the principles of the moral law is as unalterable as the moral law itself.

SEVENTH. *It is a ridiculous and absurd dream to suppose that Human Governments can ever be dispensed with in the present world.*

1. Because such a supposition is entirely inconsistent with the nature of human beings.

2. It is equally inconsistent with their relations and circumstances.

3. Because it assumes that the necessity of government is founded alone in human depravity; whereas the foundation of this necessity is human ignorance, and human depravity is only an additional reason for the existence of human governments. The primary idea of law is to teach; hence law has a *precept*. It is authoritative, and therefore has a penalty.

4. Because it assumes that men would always agree in judgment, if their hearts were right, irrespective of their degrees of information.

5. Because it sets aside one of the plainest and most unequivocal doctrines of revelation.

Obj. I. The kingdom of God is represented in the Bible as subverting all other kingdoms.

Ans. This is true, and all that can be meant by this is, that the time shall come when God shall be regarded as the supreme and universal sovereign of the universe; when his law shall be regarded as universally obligatory; when all kings, legislators, and judges shall act as his servants, declaring, applying, and administring the great principle of his law to all the affairs of human beings. Thus God will be the supreme sovereign, and earthly rulers will be governors, kings, and judges under him, and acting by his authority, as revealed in the Bible.

Obj. II. It is objected that God only providentially establishes human governments, and that he does not approve of their selfish and wicked administration; that he only uses them providentially, as he does Satan for the promotion of his own designs.

Ans. 1. God no where commands mankind to obey Satan, but he does command them to obey magistrates and rulers.

Rom. 13: 1. 'Let every soul be subject unto the higher powers: for there is no power but of God: the powers that be are ordained of God."

1 Pet. 2: 13, 14. 'Submit yourselves to every ordinance of man for the Lord's sake: whether it be to the king, as supreme; or unto governors, as unto them that are sent for the punishment of evildoers, and for the praise of them that do well.'

2. He no where recognizes Satan as his servant, sent and set by him to administer justice and execute wrath upon the wicked; but he does this in respect to human governments.

Rom. 13: 2—6. 'Whosoever therefore resisteth the power, resisteth the ordinance of God; and they that resist shall receive to themselves damnation. For rulers are not a terror to good works, but to the evil. Wilt thou then not be afraid of the power? Do that which is good, and thou shalt have praise of the same. For he is the minister of God to thee for good. But if thou do that which is evil, be afraid: for he beareth not the sword in vain: for he is the MINISTER OF GOD, a revenger to execute wrath upon him that doeth evil. Wherefore ye must needs be subject, not only for wrath, but also for conscience' sake. For, for this cause pay ye tribute also: for they are God's ministers, attending continually upon this very thing.'

3. It is true indeed that God approves of nothing that is ungodly and selfish in human governments. Neither did he approve of what was ungodly and selfish in the Scribes and Pharisees; and yet Christ said to his disciples, "The Scribes and Pharisees sit in Moses' seat. Therefore whatsoever things they command you, that observe and do; but go ye not after their works, for they say, and do not." Here the plain common sense principle is recognized, that we are to obey when the requirement is not inconsistent with the moral law, whatever may be the character or the motive of the ruler. We are always to obey heartily as unto the Lord, and not unto men, and render obedience to magistrates for the honor and glory of God, and as doing service to him.

Obj. III. It is objected that Christians should leave human governments to the management of the ungodly, and not be diverted from the work of saving souls to intermeddle with human governments.

Ans. 1. This is not being diverted from the work of saving souls. The promotion of public and private order and happiness is one of the indispensable means of saving souls.

2. It is nonsense to admit that Christians are under an obligation to obey human government, and still have nothing to do with the choice of those who shall govern.

Obj. IV. It is objected that we are commanded not to avenge ourselves, that "Vengeance is mine, and I will repay, saith the Lord." It is said, that if I may not avenge or redress my own wrongs in my own person, I may not do it through the instrumentality of human government.

Ans. 1. It does not follow that because you may not take it upon you to redress your own wrongs by a summary and personal infliction of punishment upon the transgressor, that human governments may not punish them.

2. Because all *private* wrongs are a *public* injury; and irrespective of any particular regard to your personal interest, magistrates are bound to punish crime for the public good.

3. It does not follow, because that while God has expressly for

bidden you to redress your own wrongs by administering personal and private chastisement, he has expressly recognized the right and made it the duty of the public magistrate to punish crimes.

Obj. V. It is objected that love is so much better than law as that where love reigns in the heart, law can be universally dispensed with.

Ans. 1. This supposes that if there is only love there need be no rule of duty.

2. This objection overlooks the fact that law is in all worlds the rule of duty, and that legal sanctions make up an indispensable part of that circle of motives that are suited to the nature, relations, and government of moral beings.

3. The law requires love; and nothing is law, either human or divine, that is inconsistent with universal benevolence. And to suppose that love is better than law, is to suppose that obedience to law sets aside the necessity of law.

Obj. VI. It is objected that Christians have something else to do besides meddle with politics.

Ans. 1. In a popular government politics are an indispensable part of religion. No man can possibly be benevolent or religious without concerning himself to a greater or less extent with the affairs of human government.

2. It is true that Christians have something else to do than to go with a party to do evil, or to meddle with politics in a selfish or ungodly manner. But they are bound to meddle with politics in popular governments, for the same reason that they are bound to seek the universal good of all men.

Obj. VII. It is said that human governments are no where expressly authorized in the Bible.

Ans. 1. This is a mistake. Both their existence and lawfulness are as expressly recognized in the above quoted scriptures as they can be.

2. If God did not expressly authorize them, it would still be both the right and the duty of mankind to institute human governments, because they are plainly demanded by the necessities of human nature. It is a first truth, that whatever is essential to the highest good of moral beings in any world, they have a right and are bound to do. So far, therefore, are men from needing any express authority to establish human governments, that no possible prohibition could render their establishment unlawful. It has been shown, in these lectures on moral government, that moral law is a unit—that it is that rule of action which is in accordance with the nature, relations, and circumstances of moral beings—that whatever is in accordance with, and demanded by the nature, relations, and circumstances of moral beings, is obligatory on them. It is

moral law, and no power in the universe can set it aside: Therefore, were the scriptures entirely silent on the subject of human governments, and on the subject of family government, as it actually is on a great many important subjects, this would be no objection to the lawfulness, and expediency; necessity, and duty of establishing human governments.

Obj. VIII. It is said that human governments are founded in and sustained by force, and that this is inconsistent with the spirit of the gospel.

Ans. 1. There cannot be a difference between the *spirit* of the Old and New Testaments, or between the *spirit* of the law and the gospel, unless God has changed, and unless Christ has undertaken to make void the law, through faith, which cannot be.

Rom. 3 : 31. 'Do we then make void the law through faith? God forbid: yea, we establish the law.'

2. Just human governments, and such governments only are contended for, will not exercise force unless it is demanded to promote the highest public good. If it be necessary to this end, it can never be wrong. Nay, it must be the duty of human governments to inflict penalties, when their infliction is demanded by the public interest.

Obj. IX. It is said that there should be no laws with penalties.

Ans. This is the same as to say there should be no law at all; for that is no law which has no penalty, but only advice.

Obj. X. It is said that church government is sufficient to meet the necessities of the world, without secular or state governments.

Ans. 1. What! Church governments regulate commerce, make internal improvements, and undertake to manage all the business affairs of the world!

2. Church government was never established for any such end; but simply to regulate the spiritual, in distinction from the secular concerns of men—to try offenders and inflict spiritual chastisement, and never to perplex and embarrass itself with managing the business and commercial operations of the world.

Obj. XI. It is said that were all the world holy, legal penalties would not be needed.

Ans. Were all men perfectly holy, the *execution* of penalties would not be needed; but still, if there were law, there would be penalties; and it would be both the right and the duty of magistrates to inflict them, should their execution be called for.

Obj. XII. It is asserted that family government is the only form of government approved of God.

Ans. This is a ridiculous assertion:

1. Because God as expressly commands obedience to magistrates as to parents.

2. He makes it as absolutely the duty of magistrates to punish crime, as of parents to punish their own disobedient children.

3. The right of family government is not founded in the arbitrary will of God, but in the necessities of human beings; so that family government would be both allowable and obligatory, had God said nothing about it.

4. So, the right of human government has not its foundation in the arbitrary will of God, but in the necessities of human beings. The larger the community the more absolute the necessity of government. If, in the small circle of the family, laws and penalties are needed, how much more in the larger communities of states and nations. Now, neither the ruler of a family, nor of any other form of human government, has a right to legislate arbitrarily, or enact, or enforce any other laws, than those that are in accordance with the nature, relations, and circumstances of human beings. Nothing can be law in heaven—nothing can be law on earth—nothing can be obligatory on moral beings, but that which is founded in the nature, relations, and circumstances of moral beings. But human beings are bound to establish family governments, state governments, national governments, and, in short, whatever government may be requisite for the universal instruction, government, virtue, and happiness of the world.

5. All the reasons, therefore, for family government, hold equally in favor of state and national governments.

6. There are vastly higher and weightier reasons for governments over states and nations, than in the small communities of families.

7. Therefore, neither family nor state governments need the express sanction of God, to render them obligatory; for both the right and duty of establishing and maintaining these governments would remain, had the Bible been entirely silent on the subject. But on this, as on many other subjects, God has spoken and declared, what is the common and universal law, plainly recognizing both the right and duty of family and human governments.

8. Christians, therefore, have something else to do, than to confound the right of government with the abuse of this right by the ungodly. Instead of destroying human governments, Christians are bound to reform them.

9. To attempt to destroy, instead of reform human governments, is the same in principle as is often plead by those who are attempting to destroy, rather than reform the Church. There are those, who, disgusted with the abuses of Christianity practiced in the Church, seem bent on destroying the Church altogether, as the means of saving the world. But what mad policy is this!

10. It is admitted that selfish men need and must have the restraints of law; but that Christians should have no part in restraining them by law. But suppose the wicked should agree among

themselves to have no law, and therefore should not attempt to restrain themselves nor each other by law; would it be neither the right nor the duty of Christians to attempt their restraint, through the influence of wholesome government?

11. It is strange that selfish men should need the restraints of law, and yet that Christians have no right to meet this necessity, by supporting governments that will restrain them. What is this but admitting, that the world really needs the restraints of governments—that the highest good of the universe demands their existence; and yet, that it is wicked for Christians to seek the highest good of the world, by meeting this necessity in the establishment and support of human governments! It is right and best that there should be law. It is necessary that there should be. Therefore, universal benevolence demands it; but it is wicked in Christians, to have any thing to do with it! This is singular logic.

LECTURE XLII.

MORAL GOVERNMENT.—No. 21.

HUMAN GOVERNMENTS ARE A PART OF THE MORAL GOVERNMENT OF GOD.—NO. 2.

In this lecture I shall show:

FIRST. The reasons why God has made no particular form of Church or State Governments universally obligatory.

SECOND. The particular forms of Church and State Government must and will depend upon the intelligence and virtue of the people.

THIRD. The true basis on which the right of Human Legislation rests.

FOURTH. That form of Government is obligatory, that is best suited to meet the necessities of the people.

FIFTH. Revolutions become necessary and obligatory, when the virtue and intelligence, or the vice and ignorance of the people demand them.

SIXTH. In what cases Human Legislation is valid, and in what cases it is null and void.

SEVENTH. In what cases we are bound to disobey Human Governments.

FIRST. *The reasons why God has made no form of Church or State Government universally obligatory.*

1. That God has no where in the Bible given directions in regard to any particular form of church or secular government, is a matter of fact.

2. That he did not consider the then existing forms, either of church or state government, as of perpetual obligation, is also certain.

3. He did not give directions in regard to particular forms of government, either church or state:

(1.) Because no such directions could be given, without producing great revolutions and governmental opposition to Christianity. The governments of the world are and always have been exceedingly various in form. To attempt, therefore, to insist upon any particular form, as being universally obligatory, would be calling out great national opposition to religion.

(2.) Because, that no particular form, of church or state government, either now is, or ever has been, suited to all degrees of intelligence, and states of society.

(3.) Because the forms of both church and state governments, need to be changed, with any great elevations or depressions of society in regard to their intelligence and virtue.

SECOND. *The particular forms of Church and State Government, must and will depend upon the virtue and intelligence of the people.*

1. Democracy is self-government, and can never be safe or useful, only so far as there is sufficient intelligence and virtue in the community to impose, by mutual consent, salutary self-restraints, and to enforce by the power of public sentiment, and by the fear and love of God, the practice of those virtues which are indispensable to the highest good of any community.

2. Republics are another and less perfect form of self-government.

3. When there are not sufficient intelligence and virtue among the people, to legislate in accordance with the highest good of the state or nation, then both democracies and republics are improper and impracticable, as forms of government.

4. When there is too little intelligence and virtue in the mass of the people, to legislate on correct principles, monarchies are better calculated to restrain vice and promote virtue.

5. In the worst states of society, despotisms, either civil or military, are the only proper and efficient forms of government.

6. When virtue and intelligence are nearly universal, democratic forms of government are well suited to promote the public good.

7. In such a state of society, democracy is greatly conducive to the general diffusion of knowledge on governmental subjects.

8. Although in some respects less convenient and more expensive, yet in a suitable state of society, a democracy is in many respects the most desirable form, either of church or state government:

(1.) It is conducive, as has been already said, to general intelligence.

(2.) Under a democracy, the people are more generally acquainted with the laws.

(3.) They are more interested in them.

(4.) This form of government creates a more general feeling of individual responsibility.

(5.) Governmental questions are more apt to be thoroughly discussed and understood before they are adopted.

(6.) As the diffusion of knowledge is favorable to individual and public virtue, democracy is highly conducive to virtue and happiness.

9. God has always providentially given to mankind those forms of government that were suited to the degrees of virtue and intelligence among them.

10. If they have been extremely ignorant and vicious, he has restrained them by the iron rod of human despotism.

11. If more intelligent and virtuous, he has given them the milder forms of limited monarchies.

12. If still more intelligent and virtuous, he has given them still more liberty, and providentially established republics for their government.

13. Whenever the general state of intelligence has permitted it, he has put them to the test of self-government and self-restraint, by establishing democracies.

14. If the world ever becomes perfectly virtuous both church and state governments will be proportionally modified, and employed in expounding and applying the great principles of moral law, to the spiritual and secular concerns of men.

15. The above principles are equally applicable to church and state governments. Episcopacy is well suited to a state of general ignorance among the people. Presbyterianism, or Church Republicanism is better suited to a more advanced state of intelligence and the prevalence of Christian principle. While Congregationalism, or spiritual Democracy, is best suited and only suited to a state of general intelligence, and the prevalence of Christian principle.

16. God's providence has always modified both church and state governments, so as to suit the intelligence and virtue of the people. As churches and nations rise and fall in the scale of virtue and intelligence, these various forms of government naturally and necessarily give place to each other. So that ecclesiastical and state despotism, or liberty, depends naturally, providentially, and necessarily upon the virtue and intelligence of the people.

17. God is infinitely benevolent, and from time to time, gives the people as much liberty as they can bear.

THIRD. *The true basis on which the right of Human Legislation rests.*

Under this head, I need only to repeat what has already been said in substance in these lectures, that the right of human legislation is founded in the necessities of mankind. The nature and ignorance of mankind lie at the foundation of this necessity. Their wickedness, the multiplicity and variety of their wants, are additional reasons, demanding the existence of human governments. Let it be understood, then, that the foundation of the right of human governments lies not in the arbitrary will of God; but in the nature, relations, and circumstances of human beings.

FOURTH. *That form of Government is obligatory, that is best suited to meet the necessities of the people.*

1. This follows as a self-evident truth, from the consideration, that it is necessity alone that creates the right of human government. To meet these necessities, is the object of government; and that government is obligatory and best, which is demanded by the circumstances, intelligence, and morals of the people.

2. Consequently, in certain states of society, it would be a Christian's duty to pray for and sustain even a military despotism; in a certain other state of society, to pray for and sustain a monarchy. And in other states, to pray for and sustain a republic; and in a still more advanced stage of virtue and intelligence, to pray for and sustain a democracy; if indeed a democracy is the most wholesome form of self-government, which may admit a doubt.

FIFTH. *Revolutions become necessary and obligatory, when the virtue and intelligence or the vice and ignorance of the people demand them.*

1. This is a thing of course. When one form of government fails to meet any longer the necessities of the people, it is the duty of the people to revolutionize.

2. In such cases, it is in vain to oppose revolution; for in some way the benevolence of God will bring it about. Upon this principle alone, can what is generally termed the American Revolution be justified. The intelligence and virtue of our Puritan fore-fathers rendered a monarchy an unnecessary burden, and a republican form of government both appropriate and necessary. And God always allows his children as much liberty as they are prepared to enjoy.

3. The stability of our republican institutions must depend upon the progress of general intelligence and virtue. If in these respects the nation falls, if general intelligence, public and private virtue sink to that point below which self-control becomes impossible, we must fall back into monarchy, limited or absolute; or into a civil or military despotism; just according to the national standard of intelligence and virtue. This is just as certain as that God governs the world, or that causes produce their effects.

4. Therefore, it is the maddest conceivable policy, for Christians to attempt to uproot human governments, while they ought to be engaged in sustaining them, upon the great principles of the moral

law. It is certainly stark nonsense, if not abominable wickedness, to overlook, either in theory or practice, these plain, common sense, and universal truths.

SIXTH. *In what cases Human Legislation is valid, and in what cases it is null and void.*

1. Human legislation is valid, when called for by the necessities—that is—by the nature, relations and circumstances of the people.

2. Just that kind and degree of human legislation which are demanded by the necessities of the people are obligatory.

3. Human legislation is utterly null and void in all other cases whatsoever; and I may add, that divine legislation would be equally null and void; unless demanded by the nature, relations, and necessities of human beings. Consequently human beings can never legislate in opposition to the moral law. Whatever is inconsistent with supreme love to God and equal love to our neighbor, can by no possibility be obligatory.

SEVENTH. *In what cases we are bound to disobey Human Governments.*

1. We may yield obedience, when the thing required does not involve a violation of moral obligation.

2. We are bound to yield obedience, when legislation is in accordance with the law of nature.

3. We are bound to obey when the thing required has no moral character in itself; upon the principle, that obedience, in this case, is a less evil than revolution or misrule. But—

4. We are bound in all cases to disobey, when human legislation contravenes moral law, or invades the rights of conscience.

223 His exegesis.